Multicultural Acquisitions

The Acquisitions Librarian Series:

Multicultural Acquisitions

Karen Parrish, MLS
Bill Katz, PhD

Editors

The Haworth Press, Inc.
New York · London · Norwood (Australia)

Multicultural Acquisitions has also been published as *The Acquisitions Librarian,* Numbers 9/10 1993.

The Haworth Press, Inc., 10 Alice Street, Binghamton, NY 13904-1580 USA

Library of Congress Cataloging-in-Publication Data

Multicultural acquisitions / Karen Parrish, Bill Katz editors.
    p. cm.
    ISBN 1-56024-451-8 (acid free paper)
    1. Libraries–United States–Special collections–Minorities. 2. Libraries and minorities–United States 3. Pluralism (Social Sciences)–United States. I. Parrish, Karen. II. Katz, Bill.
Z688.M84M85 1993
027.6'3–dc20   93-7657
                                                                  CIP

INDEXING & ABSTRACTING

Contributions to this publication are selectively indexed or abstracted in print, electronic, online, or CD-ROM version(s) of the reference tools and information services listed below. This list is current as of the copyright date of this publication. See the end of this section for additional notes.

- *Current Awareness Bulletin*, Association for Information Management, Information House, 20-24 Old Street, London, EC1V 9AP, England

- *Educational Administration Abstracts*, Sage Publications, Inc., 2455 Teller Road, Newbury Park, CA 91320

- *Foreign Library and Information Service*, China Sci-Tech Book Review, Library of Academia Sinica, 8 Kexueyuan Nanlu, Zhongguancun, Beijing 100080, People's Republic of China

- *Index to Periodical Articles Related to Law*, University of Texas, 727 East 26th Street, Austin, TX 78705

- *Information Reports & Bibliographies*, Science Associates International, Inc., 465 West End Avenue, New York, NY 10024

- *Information Science Abstracts*, Plenum Publishing Company, 233 Spring Street, New York, NY 10013-1578

- *INSPEC Information Services,* Institution of Electrical Engineers, Michael Faraday House, Six Hills Way, Stevenage, Herts SG1 2AY, England

- *Library & Information Science Abstracts (LISA),* Bowker-Saur Limited, 60 Grosvenor Street, London, W1X 9DA, England

- *Library Literature,* The H.W. Wilson Company, 950 University Avenue, Bronx, NY 10452

- *The Informed Librarian,* Infosources Publishing, 140 Norma Road, Teaneck, NJ 07666

SPECIAL BIBLIOGRAPHIC NOTES

related to indexing and abstracting

☐ indexing/abstracting services in this list will also cover material in the "separate" that is co-published simultaneously with Haworth's special thematic journal issue or DocuSerial. Indexing/abstracting usually covers material at the article/chapter level.

☐ monographic co-editions are intended for either non-subscribers or libraries which intend to purchase a second copy for their circulating collections.

☐ monographic co-editions are reported to all jobbers/wholesalers/approval plans. The source journal is listed as the "series" to assist the prevention of duplicate purchasing in the same manner utilized for books-in-series.

☐ to facilitate user/access services all indexing/abstracting services are encouraged to utilize the co-indexing entry note indicated at the bottom of the first page of each article/chapter/contribution.

☐ this is intended to assist a library user of any reference tool (whether print, electronic, online, or CD-ROM) to locate the monographic version if the library has purchased this version but not a subscription to the source journal.

☐ individual articles/chapters in any Haworth publication are also available through the Haworth Document Delivery Services (HDDS).

Multicultural Acquisitions

CONTENTS

AT THE ACADEMIC LEVEL

THE GOVERNMENT

FOR OTHER CULTURES

ABOUT THE EDITORS

Karen Parrish, MLS, became interested in other cultures and our attitudes toward them when she lived in Sidi Yahia, Morocco, where she worked in a Navy library from 1969 to 1971. Currently, she is an itinerant librarian (school media specialist) for Washington, Warren, Hamilton, and Essex County BOCES in upstate New York.

Bill Katz, PhD, is affiliated with the School of Information Science and Policy of the State University of New York at Albany, Nelson A. Rockefeller College of Public Affairs and Policy, Draper Hall, 113, 135 Western Avenue, Albany, NY 12222.

Introduction

Karen Parrish

With the arrival of a global economy, it has become more and more important that our population, both young and old, be aware of, respectful of, and knowledgeable about other cultures. Whether it is a Hispanic first grader in New York City seeking information about her Puerto Rican heritage or a Los Angeles businessman inquiring about the customs of a client from China, it is the responsibility of the information specialists to provide accurate references to answer these questions.

We have compiled what we hope is a broad basis for all levels of librarianship to develop collections addressing multiculturalism. The articles are as diverse as our topic. They represent a multitude of perspectives from the graduate student to a variety of professional information and school media specialists to authors and editors.

We open with a general chapter about multiculturalism and libraries. This is followed by a section dealing with the younger segment of our society, examining the importance and problems of getting materials on our diverse populace into the hands of our youth. Next, we include the situation at the academic level. This covers the availability of materials to students for research as well as how the subject is handled in training future librarians. One succeeding article deals with the issue in regard to government documents. We conclude with pieces about several individual cultural and subcultural groups.

[Haworth co-indexing entry note]: "Introduction," Parrish, Karen Co-published simultaneously in *The Acquisitions Librarian* (The Haworth Press, Inc.) No. 9/10, 1993, pp. 1-2; and: *Multicultural Acquisitions* (ed: Karen Parrish and Bill Katz) The Haworth Press, Inc., 1993, pp. 1-2. Multiple copies of this article/chapter may be purchased from The Haworth Document Delivery Center. Call 1-800-3-HAWORTH (1-800-342-9678) between 9:00 - 5:00 (EST) and ask for DOCUMENT DELIVERY CENTER.

Our goal is not to provide an all inclusive answer to creating multicultural collections. Our goal is to make librarians aware of the issue and its importance. Our goal is to give points to consider when approaching the subject of multiculturalism. Our goal is to make you think–think about the importance of a multicultural approach to librarianship–think about providing information to a global population.

IN GENERAL

Multiculturalism and Library Services

Gillian D. Leonard

SUMMARY. In this paper multiculturalism is considered in relation to education and public library services. Following a brief review of the historical relationship between libraries and minorities, the current debate concerning multiculturalism in education is discussed. Issues relevant to education and librarianship are identified. The position presented is that libraries have a responsibility to provide services and materials appropriate to the communities they serve, but must remain neutral in response to social issues. The implications of various multicultural approaches to library service are examined.

INTRODUCTION

The provision of multicultural library services and programs has been of increasing concern to many librarians, as well as to ALA as

Address correspondence to: Gillian D. Leonard, 3 Center Street, Apt. D., Green Island, NY 12183.

[Haworth co-indexing entry note]: "Multiculturalism and Library Services," Leonard, Gillian D. Co-published simultaneously in *The Acquisitions Librarian* (The Haworth Press, Inc.) No. 9/10, 1993, pp. 3-19; and: *Multicultural Acquisitions* (ed: Karen Parrish and Bill Katz) The Haworth Press, Inc., 1993, pp. 3-19. Multiple copies of this article/chapter may be purchased from The Haworth Document Delivery Center. Call 1-800-3-HAWORTH (1-800-342-9678) between 9:00 - 5:00 (EST) and ask for DOCUMENT DELIVERY CENTER.

3

evidenced by their report, *Addressing Ethnic and Cultural Diversity: A Report on the Activities of the American Library Association 1986-1989*.[1] In this report over 40 preconference and conference programs are described as well as various projects and publications related to cultural diversity. Also included is ALA's Minority Concerns Policy which focuses on the needs of African-Americans, Hispanic Americans, Asian Americans and Native Americans. In a general sense this report, which will be discussed in greater detail, reflects ALA's commitment to addressing the needs of an ethnically and culturally diverse nation.

While the multiculturalist approach to library service is clearly endorsed by ALA, multiculturalism has been and continues to be a hotly debated issue. Multiculturalism today covers a wide range of philosophies. Milton J. Gold defines multiculturalism rather broadly as "the respect shown to the varied cultures and ethnic groups which have built the United States and which continue today to contribute to its richness and diversity."[2] It represents an increasing shift away from the idea of America as a "melting pot," toward cultural pluralism in which ethnic and cultural diversity is embraced. Critics fear that it has gone too far; that in its more radical forms multiculturalism promotes separatism and is antithetical to the values upon which America was founded. As Diane Ravitch writes, "Almost any idea, carried to its extreme can be made pernicious, and this is what is happening now to multiculturalism."[3] In the meantime multiculturalist thought is having a noticeable effect on many of our public institutions. While most of the changes have occurred in education, multiculturalism has significant implications for public libraries which must now contend with questions relating not only to the provision of special services but the role of the library and librarian in relation to social change. There is a growing demand for libraries to provide multicultural materials and services. However, the assumed benefits of certain targeted efforts should be examined closely. The position presented here is that public libraries have a responsibility to maintain a neutral position in response to social issues while at the same time providing services and materials appropriate to the communities they serve. Following a brief overview of the historical relationship between minorities and libraries this discussion will be primarily concerned with the debate over multiculturalism in education and the implications of multiculturalism thought for public libraries.

LIBRARIES AND MINORITIES: A HISTORICAL PERSPECTIVE

It is commonly felt that early immigrants from Europe assimilated into this country with relative ease while blacks, Hispanics, Native Americans and Asians have been to varying degrees less successful. Reflecting the values of the period, libraries in the middle part of the nineteenth century made no apparent effort to assist these groups. As Nauratil notes,

> In the midnineteenth century, which saw the beginnings of the Public library movement, most black Americans still had the legal status of chattels, and American Indians were widely considered vermin worthy only of extermination. Both Asian immigrants and Chicanos born in U.S. territory were objects of hostility and scorn. The democratic and humanitarian rhetoric upon which public libraries were founded was rarely extended to include these segments of the population.[4]

Though public library assistance to immigrants in the form of "Americanization" programs was extensive, Nauratil states, "If library service available to black Americans was severely restricted and uneven prior to World War I, it was almost nonexistent for members of other minority groups."[5] MacCann suggests that these groups were not only ignored but that "inequities in library service were produced with conscious intent . . . as librarians set policies to encourage basic educational opportunities for immigrants and discourage availability for Blacks."[6] Clearly, progress has been slow and inconsistent. For example, as Cain points out, publications of the Public Library Inquiry which identified the libraries "natural audience" as the educated and economically advantaged, somewhat "overshadowed" the 1943 *Post-War Standards for Public Libraries* and *The National Plan for Public Library Service* both of which displayed "an early orientation toward what would later be called outreach."[7] However to suggest that librarians had a professional agenda which was consciously designed to exclude blacks misses the point that libraries tend to mirror the values of the societies in which they exist. As Alexander states, "Contrary to the view held by progressive librarians, libraries are reflectors of society rather than agents of change."[8]

During the 1930s and 1940s libraries began to place less emphasis upon programs for immigrants. McMullen suggests three possible reasons for this. First, immigrants who arrived in America just before or after World War II were able to take advantage of programs already in place and as a result assimilated without any great difficulty. Second, the number of immigrants had already reached its peak. Finally "Americanization" was no longer regarded as primary to the successful absorption of people from other countries.[9] At the same time, the black civil rights movement began to take hold. By the 1950's Cain suggests that democracy had replaced Americanization as the principal upon which library service was to be based.[10]

Passage of the Library Services Act in 1956 provided the first direct federal funding for libraries.[11] It also paved the way for gradual progress in library services not only for blacks but for Native Americans, Hispanics and Asians over the next decades. Still, the great majority of public library patrons continue to be white, middle class and fairly well-educated. The question is, how best to serve the needs of those who do not fit this profile. Currently, a great deal of thought and effort is being directed toward the provision of multicultural library services. In order to fully comprehend arguments for and against various services it will be important to consider them in relation to the wider debate that is currently focused on education.

MULTICULTURALISM AND EDUCATION: THE CURRENT DEBATE

Arguments for and against the provision of multicultural library services are related to the current debate over multiculturalism in education. Moreover, public libraries have traditionally been conceived (at least in theory) as institutions in which self-education could be attained. Alexander suggests that prior to the advent of the multicultural approach to library services, multiculturalism was already a "key concept in a number of other professions, notably education. . . . As a sister profession, education is still far in advance of Librarianship on this issue, primarily because of Black community pressure."[12] Though Alexander wrote this in England nearly a decade ago, these observations still apply in America today. Education continues to be somewhat in advance of librarianship in the multicultural arena and black educators are still at the forefront of the movement.

In 1989, New York State Education Commissioner, Thomas Sobol, appointed a task force to review the social studies curriculum in New York State public schools. Though major modifications of the curriculum in 1987 were intended to emphasize multicultural awareness, the report released by Sobol's task force, indicated that the social studies program was still largely rooted in "Eurocentric" thought. The report, which was called *A Curriculum of Inclusion,* became instantly controversial with it's widely quoted opening statement: "Afro-Americans, Asian Americans, Puerto Ricans/Latinos and Native Americans have all been victims of intellectual and educational oppression that has characterized the culture and institutions of the United States and the European American World for centuries."[13]

In 1991, a new committee was appointed to once again review the social studies program. This review resulted in a second report entitled, *One Nation, Many Peoples: A Declaration of Cultural Independence.*[14] Though generally considered less controversial than its predecessor, this report was still widely criticized. Paul Gray offers the following comments:

> The most revolutionary changes propounded by the Sobol panel . . . rest on a series of buried premises that are offered, sometimes glancingly, as assumptions shared by Americans. But are they? Does everyone agree that 'education should be a source of strength and pride' for diverse ethnic groups? How about the notion that teaching individuals to fulfill their own abilities is secondary to training them to participate in 'cultural interdependence'? Or that U.S. children should view themselves as citizens of the world rather than of America? Are we all on the same page when it comes to the classroom as a training ground for 'social action'?[15]

While this second report was an attempt to recommend ways in which students might better understand the histories and cultures of the various groups that co-exist in this country, critics point to the danger of emphasizing cultural diversity to the exclusion of those aspects of American culture that we all share. Diane Ravitch contrasts the "particularist path marked out by the Sobol report"[16] with the concept of pluralism.

> As a result of the political and social changes of recent decades, cultural pluralism is now generally recognized as an organizing principle of this society. In contrast to the idea of the melting pot, which promised to erase ethnic and group differences, children now learn that . . . America has provided a haven for many cultural groups and has allowed them to maintain their cultural heritage or assimilate, or–as is often the case–to do both; . . .They learn that cultural pluralism is one of the norms of a free society. . . .
> Today, pluralistic multiculturalism must contend with a new particularistic multiculturalism. The pluralists seek a richer common culture; the particularists insist that no common culture is possible or desirable.[17]

Paul Gray suggests that, "Ultimately, multicultural thinking, for all its nods toward pluralism and diversity, can lead to several regressive orthodoxies. One is the notion that truth is forever encapsulated within collective identities, that what white males or females or blacks or Hispanics or Asians know about their experiences can be communicated only imperfectly to people beyond their pales."[18] It is just this form of multiculturalism that Ravitch objects to; a way of thought that encourages minorities to believe that, "the culture in which they live is not their own culture even though they were born here . . . " and which "throws into question the very idea of American public education," which exists "to teach children the skills and knowledge they need to succeed in American society . . ."[19]

It has been suggested that the Sobol commission proposals will result in the teaching of certain historical inaccuracies and that the unifying effect that is fostered by a recognition of a shared history is now being replaced by another objective which is to improve the self-esteem of various minority groups. In *The Disuniting of Ameri-*

ca, Arthur M. Schlesinger, Jr. writes, "The use of history as therapy means the corruption of history as history . . . Even if history is sanitized in order to make people feel good, there is no evidence that feel-good history promotes ethnic self-esteem and equips students to grapple with their lives."[20] Similarly, Ravitch questions the premise that self-esteem is the direct result of learning about the accomplishments of ones ancestors, rather, "For most children, self-esteem–the self-confidence that grows out of having reached a goal–comes not from hearing about the monuments of their ancestors but as a consequence of what they are able to do and accomplish through their own efforts."[21]

Any version of history will probably reflect a bias of some sort and charges of "Eurocentrism" concerning history as it has been taught in this country are, in many cases, well grounded. However the need to represent the achievements of minorities has given rise to some dubious reinterpretations of the past. For example in New York State the curriculum guide for eleventh grade American history now lists the Iroquois political system as one of three apparently equal influences on the United States Constitution, the other influences being 17th and 18th Century Enlightenment thought and Colonial experience. The fact that no other state subscribes to this particular theory has been attributed by some to the political clout that the Iroquois in New York State have achieved.[22] As Schlesinger states, "Europhobia makes for some very bad history."[23] Schlesinger, who served on the Sobol commission, has been highly critical of multiculturalism, particularly in its more radical forms. He points out that "for most Americans ethnicity is not the defining experience."[24] Moreover, enhanced self-esteem is an unlikely outcome "when you discover that you have fallen for a series of 'therapeutic' absurdities . . . The plight of inner-city Americans is indeed appalling, Schlesinger states, and to fight for themselves they need the best education we can deliver them, not a pack of anodyne lies."[25]

For most critics of the current multicultural movement the point is not that the culturally pluralistic nature of this country should be ignored but rather that we recognize the destructive implications of those forms of multiculturalism that insist upon identifying solely with ones ethnic past and that require history to be revised in the interests of any one group. The past is the past, and the fact that history has been written the way it has may be of interest in itself. Attempts to make known the achievements of those who have been overlooked in history (whether they be black, female, Hispanic or whatever) are certainly justified, however distorting the influence of any group or person is not the answer.

MULTICULTURAL LIBRARY SERVICES

As previously noted, arguments for and against the provision of multicultural library services are related to the current debate over multiculturalism in education. First there is the question of purpose. Just as the Sobol report suggests that "education should be a source of strength and pride,"[26] for ethnic groups, the ALA report states that it is the libraries role to "empower minority people."[27] Mac-Cann reiterates the "empowerment" theme, suggesting that "Service to the empowered mainstream and the still unempowered 'minority' groups will remain dissimilar in the future unless we search deeply for underlying causes within our everchanging, but nonetheless tangible and traceable, social processes."[28] It is clearly the responsibility of public libraries to provide equal service and equal access to information, but discussions concerning the "empowered" and the "unempowered" tend to suggest that, like our educational system, our public libraries have been founded upon a "Eurocentric" base which needs to be overthrown. In education, "Eurocentrism" has come under heavy attack while major revisions of curriculum have been instituted in many areas. In 1981 Gundara and Warwick suggested a similar transformation for libraries. They asserted that the "Eurocentric library structure" should be cast aside and that multicultural library service "demands total re-orientation of attitudes, values and priorities on the part of the authorities in terms of stock, staff and the nature of services."[29] The question is, what is the role of the library and the librarian in relation to social and political issues? Arguments concerning this question tend to hinge on the concept of the library as a neutral institution with access to information being the primary objective versus a more active role in the movement toward social change. As MacCann writes,

One faction of the profession has considered social responsibility vis-à-vis libraries as an abrogation of the librarians's alleged neutrality in the selection of books. The concept is seen by this group as linked with censorship. Another faction sees no inherent contradiction between the concept of social responsibility and the concept of intellectual freedom. Individuals in this group often stress the libraries position within a broader social context.[30]

David Berninghausen is frequently cited as a proponent of the former philosophy and is quoted by MacCann as follows:

Vital though they are, it is essential that librarians in their professional activities, shall view such issues as subordinate to the issue of intellectual freedom, for, unless men have access to all varieties of expression as to the facts, theories, and alternative solutions to those problems, they will be unable to apply their powers of reason toward their resolution.[31]

In ALA's report, the issue of censorship is addressed as is the related idea that neither "advocacy" nor the promotion of causes can co-exist with the concept of intellectual freedom. The report states, "Intellectual freedom, the essence of equitable library services, promotes no causes, furthers no movements, and favors no viewpoints. It only provides for free access to all expressions of ideas through which any and all sides of a question, cause or movement may be explored."[32] "ALA Policies and Guidelines Focusing on Minorities" further states, "Nothing in the Resolution on Prejudice, Stereotyping, and Discrimination authorizes censoring, expurgation, or labeling of materials. Actions and programs to raise the awareness of library users to any problem or condition would be not in conflict with the Library Bill of Rights when they are free of any element of advocacy."[33] My own suggestion is that there is a fine line between advocacy and "empowerment." While it is not my intent to imply that there is anything inherently wrong with the report's objectives, I do think that they carry certain contradictory ideas which are worth considering. For example, the implementation of ALA's Policy Objectives involves a list of guidelines which include: "Promoting the publication, production, and purchase of print and non-print materials that present positive role models of cultural minorities."[34] At first glance this seems like a reasonable and worthy proposal, however what does this suggest about material that doesn't fit that criteria. Much is written on individuals from all racial and cultural backgrounds who would not necessarily be considered "positive role models." Does this imply that the publication and purchase of such material might be discouraged, or at least, that it might not be promoted, simply because it presents a negative image? Apart from these questions, if the role of libraries is to "enable minorities to participate fully in a democratic society,"[35] perhaps we should ask, what are the actual needs of minorities in relation to libraries and how can these needs best be served?

The ALA report also emphasizes the provision of multilingual materials and services. Though it is not the role of libraries to determine what is or is not in the best interests of any given group, the implications concerning various services are worth thinking about. For example, is it truly in the best interests of a Hispanic community to provide extensive bilingual services and a large bilingual collection. Or are such services, in the long run subtly debilitating to the very population they were meant to serve. In this country there is perhaps no skill that is more important than a proficiency in English. ESL classes which are increasingly common in public libraries are clearly a useful service. While it may seem like a good idea to attempt to accommodate diversity in our public schools and libraries through increases in bilingual materials and services, accommodation of this sort is not the norm in many other areas of American life. While multiculturalist thought clearly indicates that not enough accommodating has gone on, the reality in this country at this time is this; achievement, in any significant sense, is highly dependent upon speaking and reading English and to pretend anything else is falsification. Nauratil states, "Library service should not be a privilege conditional upon some behavioral change on the part of the user, such as developing a proficiency in English or attaining social mobility . . . the socially responsive librarian would argue further that if the socioeconomic position of the community is one resulting from social injustice, the library has a mandate to take part in the struggle against that injustice."[36] Nauratil's comments have a number of implications beginning with the role of the librarian as social activist. However, if social activism has been determined to be a role for the library, the "struggle" should not be at the expense of those it was meant to assist. For example, from a multiculturalist perspective it is perhaps unfortunate that in this country little provision is made for languages other than English. But to reinforce the idea of language as a source of cultural identity, without focusing on the needs of minorities to master English, is clearly not going to "empower" anyone. Schlesinger states, "There are those, for example, who argue that blacks should not be taught standard English, that they should be taught black English. If there is anything that is going to disable people for a role in American society, it would be to speak a separate dialect."[37] Speaking specifically about bilingual education Schlesinger points out:

> The presumed purpose is transitional: to move non-English-speaking children as quickly as possible from bilingual to all-English classes . . .
>
> Alas, bilingualism has not worked out as planned: rather to the contrary. Testimony is mixed, but the indications are that bilingual education retards rather than expedites the movement of Hispanic children into the English-speaking world and that it promotes segregation more than it does integration. Bilingualism shuts doors. It nourishes self-ghettoization, and ghettoization nourishes racial antagonism.[38]

The argument in response to this view is that Hispanics should not be forced into the English speaking world in the first place; that the English-speaking world should adjust to their needs. But to prepare Hispanic children for a world that at this time doesn't exist seems a serious disservice. Benavides discusses multicultural/bilingual education in relation to the role of public libraries. The rationale he presents is that having "jumped from an agricultural society to a postindustrial-high technology society in record time,"[39] it is no longer possible for those with limited English language capabilities to assimilate successfully into the workforce, that the attainment of an education, "signifies no less than Hispanic children's entry into the world of opportunity."[40] Yet Benavide's emphasis is not on language skills; nowhere does he mention the importance of acquiring a proficiency in English. Instead he argues for the provision of bilingual education without any indication of at what point, if ever, the transition to English should be made. The role of libraries, he suggests, is largely related to hiring bilingual librarians and other staff members from the community and providing outreach services. Yet all of this somehow seems to miss the point that in this country the dominant language is English and the ability to function in our society is very much determined by ones language skills. As Schlesinger states, "Using some language other than English dooms people to second-class citizenship in American society."[41] The idea that bilingualism handicaps those it attempts to help is rarely addressed by its proponents. Nauratil states,

> A liberal argument against providing special services to blacks and members of other racial minorities is expressed as a reluctance to segregate or 'ghettoize.' Those espousing this seemingly egalitarian point of view conveniently ignore the fact that in America, racial minorities are already ghettoized . . . The purpose of specialized collections and programs is never to exclude targeted clientele from general library services, but to offer a greater range of choices.[42]

While few would disagree with the idea of offering the greatest range of choice possible, arguing that minorities are already ghettoized, seems to suggest that we needn't worry about making a bad situation worse.

In addition to the special services mentioned thus far, minorities are often suggested to have special information needs that must be addressed within the library setting. Nauratil offers the following examples of minority information needs:

> In addition to information on housing, employment, health care, government benefits and so on, often needed by the poor, people of color also require information related to their racial status. The library should be able to provide information on how to file a discrimination complaint, for example, or how to obtain genetic counseling to deal with such race specific diseases as sickle cell anemia. Recent immigrants will require information on all aspects of American life; factual materials, even if disillusioning are of more help than is propaganda.[43]

A study by the Center for Policy Development in California concluded that the information needs of minorities "do not differ primarily because of race or ethnicity, but rather because of an individuals life situation which may include factors *associated* with race or ethnicity, such as cultural experiences, language, literacy, recent arrival in the United States, socioeconomic status, education, and most generally, levels of acculturation."[44] The information needs identified by librarians as most important to minorities (indicated through day to day observation, demographic data and needs assessment studies) were listed in order of importance as the following: survival needs, education, life skills, legal and political needs, assimilation needs, ethnic heritage needs, and entertainment needs.[45] It was also found that reference services targeted specifically at meeting minority information needs were utilized very little while minority librarians tended to rely more heavily on "informal networks of information."[46]

Librarians have a responsibility to do whatever they can to assist patrons in finding whatever information they require; this falls within the scope of their normal duties. The information requests of minority groups should pose no special problems to a competent librarian. A reference librarian, for example, should be responsive to whatever factors effect the reference interview whether it be the patrons age, their grasp of English, etc., from whatever clues are provided in what is generally a very brief period of time. It means that the librarian must assess the situation quickly and act accordingly. This should be viewed as part of a librarians basic duties, not as something pertaining specifically to minorities but extending to all people.

The question is, why are the information requirements of minorities viewed as different from those of other library patrons, or perhaps better put, why is it so often suggested that in responding to related queries, the librarian is providing a special (i.e., multicultural) service? Nauratil's examples of information needs specific to blacks bring to mind several questions. Why is providing information on sickle cell anemia any different than information on cancer? Information on filing discrimination suits should clearly be available to all patrons, but is this information to be filed in a special "Minority Concerns Section"? Further, it is unlikely that filing discrimination suits is a daily event in the lives of most black patrons. Like other members of the public library's clientele black patrons have many interests and concerns that have nothing to do with their racial or cultural background. Thinking back over my own admittedly somewhat limited experience working on a reference desk of a public library it seems that relatively few questions posed by black patrons were related to their racial or cultural identities. More often, like most patrons, their questions were connected with school, business, or home related projects. The point is that the content of the question doesn't really matter, the librarians responsibility is to answer it or at least to locate a source that will. Librarians do of course have to be sensitive to whatever factors effect the reference interview whether it be the patrons age, their grasp of English, a handicap, or anything that might effect the type, level or form of information provided. Cues of this sort must generally be recognized within a very brief period of time. It means that the librarian must assess the situation quickly and act accordingly. This is the librarians job, to assess the situation, to respond, and to treat all patrons equally.

Also emphasized in ALA's report is the need to recruit minority librarians. There is certainly evidence to suggest that minority groups have been discouraged from entering this profession as they have been discouraged from many others and that it is time this situation was corrected. However there seems to be an implication that for minority patrons, the best possible service depends upon the recruitment of librarians who are racially or culturally similar. For example, though I am a white female I do not feel it necessary in an unfamiliar library to seek out a white female librarian, nor would I feel it necessary if I had a question about Harriet Tubman to seek out a black librarian. I would assume that any capable reference librarian could direct me to appropriate sources. Moreover, it would be absurd to assume that a black librarian necessarily knows anything more about Harriet Tubman than I do.

This is not to suggest that efforts should not be made to recruit members of minority groups into library schools. There are many reasons why this is a good idea. However, the assumption that reference service to minorities will automatically be improved by these efforts should be examined closely. As librarians, we should be attempting to provide the best service possible to all patrons regardless of racial or cultural differences. We should all know the best sources in our libraries for information on Harriet Tubman and sickle cell anemia, not because we are providing multicultural services but because these are *basic* services.

CONCLUSION

It is the responsibility of public libraries to provide materials and services relevant to the needs of the communities they serve. If a community has a large Hispanic or Asian community, obviously attempts should be made to provide whatever services and materials that community wants. It is not my intent to suggest that specialized services are never appropriate, that bilingual materials should not be purchased, or that members of minority groups should not be encouraged to become librarians. Rather, the purpose of this discussion was to examine multiculturalism in education and librarianship; to question the role of public libraries in relation to social change, and finally, to debate some of the assumed benefits of various efforts that have been undertaken on behalf of minorities. The issue of advocacy in public libraries is worth close examination. The merit of the cause is not the point; it is important that public libraries remain neutral in relation to social issues at the same time that the needs of minority groups are addressed. In other words, assisting in the "empowerment" of any group has numerous implications which public institutions would do well to avoid. The point is not that cultural diversity be ignored but that the implications of multiculturalism for public institutions be fully understood. Blind acceptance of multiculturalism is not the answer.

REFERENCES

1. Sibyl E. Moses, ed. and comp., *Addressing Ethnic and Cultural Diversity: A Report on Activities of the American Library Association. 1986-1989.* (Chicago: American Library Association, 1990.)

2. Milton J. Gold, "Pressure Points in Multicultural Education," in *In Praise of Diversity: A Resource Book for Multicultural Education,* ed. Milton J. Gold, Carl A. Grant and Harry N. Rivlin (Washington, D. C.: Teacher Corps: Association of Teacher Educators, 1977), cited by Alfredo H. Benavides, "Social Responsibility: A Bilingual/Multicultural Perspective," in *Social Responsibility and*

Librarianship: Essays on Equality, ed. Donnarae MacCann (Jefferson, N.C.: McFarland and Co., 1989), p. 44.

3. Diane Ravitch, "Multiculturalism," *American Scholar* 59 (Summer 1990): 340.

4. Marcia J. Nauratil, *Public Libraries and Nontraditional Clienteles: The Politics of Special Services,* New Direction in Librarianship, no. 8 (Westport, Conn.: Greenwood Press, 1985), p. 109.

5. Ibid., p. 111.

6. Donnarae MacCann, "Libraries for Immigrants and 'Minorities': A Study in Contrasts" in *Social Responsibility and Librarianship: Essays on Equality,* p. 97.

7. Charlene Cain, "Public Library Service to Minorities," in *Adult Services: An Enduring Focus for Public Libraries,* ed. Kathleen M. Heim and Danny P. Wallace (Chicago: American Library Association, 1990), p. 216.

8. Ziggi Alexander, *Library Services and Afro-Caribbean Communities.* (London: Holmes McDougall Books, 1982), p. 51.

9. Haynes McMullen, "Service to Ethnic Minorities Other than Afro-Americans and American Indians," in *A Century of Service: Librarianship in the United States and Canada* cited by Cain, "Public Library Service to Minorities," p. 215.

10. Cain, "Public Library Service to Minorities," p. 217.

11. Ibid., p. 218.

12. Alexander, *Library Services and Afro-Caribbean Communities.* pp. 5-6.

13. New York State Special Task Force on Equity and Excellence in Education. *A Curriculum of Inclusion: Report of the Commissioner's Task Force on Minorities: Equity and Excellence* (ERIC Document Reproduction Service, ED 338 535, 1989), p. 6.

14. New York State Education Department, Albany, *One Nation, Many Peoples: A Declaration of Cultural Independence. The Report of the New York State Social Studies Review and Development Committee* (ERIC Document Reproduction Service, ED 338 536, 1991).

15. Paul Gray, "Whose America?" *Time,* 8 July 1991, p. 14.

16. Ravitch, "Multiculturalism," p. 351.

17. Ibid., pp. 339-340.

18. Gray, "Whose America?" p. 17.

19. Ravitch, "Multiculturalism," p. 351.

20. Arthur M. Schlesinger Jr., *The Disuniting of America* (New York: W.W. Norton & Co., 1992), p. 93.

21. Ravitch, "Multiculturalism," p. 351.

22. Ibid., p. 347; See Schlesinger, *The Disuniting of America,* p. 96. and Ravitch, "Multiculturalism," p. 354.

23. Arthur M. Schlesinger, Jr., in an interview with Frederic Smoker, "What Should We Teach Our Children About American History?" *American Heritage,* February/March 1992, p. 50.

24. Ibid., p. 52.

25. Ibid., p. 50.

26. The New York State Education Department, *One Nation, Many Peoples*, p. 1.

27. Moses, *Addressing Ethnic and Cultural Diversity*, p. 16.

28. Donnarae MacCann, "Libraries for Immigrants and 'Minorities': A Study in Contrasts," in *Social Responsibility in Librarianship*, p. 113.

29. Jaswinder Gundara and Ronald Warwick. "Myth or Reality," *Assistant Librarian* 74 (May 1981): p. 69, cited by Christine Talbot, "What is a Multicultural Library Service? *Library Association Record* 92 (July 1990): p. 501.

30. Donnarae MacCann, Introduction to *Social Responsibility in Librarianship*, pp. 1-2.

31. David Berninghausen, "Social Responsibility vs. The Library Bill of Rights," *Library Journal* 97 (November 15, 1972): 3675, cited by MacCann, *Social Responsibility in Librarianship*, p. 2.

32. Moses, *Addressing Ethnic and Cultural Diversity*, p. 23.

33. Ibid., p. 17.

34. Ibid., p. 16.

35. Ibid.

36. Nauratil, *Public Libraries and Nontraditional Clienteles*, p. 123.

37. Schlesinger, "What Should We Teach Our Children About American History?" p. 47.

38. Schlesinger, *The Disuniting of America*, p. 108.

39. Alfredo H. Benavides, "Social Responsibility: A Bilingual/Multicultural Perspective," in *Social Responsibility in Librarianship*, p. 48.

40. Ibid., p. 49.

41. Schlesinger, *The Disuniting of America*, p. 108.

42. Nauratil, *Public Libraries and Nontraditional Clienteles*, p. 120.

43. Ibid., p. 121.

44. David B. Carlson et al., *Adrift in A Sea of Change: California's Public Libraries Struggle to Meet the Information Needs of Multicultural Communities*, Partnerships for Change Series, no. 2 (Center for Policy Development, 1990) p. 32.

45. Ibid., p. 25.

46. Ibid., vi.

Reference Sources
and American Ethnic Groups:
A Critical Mini-Overview

Vladimir F. Wertsman

SUMMARY. America is by its very nature of historical formation and development a multiethnic, multicultural and multilingual society, and in the last two decades an upsurge of general interest in ethnicity has stimulated publishers to substantially increase the production of books devoted to ethnic Americans.

However, a closer examination of publisher's output–over 20 noted titles ranging from encyclopedias and specialized titles covering ethnic organizations, institutions, periodicals, statistics and book series by leading publishers–reveals that the overall picture is still far from being satisfactory. The truth is that, with very few exceptions, reference books are either outdated, incomplete by leaving many ethnic groups without coverage, or confusing.

There is a profound need for a comprehensive encyclopedia of American ethnic groups *covering all groups* (small and large) with balanced entries, and using latest census data (1990) combined with ethnic organizations sources. Publishers should also publish a handbook and brochures covering all American ethnic groups, and thus make the American ethnic mosaic accessible to all levels and specific needs of vicinities, districts, regions, states.

Vladimir F. Wertsman is Senior Librarian, Mid-Manhattan Library, The New York Public Library, 455 Fifth Avenue, New York, NY 10016.

[Haworth co-indexing entry note]: "Reference Sources and American Ethnic Groups: A Critical Mini-Overview," Wertsman, Vladimir F. Co-published simultaneously in *The Acquisitions Librarian* (The Haworth Press, Inc.) No. 9/10, 1993, pp. 21-27; and: *Multicultural Acquisitions* (ed: Karen Parrish and Bill Katz) The Haworth Press, Inc., 1993, pp. 21-27. Multiple copies of this article/chapter may be purchased from The Haworth Document Delivery Center. Call 1-800-3-HAWORTH (1-800-342-9678) between 9:00 - 5:00 (EST) and ask for DOCUMENT DELIVERY CENTER.

INTRODUCTION

America has been by its very nature of historical formation and development a "teaming of nations"(Walt Whitman), a multiethnic, multicultural and multilingual society. Despite the continuous and irreversible effects of the "melting pot" factor (acculturation, assimilation, mixed marriages) several dozens of millions Americans have preserved–in various degrees–not only the customs and religion of their predecessors, but also the costumes, popular art and music, and especially the languages of their parents, grand or grand-grand parents who came virtually from all continents. America is, in essence, an ethnic microcosm of the entire world.

During the last two decades, an upsurge of general interest in ethnicity (search for ethnic roots, manifestations of ethnic pride in various forms, inclusion of ethnic studies in high school and college curricula) have stimulated publishers to substantially increase the production of books devoted to ethnic Americans. However, a closer examination of publisher's output reveals that presently coverage on American ethnic groups–as shown in continuation–is still far from being satisfactory.

ENCYCLOPEDIAS

Encyclopedia Americana (Grollier, 1991) and *World Book Encyclopedia* (World Book, 1991), so popular among adult and student researchers, have only very small "ethnic group" entries. The same is true of *New Book of Knowledge* (Grollier, 1991), and *Academic American Encyclopedia* (Grollier, 1990), both used by younger readers, while *International Encyclopedia* (Lexicon Publications, 1977) and *Merit Student's Encyclopedia* (Macmillan, 1991) have no entries at all. In addition, some information is incomplete or wrong. For instance, the Americana correctly shows that "ethnic groups are especially numerous in countries inhabited by people of different national origins" and yet makes no express, or at least SEE reference to the USA population, and in the section dealing with the American people uses 1970 Census data. World Book considers that in our country the term ethnic group refers "especially to nationality groups that immigrated to America since about 1840" even though it is well known long before that date America's population already encompassed Blacks, Native Americans, Spanish, French, Dutch, German, Scottish, Irish, Polish and other groups. The most comprehensive reference tool on ethnic Americans is *Harvard Encyclopedia of American Ethnic Groups* (Belknap Press, 1980) covering over 100 groups and certainly marking an important scholarly achievement, but some entries are not balanced (too large or too small). For example, Indonesians are treated only in a few lines, while other small groups (Cossacks) are given extensive space. Then, Mormons are treated like an ethnic group even though they constitute a religious body. Central and South Americans are treated in one generic entry rather than treating each group (e.g., Salvadorian Americans, Ecuadorian Americans, Brazilian Americans, etc.) separately as were so many European groups. Finally, the book is based on 1970 Census data, therefore, 20 years behind the latest (1990) census.

SPECIALIZED REFERENCE

Building Ethnic Collections: An Annotated Guide for School Media Centers and Public Libraries (Libraries Unlimited, 1977), edited by L. Buttlar and L. Wynar, covers over 50 ethnic groups, but several groups are treated generically (e.g., Arab Americans, Asian Americans, Slavic Americans, etc.) instead of being individualized as were the majority of included groups.

S. Bernardo's *Ethnic Almanac* (Doubleday, 1981) with short coverage of over 40 ethnic groups (some statistics, noted ethnics, short sketches, bibliography and trivia) and still useful to some extent, is based on 1970 Census data and its methodology is debatable.

S. Cardasco's *American Ethnic Groups, The European Heritage: A Bibliography of Doctoral Dissertations Completed at American Universities* (Scarecrow, 1981) lists 1,400 dissertations covering over 30 groups from various parts of Europe, but many entries consist of only author and title without any annotation.

R. Georges covers 56 groups (42 European, 13 Asian, 1 African) in his valuable *American and Canadian Immigrant Ethnic Folklore: An Annotated Bibliography* (Garland, 1982), but it leaves room for a companion volume for coverage of dozens of other ethnic groups which were not included.

Ethnic Studies in Higher Education: State of the Art and Bibliography (American Association of State College Universities, 1972) is obviously dated.

ORGANIZATIONS AND INSTITUTIONS

L. Wynar's *Guide to Ethnic Museums, Libraries, and Archives in the United States (*Kent State University, School of Library Science 1978) (and *Encyclopedic Directory of Ethnic Organizations (*Libraries Unlimited, 1975) although covering 60 and respective 70 groups, are obsolete, and newer editions are long overdue.

Ethnic Information Sources of the United States (Gale, 1983), Paul Wasserman, ed., with its ample coverage of about 100 groups (organizations, cultural institutions, programs, libraries, firms, travel agencies, and bibliographic sources) is outdated for a long time, and no effort has been made to issue a new, revised and improved edition.

Presently, the only and best source of information, compared to all previous items, is *Encyclopedia of Associations (*Gale, 1991) covering over 100 groups, with addresses, telephones, and short descriptions of their activities and purpose. However, one has to be aware that many ethnic organizations are not included because they did not answer editorial questionnaires or were not interested for other reasons.

PERIODICALS

The seventh edition of *Magazines for Libraries* (New York: R.R. Bowker, 1992) has several sections of interest. All include individual descriptive and evaluative annotations of basic periodicals covering various ethnic groups, such as Asian Americans. The guide is invaluable for intelligent selection of the best periodicals.

Standard Periodical Directory (Oxbridge, 1992) lists hundreds of ethnic periodicals and covers over 60 ethnic groups arranged in alphabetical order. It is regrettable not only that several dozens of groups were overlooked, but also the inclusion of erroneous information. For instance, the Romanians figure with only 2 periodicals, and over a dozen of Romanian titles were mixed up with Russian titles under the heading "Russians" (pp. 558-59). On the other hand, there are only few Russian titles, even though this group was extremely prolific in the last two decades (at least 50-60 active periodicals).

The *Editor and Publisher International Year Book* (Editor and Publisher, 1991) has a section "Ethnic Newspapers Published in the United States" which covers only 35 groups and these very superficially. *The Ethnic Press in the United States: A Historical Analysis and Handbook* (Greenwood, 1987), S. Miller, ed., has good background coverage and bibliographies, but it is limited to only 27 groups, mostly of European origin. Also covering 30 European American groups (interesting articles, statistics and bibliographies) is D. Hoerder's *The Immigrant Labor Press in North America, 1840's-1970's: An Annotated Bibliography* (Greenwood, 1987) consisting of a three volume set, with relevant indexes. L. Wynar's *Encyclopedic Directory of Ethnic Newspapers and Periodicals in the United States* (Libraries Unlimited, 1976) is outdated and covers only 50 groups, some generically (Asian, Scandinavian, Spanish, etc.).

BOOK SERIES ON INDIVIDUAL GROUPS

Oceana published "Ethnic Chronology Series" encompassing over 30 ethnic groups, and destined for high school and junior college students. Each volume contains a chronology of main events, relevant documents, bibliography, statistics and other materials. Gale Research put out "Ethnic Studies Information Series"– with ample annotated bibliographies and other materials of interest to scholars and college students–but discontinued it after covering only 7 groups (mostly European).

Facts on File issued "Teacher's Guide for Lerner Ethnic Studies Library" series for junior high school students, but covered only two dozen groups (background, immigration, contributions to America, illustrations), while Learner produced "In America Series" with similar information covering over 30 groups only. Millbrook, which recently (1991) published *Ethnic America* four volume set, part of "American Scene Series," encompasses very short, confusing and some even ethnically offensive sketches *(Booklist,* January 15, 1992, p. 935).

The most ample coverage (number of covered ethnic groups) is currently offered by Chelsea House in its "People of North America Series" dealing with several dozen groups, their immigration, settlement, contributions, bibliographies, plus illustrations. Some groups, such as Iberian Americans, are treated generically or ethnicity is confused with country of origin. Perhaps what is needed is the devoting of a book to each group (e.g. Spanish, Portuguese).

STATISTICS

Statistical Abstracts and U.S. Census data recorded immigrants by country of origin, completely disregarding the ethnic composition of immigrants. For instance, let's take Russia (formerly U.S.S.R.). The fact that during a given year a country figures with a specific number of immigrants does not mean that all were Russians, even though they were born in Russia. Among the immigrants from Russia were Ukrainians, Jews, Georgians, Armenians, and other ethnics. To equate the number of immigrants from a given country with the number of ethnics of the same country is wrong and misleading. On the other hand, figures provided by ethnic organizations are also not completely accurate. They tend to exaggerate the numeric composition of their communities. Therefore, the researchers must try to combine official United States statistics, with ethnic sources, and with other independent sources to arrive at more or less objective conclusions, especially in cases of mixed marriages, when children may adopt the ethnic affiliation of either of the parents, or opt to be just an American.

We the People of America: An Atlas of America's Ethnic Diversity (Macmillan, 1988), J.P. James and E. James, eds., identifying American ethnic groups with statistical data, both on national and regional scales, as well as in important cities, is based on 1980 U.S. Census data, and, therefore outdated in light of the last (1990) statistics.

CONCLUSION

Most reference books on American ethnic groups–with very few exceptions–are either outdated, incomplete by leaving many groups without coverage, or confusing (ethnicity is confused with country of origin, and in some cases ethnicity is limited only to some minorities);

- There is a profound need for a comprehensive encyclopedia of American ethnic groups, *covering all groups (*well over 150) from A to Z, with balanced entries (no group is too small to be recorded) and relevant bibliographies, and statistical data culled from the 1990 Census data combined with ethnic organization sources;
- A condensed version of the encyclopedia (in the form of a handbook) should be produced for high school and college students, so that the American ethnic mosaique be easier accessible;
- Each ethnic group (large or small) should also be covered in a series of brochures (a brochure for each group) so that schools could select materials covering the specific needs of a given neighborhood, district, region, state, etc. No ethnic group is too small to be neglected as long as it has its own heritage, culture and specific forms of expression;
- Publishers should be encouraged–via grants and by combining resources with interested organizations–to publish more on ethnic groups, both quantatively and qualitatively.

Developing Media Collections to Serve Multicultural/Multiethnic Communities

Barbara L. Flynn

SUMMARY. This article focuses on the necessity for building well-rounded media collections as a means of promoting multicultural/multiethnic understanding and appreciation. Beginning with a definition of the term "multicultural," it then moves on to the need for a media collection to supplement the already established print collections of the library. Guidelines for the selection of multicultural/multiethnic media are included. While no specific 16mm film or videocassette titles are given in the article, the listing of resource guides and review media will give readers the information needed to locate the materials needed to build strong collections.

INTRODUCTION

As recent census figures demonstrate, the United States currently is home to the greatest number of foreign born individuals in its history.[1] This change in the population make-up of our cities and

Barbara L. Flynn is Administrative Librarian, Park Forest Public Library, 400 Lakewood, Park Forest, IL 60466.

[Haworth co-indexing entry note]: "Developing Media Collections to Serve Multicultural/Multiethnic Communities," Flynn, Barbara L. Co-published simultaneously in *The Acquisitions Librarian* (The Haworth Press, Inc.) No. 9/10, 1993, pp. 29-40; and: *Multicultural Acquisitions* (ed: Karen Parrish and Bill Katz) The Haworth Press, Inc., 1993, pp. 29-40. Multiple copies of this article/chapter may be purchased from The Haworth Document Delivery Center. Call 1-800-3-HAWORTH (1-800-342-9678) between 9:00 - 5:00 (EST) and ask for DOCUMENT DELIVERY CENTER.

towns across the country offers new challenges to libraries and librarians as we try to meet the information needs of these new residents. While this is true all across the country, it is particularly true in our large urban areas such as Los Angeles, Miami, Washington, D.C., and Chicago, among others, which have seen the greatest influx of newcomers between 1980 and 1990.

As we attempt to serve these diverse populations, we face a two-fold task. The first is to supply information and materials in both English and the native language of each ethnic group. The second is to provide information on all ethnic groups to all library users. Not only is it necessary to provide the printed word, but also the adjunct media services that help to present the whole picture. It is the provision of these materials (specifically videocassettes and 16mm film programs) that is the focus of this article.

SCOPE OF THE ARTICLE

This article will cover the following points:

1. A definition of the term multicultural/multiethnic. This definition will be the operative one throughout the article. The various sources used to formulate this definition will also be cited.
2. A discussion of the need for well-rounded media collections which will serve as a supplement to the already established print collections. (For the purposes of this article, I use the term "media" to refer to videocassettes and 16mm films only.) This is not meant to convey the idea that non-print collections do not already exist in the majority of libraries. They do. My intent here is to highlight sources of multicultural/multiethnic videocassette and 16mm film programs. These programs can be used to strengthen already existing collections and to build others.
3. In addition to highlighting sources of multicultural/multiethnic programs, review sources for these programs will also be listed. Some basic guidelines for selection will also be included.

The article will conclude with a bibliography of resources, including both sources of materials and review sources.

This is in no way meant to be the final word on building multicultural/multiethnic media collections. In writing this article I have drawn on the work done by others over the years. What follows is meant to be a very basic approach to multicultural/multiethnic media collection building. The reader will find, when consulting the references and resources listed, a wealth of materials and information from which to build a media collection.

DEFINING MULTICULTURAL/MULTIETHNIC

There has been much discussion in the literature of just which groups of people we are and are not speaking of when we use the word multicultural. While many people seem to feel that the term multicultural encompasses four groups: African-American, Asian-American, Hispanic-American, and Native American, others do not agree. It is true that these four ethnic groups were the focus of the *Report of the Task Force on Library and Information Service to Cultural Minorities*. It is also true, however, that the report made it a point to mention the necessity for libraries to provide for the information needs of other minority groups.[2] This is in keeping with the mission of libraries to provide for the information needs of all of its users.

The U.S. Commission on Civil Rights, in a 1981 statement about civil rights and Euro-Ethnic Americans stressed the fact that American society is "multiracial, multifaith, multicultural, and multilingual."[3] This takes in all the various ethnic groups in America.

Speaking at a forum entitled "The Multicultural Library: The Way of the Future," Danilo H. Figueredo, Director of the Bloomfield College Library (New Jersey), also addressed the definition of multicultural, stating that a multicultural framework encompassed more than just minority groups. In his view, "a multicultural society includes everyone."[4]

Patricia Beilke, writing in the Spring, 1992 issue of the EMIE Bulletin, called attention to the various definitions of the word multicultural currently in use, and stressed that we must be aware of all these varied definitions in order to better understand various groups and their viewpoints.[5]

All of this points out very clearly that there is no one easy definition for the term multicultural. For the purposes of this article, I have taken the broadest, most inclusive definition of multicultural, and have included the term multiethnic as a further clarifier. Thus, multicultural/multiethnic includes people of all races and ethnic groups.

THE NEED FOR MEDIA COLLECTIONS

The need for strong media collections has been stressed again and again, most recently by Phyllis Levy Mandell in her "Cultural Diversity Videos Part 1–African Americans." Writing in the introduction to that work, she stresses the need for "visual documentation of our multicultural diversity," saying that these programs are necessary in our libraries to a greater extent than ever before.[6]

These sentiments are echoed in a statement made by the Regional Director of B'nai B'rith (San Francisco), speaking during the hearings of the Task Force on Library and Information Services to Cultural Minorities which were held at the American Library Association Conference in San Francisco, CA, in 1981. In her remarks she spoke of the need to build positive feelings for all ethnic groups and to celebrate the things we share in common rather than dwelling on the things that are different.[7]

Visual media allows us to see other groups, not only read about them. It is in the seeing that each group becomes more real and their similarities and differences to all other groups more easily recognized and, hopefully, appreciated and understood.

We are a visually oriented society. Whether we like it or not, many people who rarely read a book watch television or prerecorded videocassette programs. There is a wealth of material on videocassette (and 16mm film) covering a multitude of subjects. People of all ages and all economic and social groups make use of these materials. They learn how to remodel a kitchen, care for a new puppy, or plant a garden. They visit the world from the comfort of an easy chair. They learn more about science, politics, or finance. They explore the world of history, or learn about the life of a famous figure in history, all through the convenience of a VCR.

Videocassettes and 16mm films enable the viewer to go beyond the printed word, and to further examine or study a subject or topic of interest. In so doing, new facts, not yet in book form, might be presented, for video in particular has a timeliness that books find it hard to match, due to the length of time for publication.

In addition, visual media has a language, indeed, is a language all its own. It can be enjoyed, and to a great extent understood, regardless of its spoken language. This enables it to cross barriers of illiteracy, etc., and provide information for those unable to read well, or for those with a limited grasp of written English.

Another point that cannot be overlooked when underscoring the need for media as well as print materials are the special characteristics of media, one of which has already been mentioned briefly, its appeal to nonreaders. But the most important is the fact that visual media is able to present some information better than the printed word. Think of the visual beauty of the Grand Canyon, the might of a volcano, the destructive power of a rampaging mob. However one might verbally describe such things or events, most of us would agree that nothing can surpass seeing them; a visual makes such a lasting impression.[8]

EVALUATION OF MATERIALS

Videocassettes and 16mm films require the same careful assessment as books. Librarians are obligated to respond to the needs of their communities with materials that provide the information required, and do so in the best possible way. Writing in the February, 1992 issue of *Wilson Library Bulletin,* Shelley Quezada addresses this need, and then goes on to talk about the importance of having materials available all year long, not just making them available for special events, i.e., to commemorate a birthday, or an event in history. She sees this type of event or programming as "cultural tourism" which gives limited attention to the needs of the ethnic or minority population being served.[9]

Keeping in mind this necessity for careful assessment of videocassette and/or 16mm films, the following are some cautions and guidelines to observe when choosing multicultural/multiethnic materials for a collection (or for programming).

Evaluation Guidelines

1. What is the intent of the filmmaker–why has this program been produced, and what does the filmmaker hope to accomplish?
2. Is the program well made?
3. What is the theme? What values are being presented?
4. What is the intended audience?
5. Does the program give a true representation of the groups portrayed? Does it portray the good qualities of a specific group as well as any weak points? Is it a realistic portrayal of all concerned?
6. Does the program avoid stereotypes of either persons or themes?
7. Does the language avoid artificial or stereotypical dialects or idioms? Is the dialogue free of derogatory words or phrases? Does it avoid condescension?
8. Are the visuals free of inaccuracies and/or distortions? How do the people dress? What do their houses look like, and so on.
9. Are the distinctive qualities of each group shown, but not in a stereotyped fashion?
10. Is there a good ethnic balance in the production?
11. Does the presentation of each group reinforce positive images?[10]

Using these guidelines, in conjunction with printed reviews and the information given in various resource guides will help to insure that the library media collection will be of value to users, promoting positive images of all ethnic groups and helping to erase both conscious and unconscious stereotypes.

A WORD ABOUT RESOURCE GUIDES AND REVIEW MEDIA

The following listing of resource guides/review media is broken down into three parts: Resource Guides–General, Resource Guides–Specific, and Review Media. A few words of explanation about each may be in order.

General resource guides include entries in all subject areas. In addition to a title listing for each entry, information is also given as to running time, production date, grade level, producer, and distributor. An annotation is included. This may be brief, as in the case of the *Film and Video Finder*, or longer, as in the *Educational Film and Video Locator.*

Specific resource guides include only programs on a specific subject. The same general information is given for each title. Some of the volumes in this section are filmographies only, that is, they list only program titles with little other commentary or explanation. Some sources, such as *Latino Materials: A Multimedia Guide for Children and Young Adults* contains essays as well as filmographies.

Finally, review media contains a listing of various periodicals and other sources and is a good place to start when looking for reviews of multicultural/multiethnic materials. It is important to remember that these lists are merely places to start–they are not the only materials available. In choosing specific resource guides, I have taken care to be sure that no title cited is more than 20 years old. The need for retrospective collections means that one must have access to the old as well as the new, hence the inclusion of items which some might consider to be too old.

Librarians have a duty to become familiar with filmmakers, distributors, and review sources, as was so well stated by Roberto Trujillo and Linda Chavez in a recent article.[11] Beginning with the sources listed, and adding new information as it becomes available will give each librarian the tools necessary in collection building.

RESOURCE GUIDES

General

Berger, James L., ed. EDUCATORS GUIDE TO FREE AUDIO AND VIDEO MATERIALS. 38th Edition. Randolph, WI: Educators Progress Service, Inc., 1991.

BOWKER'S COMPLETE VIDEO DIRECTORY 1990. 2 vol. New York: R.R. Bowker, 1990.

Diffor, John C. and Elaine N. Diffor, eds. EDUCATORS GUIDE TO FREE FILMS. 51st Edition. Randolph, WI: Educators Progress Service, Inc., 1991.

EDUCATIONAL FILM AND VIDEO LOCATOR (of the Consortium of College and University Media Centers and R.R. Bowker), 4th Edition, 1990-1991. 2 vol. New York: R.R. Bowker, 1990.

FILM AND VIDEO FINDER. 3rd Edition. 3 vol. Medford, N.J.: Plexus Publishing Inc., (for National Information Center for Educational Media), 1991.

Monush, Barry, ed. INTERNATIONAL MOTION PICTURE ALMANAC. 61st Edition. New York: Quigley Publishing Company, Inc., 1991.

Monush, Barry, ed. INTERNATIONAL TELEVISION AND VIDEO ALMANAC. 36th Edition. New York: Quigley Publishing Company, Inc., 1991.

Weiner, David J., ed. THE VIDEO SOURCE BOOK. 2 vol. Detroit: Gale Research Inc., 1990.

Specific

American Film Institute. THE NATIVE AMERICAN IMAGE ON FILM: A PROGRAMMER'S GUIDE. Washington, D.C.. The American Film Institute, 1980.

Bataille, Gretchen M. and Charles L.P. Silet, eds. THE PRETEND INDIANS: IMAGES OF NATIVE AMERICANS IN THE MOVIES. Ames, IA: Iowa State University Press, 1980.

THE BLACK VIDEO GUIDE. St. Louis, MO: Video Publications Ltd., 1985.

Butler, Lucius A. and Chaesoon T. Youngs. FILMS FOR KOREAN STUDIES: A GUIDE TO ENGLISH LANGUAGE FILMS ABOUT KOREA. Honolulu: University of Hawaii, Center for Korean Studies, 1978.

Buttlar, Lois and Lubomyr R. Wynar. BUILDING ETHNIC COLLECTIONS: AN ANNOTATED GUIDE FOR SCHOOL MEDIA CENTERS AND PUBLIC LIBRARIES. Littleton, CO: Libraries Unlimited, Inc., 1977.

Center for Southern Folklore. AMERICAN FOLKLORE FILMS AND VIDEOTAPES, A CATALOG. Volume II. New York: R. R. Bowker, 1982.

Chavaria, Elvira, ed., CHICANO FILM GUIDE. 2nd Edition. Austin, TX: Mexican American Library Program, the University of Texas at Austin, 1983.

CHICANO RESOURCE CENTER FILM GUIDE. Revised Edition. Los Angeles County Public Library, 1983.

Cohen, David, ed. EMIE BULLETIN. Chicago: Ethnic Materials and Information Exchange Round Table of the American Library Association. (Volume 9, #3, Spring, 1992).

Cohen, David. MULTI-ETHNIC MEDIA: SELECTED BIBLIOGRAPHIES IN PRINT. Chicago: American Library Association, 1975.

Cyr, Helen W. A FILMOGRAPHY OF THE THIRD WORLD: AN ANNOTATED LIST OF 16MM FILMS. Metuchen, NJ: The Scarecrow Press, Inc., 1976.

Flores Duran, Daniel. LATINO MATERIALS: A MULTIMEDIA GUIDE FOR CHILDREN AND YOUNG ADULTS. New York: Neal-Schuman Publishers, Inc., 1979.

Grunman, Joseph and Ann Joachim. EDUCATIONAL FILM GUIDE FOR MIDDLE EASTERN STUDIES. Ann Arbor, MI: University of Michigan, The Center for Near Eastern and North African Studies, 1980.

Heider, Karl G. FILMS FOR ANTHROPOLOGICAL TEACHING. 7th Edition. Washington, D.C.: American Anthropological Association, 1983.

Hyatt, Marshall, ed. THE AFRO-AMERICAN CINEMATIC EXPERIENCE: AN

ANNOTATED BIBLIOGRAPHY AND FILMOGRAPHY. Wilmington, DE: Scholarly Resources, Inc., 1983.

Johnson, Harry A. ETHNIC AMERICAN MINORITIES. New York: R.R. Bowker, 1976.

LA RAZA IN FILMS. Oakland, CA: Latin American Library of the Oakland Public Library, 1972. Supplement, 1974.

Mandell, Phyllis Levy, comp. "Cultural Diversity Videos–Part I: African-Americans." *School Library Journal,* January, 1992, pp. 49-65.

Mandell, Phyllis Levy, comp. "Cultural Diversity Videos–Part II: Native Americans." *School Library Journal,* May, 1992, pp. 63-69.

Powers, Anne, ed. BLACKS IN AMERICAN MOVIES: A SELECTED BIBLIOGRAPHY. Metuchen, NJ: The Scarecrow Press, Inc., 1974.

Sable, Martin H. A GUIDE TO NONPRINT MATERIALS FOR LATIN AMERICAN STUDIES. Detroit: Blaine-Ethridge Books, 1979.

Sive, Mary Robinson. CHINA: A MULTIMEDIA GUIDE. New York: Neal-Schuman Publishers, Inc., 1982.

Westherford, Elizabeth, ed. NATIVE AMERICANS ON FILM AND VIDEO. New York: Museum of the American Indian, 1981.

Wiley, David S. AFRICA ON FILM AND VIDEOTAPE 1960-1981: A COMPENDIUM OF REVIEWS. East Lansing, MI: Michigan State University African Studies Center, 1982.

Review Media

BOOKLIST. ISSN 0006-7385. Editor: Bill Ott. American Library Association, 50 East Huron Street, Chicago, IL 60611. Monthly (except July & August). $56.

LANDERS FILM REVIEWS. Landers Associates, P.O. Box 300309, Escondido, CA 92030-0309. Quarterly.

LIBRARY JOURNAL. ISSN 0363-00277. Editor: John N. Berry, III. Cahners Publishing Company. Library Journal, P.O. Box 1977, Marion, OH 43305-1977. 21x/year. $74.

MEDIA REVIEW DIGEST. Ann Arbor, MI: The Perian Press, 1990. (See also previous volumes.)

MULTICULTURAL REVIEW. (Vol. 1, No. 1; January, 1992). ISSN 1058-9236. Editor: Brenda Mitchell-Powell. Greenwood Publishing Group, Inc., 88 Post Road W., P.O. Box 5007, Westport, CT 06881-5007. Quarterly. $59.

SCHOOL LIBRARY JOURNAL. ISSN 0362-8930. Editor: Lillian N. Gerhardt. Cahners Publishing Company. School Library Journal, P.O. Box 1978, Marion, OH 43305-1978. 10x/year. $63.

VIDEO LIBRARIAN. ISSN 0887-6851. Editor: Randy Pitman. Video Librarian, P.O. Box 2725, Bremerton, WA 98310. Monthly (combined in July & August). $35.

VIDEO RATING GUIDE FOR LIBRARIES. ISSN 1045-3393. ABC-Clio, Inc., 130 Cremona Drive, Santa Barbara, CA 93117. Quarterly. $110.

VOICE OF YOUTH ADVOCATES (VOYA). ISSN 0160-4201. Editor: Dorothy

M. Broderick. Scarecrow Press, Inc., Dept. VOYA, 52 Liberty Street, P.O. Box 4167, Metuchen, NJ 08840. Bi-monthly, April-February. $32.50.

WILSON LIBRARY BULLETIN. ISSN 0043-5651. Editor: Mary Jo Godwin. H.W. Wilson Company, 950 University Avenue, Bronx, NY 10452. Monthly (except July & August). $50.

CONCLUSION

All of us, librarians and non-librarians alike, must learn more about the many ethnic groups who call the United States home. We need to examine our understanding of the meaning of cultural diversity and its importance to each one of us.

As each of us learns more, we may, as Mary E. Nelles and Dorothy B. Simon said in a 1984 article about multiculturalism in libraries, begin to enjoy and really appreciate what we learn, and this enjoyment may in turn help to reduce ethnocentrism and aid in promoting international harmony.[12]

In closing, I find it necessary to comment on programs in languages other than English. In building collections, all the needs of the community should be addressed, including the desire for programs in various languages. When doing evaluation and selection, this must be kept in mind and materials in languages other than English should be included as needed. Margaret King Van Duyne and Debra Jacobs addressed this very well in their article "Embracing Diversity: One With One's Bold New Partnerships." Among other things, they point out the important boost that videos from home can bring to those who are struggling with a new country and a new way of life.[13]

Libraries can take a leading role in promoting multicultural/multiethnic understanding. Providing strong multicultural/multiethnic collections is a step in the right direction.

REFERENCES

1. Barbara Vobejda, "U.S. Profile Finds Surge in Diversity," *Chicago Sun-Times,* May 31, 1992, p. 27.

2. United States. Task Force on Library and Information Services to Cultural Minorities. *Report of the Task Force on Library and Information Services to Cultural Minorities,* 1983, p. 100.

3. U.S. Commission on Civil Rights. *Statement on the Civil Rights Issues of Euro-ethnic Americans,* January, 1981. Washington, D.C.: U.S. Government Printing Office, 1981, p. 1.

4. "Bloomfield College Hosts 'The Multicultural Library: The Way of the Future.'" *College and Research Library News,* 52:446, July/August, 1991.

5. Patricia Beilke, "Multicultural Definitions Vary, Be Wary," *EMIE Bulletin,* 9:1, Spring, 1992.

6. Phyllis Levy Mandell, "Cultural Diversity Videos–Part I: African-Americans," *School Library Journal,* January, 1991, p. 49.

7. United States. Task Force on Library and Information Services to Cultural Minorities. *Hearings.* Held at the American Library Association Annual Conference, San Francisco, CA, 1981. Statement of Rhonda Abrams, Regional Director, Anti-Defamation League of B'nai B'rith, p. 76.

8. Sheila S. Intner, "Access to Nonbook Material: Implications for Libraries." In *Unequal Access to Information Resources: Problems and Needs of The World's Information Poor.* Edited by Jovian Lang, OFM. Ann Arbor, MI: Pierian Press, 1988, p. 17.

9. Shelley Quesada, "Mainstreaming Library Services to Multicultural Populations: the Emerging Tapestry," *Wilson Library Bulletin,* 66:29, February, 1992.

10. Mary C. Austin and Esther C. Jenkins. *Promoting World Understanding Through Literature,* K-8. Littleton, CO: Libraries Unlimited, 1983, pp. 5-11.

11. Roberto G. Trujillo and Linda Chavez, "Collection Development on the Mexican-American Experience." In *Latino Librarianship: A Handbook for Professionals.* Edited by Salvador Guerena. Jefferson, NC: McFarland and Company, Inc., Publishers, 1990, p. 79.

12. Mary E. Nilles and Dorothy B. Simon, "New Approaches to the MultiLingual, Multi-Cultural Students in Your Library," *Catholic Library World,* May/June, 1984, p. 438.

13. Margaret King Van Duyne and Debra Jacobs, "Embracing Diversity: One With One's Bold New Partnerships," Wilson Library Bulletin, 66:42, February, 1992.

ADDITIONAL BIBLIOGRAPHY

Adams, Robert Mc. "Media and Multicultural Education." Address given at INFOCOMM Opening General Session, Washington, D.C., February 5, 1992.

Betancourt, Ingrid. "The Babel Myth: The English-Only Movement and Its Implication for Libraries." *Wilson Library Bulletin.* 66:38+. February, 1992.

Chavez, Linda. "Collection Development for the Spanish Speaking." In *Latino Librarianship: A Handbook for Professionals.* Edited by Salvador Guerena. Jefferson, NC: McFarland and Company, Inc., Publishers, 1990. pp. 68-77.

Fish, James. "Responding to Cultural Diversity: A Library in Transition." *Wilson Library Bulletin.* 66:34+. February, 1992.

Guerena, Salvador, ed. *Latino Librarianship: A Handbook for Professionals.* Jefferson, NC: McFarland and Company, Inc., Publishers, 1990.

Kruse, Ginny Moore. "No Single Season: Multicultural Literature for All Children." *Wilson Library Bulletin.* 66:30. February, 1992.

Mitchell-Powell, Brenda. "From the Editor." *Multicultural Review.* 1:1, January, 1992.

Price, Neville. "Cultural Differences and Library Services." *Library Association Record.* 92:377+.

Scarborough, Katharine. "Collections for the Emerging Majority." Library Journal. 116:44. June 15, 1991.

Stern, Stephen. "Ethnic Libraries and Librarianship in the U.S.: Models and Prospects." In *Advances In Librarianship*, Volume 15. Edited by Irene P. Godden. San Diego: Academic Press, Inc., 1991.

Talbot, Christine. "What is Multicultural Library Service?" *Library Association Record.* 92:501+ July, 1990.

Trujillo, Roberto G. and Yolanda J. Cuesta. "Services to Diverse Populations." In ALA *Yearbook of Library and Information Services*, Volume 14, 1989. Chicago: American Library Association, 1989.

The Genesis of *MultiCultural Review*

Brenda Mitchell-Powell

SUMMARY. *MultiCultural Review* is a personal response to a combination of professional objectives synthesized and formulated to effect cognitive and experiential change in the attitudes, perspectives, and orientations of public- and private-sector librarians, educators, and administrators charged with responding to the challenge of American cultural diversity. The conception of the *Review* is based on the hope that the presentation of information and resources in an objective forum, unencumbered by a political agenda, will facilitate and encourage dialogues and guidelines which sensitize professionals, students, scholars, and lay people to the experience and potential of pluralism.

ENCOUNTERS OF THE MULTICULTURAL KIND

Several years ago, a writer colleague telephoned my office to ask for feedback on an article she was preparing for a national book review. She expressed concern that the editor of the review, a person who she assumed brought years of personal and profession-

Brenda Mitchell-Powell was awarded a BA with honors from Simmons College, Boston, MA, in 1975. She is president of Orange Ball Corporation and publisher of Orange Ball Press (P.O. Box 3155, Westport, CT 06880), and editor-in-chief of *MultiCultural Review* (10 Bay Street, Westport, CT 06880).

[Haworth co-indexing entry note]: "The Genesis of *MultiCultural Review*," Mitchell-Powell, Brenda. Co-published simultaneously in *The Acquisitions Librarian* (The Haworth Press, Inc.) No. 9/10, 1993, pp. 41-46; and: *Multicultural Acquisitions* (ed: Karen Parrish and Bill Katz) The Haworth Press, Inc., 1993, pp. 41-46. Multiple copies of this article/chapter may be purchased from The Haworth Document Delivery Center. Call 1-800-3-HAWORTH (1-800-342-9678) between 9:00 - 5:00 (EST) and ask for DOCUMENT DELIVERY CENTER.

41

al experience to a demanding job, reacted with bafflement to a query regarding names of candidates to be interviewed for the feature.

My friend wanted to know of my experiences with the editor in question. Did I find the editor's knowledge far-ranging and intuitive? Were opinions valid and assessments sound? Could she expect encouragement and enthusiasm for suggestions of alternative perspectives and voices to those of lockstep American editors and publishers? Could this editor be trusted?

After all, she explained, although receptive to the unsolicited pitch for a feature on Hispanic-American writers, the editor had demonstrated little knowledge about or familiarity with the various cultural and literary heritages of the writers to be showcased. Preliminary editorial encounters indicated that the sum of literary familiarity was limited to mainstream corporate America's editorial and publishing experience. Understand, she quickly added, I'm sure of the level of sincerity and commitment to this feature; but I fear that the frame of reference is minimal, at best. I suspect, she continued, that my article will be an eye-opener for the editor as well as the targeted audience. With attitudes that vacillated between amazement and incomprehension, we wondered how the editor of an industry organ could be so uninformed.

My colleague and I spoke at length about the subject and intent of her proposed feature. We also spoke of the paucity of available outlets for such a feature and the necessity for a positive, broad-based professional response to what we hoped would be the first of a number of potential articles on the subject of "ethnic" literature. Our years of professional association, coupled with our friendship, eliminated the need to explain or clarify the importance of such an article-length essay in a premier publication.

Armed with the zeal of literary missionaries, we fine-tuned a design and focus for the feature. Finally, after what seemed like hours of laborious effort, we also narrowed our recommendations of author, critic, and publisher contacts to what we regarded as a reasonable number.

At the conclusion of our discussion, my friend asked why and how I was able to offer so much helpful counsel in an area of literary criticism in which I regard myself as a novice. She knows, of course, that I am a voracious reader and an information junkie, always in search of new avenues of exploration and discovery. She knows, too, that I believe knowledge is wholly dependent upon, and not merely enhanced by, constant reinforcement. I, in turn, understood that her question related more to the level of my awareness of and commitment to Hispanic literature and culture than to any personal or professional knowledge *per se*. I did not hesitate when she reiterated her question.

It's really quite simple, I quipped: You find what you seek. I've taken the time, *made* the time, to familiarize myself with the world and the people around me.

My attitude is not unique, nor does it represent either literary altruism or cultural beneficence. It is, quite simply, a demonstration of cultural and human respect.

SETTING THE STAGE

An opportunity to address the obvious need for information about and resources to multiculturalism presented itself in the form of an appeal from another colleague. In March 1991, Robert Hagelstein, president of Greenwood Publishing Group, Inc., telephoned me to request that I submit a précis for a journal which I would conceive and edit and which Greenwood would publish. Ever stimulated by a challenge, within three days, I proposed an interdisciplinary, multimedia trade journal/book review designed to showcase American cultural diversity. Shortly thereafter, I received a follow-up call advising me that my proposal had been accepted.

This symbiotic association coupled professional energies to undertake a network of goals. As a distinguished academic publisher with a long-standing commitment to multicultural studies, Greenwood was an ideal setting for the launch of a library-oriented resource. In addition, the introduction of a major reference periodical offered an opportunity to expand the educator/administrator offerings of the company's established serials department. For my part, I welcomed the chance to collaborate with a colleague and friend who enthusiastically endorsed and embraced my mission orientation. As the former editor-in-chief of *Small Press*™ magazine, I provided familiarity with both independent publishing and serial publishing. The potential range of titles and materials to be highlighted in the *Review*, therefore, would mirror the cultural inclusivity epitomized in the journal. Working on an accelerated schedule, we inaugurated the *Review* in January 1992–the year which also marks Greenwood Publishing Group's twentieth-fifth anniversary.

Key to my concept for *MultiCultural Review* is the representation of the full spectrum of ethnic, racial, and religious diversity unencumbered by a political agenda or framework. In an organic, egalitarian forum of experiences, the *Review* celebrates common bonds and various traditions while concertedly striving to heighten sensitivity, sharpen awareness, and expand collective wisdom and strength. Effecting change through education and interaction is a fundamental objective: Practical news, authoritative articles, and indispensable resources inform and engage; didactic features facilitate implementation of diversity management.

In keeping with my initial proposal, the editorial agenda planned for the first year or two of the *Review* would feature presentation and analysis of cultural diversity in the Americas: Canada, the United States, the Caribbean, and Central and South America. Incorporation of international multiculturalism would be implemented as part of a process of ongoing development during the second or third volume year. Happily, a stroke of unexpected good fortune enabled us to hasten both the original plans and schedule.

In September 1991, I was contacted by Charles T. Townley, dean of the University Library, New Mexico State University, and chair of the International Federation of Library Associations Section on Library Services to Multicultural Populations, regarding a proposal to merge the *Journal of Multicultural Librarianship* with *MultiCultural Review*. Immediately, another synergetic collaboration began, and the premiere issue of the *Review* announced the formal incorporation of our periodicals. The union of our two organizations enhances our individual and collective strengths and potentialities to more effectively and more efficiently serve our constituencies.

THE MULTICULTURAL AGENDA

The common bonds and traditions of American culture derive from an ever-expanding combination of parallel and intersecting contributions. This unique formula is the essence of the American experience. The essence of multiculturalism is the appreciation of the synergy underlying this multifacetedness.

Facilitating ways in which the process of national acculturation is expedited through the process of individual and group enculturation is essential to complete and successful integration of the varieties of American constituencies. In particular, the conscious incorporation of assorted cultural perspectives and experiences serves to instill awareness of and sensitivity to peoples and traditions typically perceived as "marginalized" or estranged from the dominant culture. This effort is organic and ongoing within "minority" communities in which successive generations of constituents strive to preserve their distinct traditions while adapting to or merging with the dominant society. The greater effort, therefore, is the implementation of a process of education which enables the society at large to recognize and acknowledge the qualitative and quantitative influences of acculturated peoples both in the creation of a common American culture and in their impact on the dominant culture.

EDUCATION: IMPLEMENTING THE PROCESS

The lessons in the education efforts described above offer a challenge to individuals and groups weaned on the concept of a narrow, idealized America. It is imperative, however, to remember that the acculturation of multiethnic and multiracial peoples has been an evolutionary American process for more than five hundred years. The dramatic demographic changes anticipated within the next generations, therefore, need not signal an abrupt eradication of an established cultural system. In all likelihood, the same gradual changes that have typified the genesis of America will continue to operate.

The assurance of a process of moderate, evolutionary adaptation, however, requires the voluntary and enthusiastic embrace of all segments of American population, with particular emphasis on the participation of those groups too often excluded from the process of engagement. Individuals and groups proactively involved in the process of constructive adaptation and accommodation share a heightened motivation to trust, support, and augment an existing system.

Multiculturalism epitomizes the embrace of American ethnic, racial, and religious diversity. Key to a full understanding of this ideology, however, is the semantic distinction between multicultural and "minority." In reaction to a tidal wave of so-called "political correctness," many critics have erroneously interpreted multiculturalism as a contemporary euphemism for "minority." This interpretation is invalid not merely for its linguistic inaccuracy, but also for its reductionist approach to the issue of diversity. In fact, multiculturalism is a factually apt descriptor of the varieties of American cultural experiences precisely because it conveys appropriate inclusivity free of the inherent biases of politically and historically loaded language.

Arguments that manipulate the term "multicultural" to defend or laud an America rigidly and exclusively defined as white, Eurocentric, and male-dominated are linguistic and political perversions of the intent of multiculturalism. Proponents of multicultural ideologies, unlike philosophical centrists of various extreme persuasions, neither seek nor desire rejection–or exclusion–of the cultural values of what has been the dominant American population. Rather, we strive to enlarge the concept of American culture to include the historical, social, and artistic legacies of *all* Americans.

More specifically, we seek to amend the reductive process of hierarchy and factionalization in which issues of exclusivity and dominance supersede considerations of content, context, and focus. The goal is a measured, inclusive perspective encompassing a broad cultural framework in which value systems are subordinated to access to and presentation of information. Simply stated, multiculturalism encompasses two bilateral objectives: elimination of categorizations and qualifications that restrict rather than expand information resources and, then, recognition and celebration of commonality based on shared national experiences which incorporate diversity.

Difficulties of Subject Access
for Information About Minority Groups

Lois Olsrud
Jennalyn Chapman Tellman

SUMMARY. Finding material in the library on ethnic or minority groups is problematic because of the variety of terms that are applied to them in different access sources. Cross references cannot be relied upon completely. This article will elaborate on some of the difficulties and will show examples of headings from the *Library of Congress Subject Headings* and from a selection of periodical indexes to illustrate this complex issue.

INTRODUCTION

An article appeared on the front page of one of our city's daily newspapers with the headline, "Black Contributors Invisible in Library."[1] The reporter tells of a junior business major at our University who was preparing a speech on black inventors for his public speaking class. The student knew that the inventor of the

Lois Olsrud is Humanities Reference Librarian, University of Arizona Library, Tucson, AZ 85721. Jennalyn Chapman Tellman is Literature/Humanities Cataloger, University of Arizona Library, Tucson, AZ 85721.

[Haworth co-indexing entry note]: "Difficulties of Subject Access for Information About Minority Groups," Olsrud, Lois and Jennalyn Chapman Tellman. Co-published simultaneously in *The Acquisitions Librarian* (The Haworth Press, Inc.) No. 9/10, 1993, pp. 47-60; and: *Multicultural Acquisitions* (ed: Karen Parrish and Bill Katz) The Haworth Press, Inc., 1993, pp. 47-60. Multiple copies of this article/chapter may be purchased from The Haworth Document Delivery Center. Call 1-800-3-HAWORTH (1-800-342-9678) between 9:00 - 5:00 (EST) and ask for DOCUMENT DELIVERY CENTER.

automatic traffic signal was a black named Garrett Morgan, and he wanted more information about this person and about other black inventors. When he asked for help, the business major was directed to some books on inventors and to a chronology on inventors and told that "anybody who is anybody is there." But Garrett Morgan was not given in that source and neither was his 1923 invention.

The newspaper article goes on to tell how disappointed the student was in not finding any information on his topic. He said, "I was told this was a research institution and yet I couldn't find any black inventors." After contacting a few black universities he was referred to books that could help him in his research on people of his racial background. He then learned of thousands of other blacks who have made substantial contributions that have changed the world.

This incident was an embarrassing one for our institution. Our Assistant University Librarian responded with a follow-up letter to the editor apologizing for failing to help the student and telling that our library does have material on African-American inventors and scientists.[2] One is a very appropriate book entitled *American Black Scientists and Inventors*.[3] We also have many reference books and other materials which deal with African-Americans including an index to periodicals on blacks with a number of articles about individual inventors, including Garrett Morgan.

PROBLEMS IN USING THE RIGHT SUBJECT TERMS

Several questions are raised from this episode. Why did we fail in providing the student with the information he needed for his research when we do have it? When he asked for assistance and did not get appropriate answers, should he have found some sources on his own (isn't that the purpose of our subject access?). But herein lies the problem—under what words should one look—Black American, Afro-American, African-American, American Black, Negro, or some kind of inverted heading such as Inventors, Black? And is it just as confusing to find material on other groups? How about Hispanics? Do we use Mexican-American, Hispanic-American, or Chicano? And what about Native Americans? Should we look under Indians, Native Americans, Indians of North America, or American Indians? And are the same headings used for finding periodical articles as for books?

This article will examine some of the problems regarding subject access for books and periodical articles for minority groups. We are limiting these groups to Afro-Americans, Hispanic Americans, American Indians, and gays and lesbians. We will not include women as a group since there are two excellent books written on this subject. These are *Women in LC's Terms: a Thesaurus of Library of Congress Subject Headings Relating to Women* by Ruth Dickstein, Victoria A. Mills, and Ellen J. Waite;[4] and *A Women's Thesaurus: an Index of Language used to Describe and Locate Information by and about Women* edited by Mary Ellen S. Capek.[5]

LIBRARY OF CONGRESS SUBJECT HEADINGS

If we look at the headings for Afro-American and Afro-Americans we can see some of the difficulties involved in finding relevant headings. When a user looks in the *Library of Congress Subject Headings,* 14th edition,[6] under the term AFRO-AMERICANS, he or she finds eight pages of headings beginning with this term, including the term AFRO-AMERICAN INVENTORS. By carefully examining headings in this list the user is also led to other relevant headings.

It should be noted that the Library of Congress uses the term AFRO-AMERICANS for works about citizens of the United States of black African descent. Works on blacks who temporarily reside in the United States, such as aliens, students from abroad, etc., are entered under BLACKS–UNITED STATES. Works on blacks outside the United States are entered under Blacks–[place].

For a user to be inclusive he must look under both the broader and narrower terms. Various terms will be used depending on the coverage of the work and judgement of the cataloger. Cataloging rules instruct the cataloger to use the most precise term available. However, there are differences from cataloger to cataloger in interpretation of content and different assumptions about the appropriate depth of analysis and representation.[7]

In some cases the user is led to broader headings, such as from AFRO-AMERICAN ACTOR to see also ACTORS, BLACK or from

AFRO-AMERICAN AGED to MINORITY AGED. Other examples include:

UNITED STATES. AIR FORCE–AFRO AMERICANS, in addition to AFRO-AMERICAN AIR PILOTS.

UNITED STATES–ARMED FORCES–AFRO-AMERICANS, in addition to AFRO-AMERICAN SOLDIERS or AFRO-AMERICAN SEAMEN.

BLACK THEOLOGY, in addition to AFRO-AMERICAN THEOLOGIANS.

There is a whole range of broader terms beginning with the word ETHNIC or MINORITY or MINORITIES that may lead to helpful material. Other helpful broader terms may be found under RACE RELATIONS; MAJORITIES; SEGREGATION; ASSIMILATION (SOCIOLOGY); DISCRIMINATION; SLAVERY; SLAVES; UNITED STATES–ETHNIC RELATIONS; and UNITED STATES–RACE RELATIONS.

In other cases, the user is led from a heading that is not used to a heading that is used. Examples include:

COOKERY, AFRO-AMERICAN instead of AFRO-AMERICAN COOKERY

BLACK ENGLISH instead of AFRO-AMERICAN DIALECT

HAIRDRESSING OF AFRO-AMERICANS instead of AFRO-AMERICAN HAIRDRESSING

BLACK MILITANT ORGANIZATIONS–UNITED STATES instead of AFRO-AMERICAN MILITANT ORGANIZATIONS

SPIRITUALS (SONGS) instead of AFRO-AMERICAN SPIRITUALS

UNITED STATES. AIR FORCE–AFRO-AMERICANS instead of AFRO-AMERICAN AIR FORCE PERSONNEL.

While there are many terms beginning with the words AFRO-AMERICAN to describe Afro-Americans of specific occupations such as AFRO-AMERICAN ARCHITECTS; AFRO-AMERICAN DENTISTS and AFRO-AMERICAN PHYSICIANS, there are also headings such as AFRO-AMERICANS IN BUSINESS; AFRO-AMERICANS IN DENTISTRY; and AFRO-AMERICANS IN MED-

ICINE. A user needs to look under both types of headings to be inclusive.

In addition, there are many headings beginning with the term BLACK such as BLACK POWER–UNITED STATES and BLACK MUSLIMS, and while there is a cross reference from the term BLACK COLLEGE GRADUATES to COLLEGE GRADUATES, BLACK and BLACK COMPOSERS to use COMPOSERS, BLACK, there is none from BLACK INVENTORS to AFRO-AMERICAN INVENTORS. The heading AFRO-AMERICAN INVENTORS has references from INVENTORS, AFRO-AMERICAN and from NE-GRO INVENTORS. A user would have to be diligent to find a general cross reference from BLACK AMERICANS to AFRO-AMERICANS to realize that the latter term is the general heading to use. Furthermore, there is a set of headings beginning with the term BLACKS, many of which may contain material of value to the user.

There are also headings beginning with the term BLACK, such as BLACK VIRGINS, that refer to certain representations of the Virgin Mary. Since there is not a scope note to indicate that this is the case, a user might think that the term refers to a non-religious topic concerning blacks.

The user should be aware that there are many relevant headings in which AFRO-AMERICANS and BLACKS can be found as sub-divisions. This is true for specific wars. However, the subdivision WARS is also used under the name of ethnic groups for works discussing collectively the wars in which the group has participated, such as AFRO-AMERICANS-WARS.

Literary collections written by members of an ethnic group are found by looking first under the literary form and then the subdivision AFRO-AMERICAN; INDIAN AUTHORS; MEXICAN-AMERICAN AUTHORS, etc. While literary collections written by members of an ethnic group are to be found in this fashion, we should know that these headings pick up only collections. There are no subject head-ings which retrieve specific works of literature by individual au-thors of an ethnic group.

The following are some relevant examples of literary collections:

AMERICAN DRAMA–AFRO-AMERICAN AUTHORS

AMERICAN FICTION–AFRO-AMERICAN AUTHORS
AMERICAN LITERATURE–AFRO-AMERICAN AUTHORS
AMERICAN POETRY–AFRO-AMERICAN AUTHORS
AMERICAN PROSE LITERATURE–AFRO-AMERICAN
AUTHORS
SERMONS, AMERICAN–AFRO-AMERICAN AUTHORS
SHORT STORIES, AMERICAN–AFRO-AMERICAN AUTHORS

Some other headings that do not begin with the terms AFRO-AMERICAN/S or BLACK/S include:

ART IN AFRO-AMERICAN UNIVERSITIES AND
COLLEGES
ART, BLACK
ARTISTS, BLACK
BAPTISTS, BLACK
CHRISTIANS, BLACK
CHURCH WORK WITH AFRO-AMERICAN YOUTH

HEADINGS FOR AFRO-AMERICANS IN PERIODICAL INDEXES

Looking for articles about ethnic groups in periodical indexes can be frustrating for several reasons. First, there is not always a thesaurus of subject headings to consult such as *Thesaurus of Psychological Index Terms*[8] and *Thesaurus of ERIC Descriptors.*[9] Second, the terms will vary from one index source to another. And third, the terminology changes over a period of years within the same index source. This remains true for on-line as well as paper versions.

For instance, when checking the *Readers' Guide to Periodical Literature* for 1945, there are no subject headings for Blacks, or Afro-Americans, or African-Americans. Instead, the terms NEGRO and NEGROES are designated. Some of the headings that year were NEGRO ATHLETES, NEGRO ENGINEERS, NEGRO MUSICIANS, NEGROES IN ART, and NEGROES IN THE UNITED STATES. Some cross references are made to more general headings such as:

NEGRO BASEBALL PLAYERS. See BASEBALL PLAYERS
NEGRO MOVING PICTURE PRODUCERS. See MOVING
PICTURE INDUSTRY
NEGRO-WHITE INTERMARRIAGE. See INTERMARRIAGE
OF RACES

But there were no cross references to individuals, so only by looking specifically under a person's name will anything be found if they are indexed. Although four articles about the singer Marian Anderson are given under her name, no references are given to her from the heading NEGRO MUSICIANS. An improvement is made in 1968 when cross references appear for individuals from a broader heading, so when users look under NEGRO AUTHORS they will find references to articles about J. Baldwin, E. Cleaver, W.E.B. DuBois, and R. Wright under their names.

A significant change is made in the 1977/78 edition when the term NEGROES is no longer used. A see reference is given: NEGROES. See BLACKS. A sample of headings here includes BLACK AIR PILOTS; BLACK PUBLIC OFFICERS; BLACK STUDENTS; and BLACK WOMEN. The latest editions continue using BLACKS to the present. It is interesting to note the increase in numbers of headings for this ethnic group. There are now headings with articles for BLACK ASTRONAUTS; BLACK COLLEGE PRESIDENTS; BLACK EXECUTIVES; BLACK FAMILY; BLACK JUDGES; BLACK MIDDLE CLASS; BLACK SURGEONS, etc.

Several other periodical indexes (including *Public Affairs Information Service (PAIS), Current Index to Journals in Education (CIJE), Social Science Index* and other Wilson indexes) made the change from NEGRO to BLACK in 1977/78. But *Psychological Abstracts* continued using NEGRO until 1981 and *Sociological Abstracts* until 1985. Both of these are presently using the term BLACK. *Current Law Index* uses AFRO-AMERICAN. Examples: AFRO-AMERICAN ATTORNEYS; AFRO-AMERICAN WOMEN, with a cross reference BLACKS (UNITED STATES) see AFRO-AMERICANS. *Music Index* also uses AFRO-AMERICAN. Examples: AFRO-AMERICAN COMPOSERS; AFRO-AMERICAN MUSIC, with no cross references.

The *Index to Black Periodicals* (formerly *Index to Periodical Articles by and about Blacks*) explains that because of its specialized scope the subject Afro-Americans and subjects starting with the word Afro-American are used infrequently. Instead, users should look under the appropriate subject heading such as RELIGION, AFRO-AMERICAN.

HEADINGS FOR HISPANIC AMERICANS

While there are many pages of headings relevant to Afro-Americans in the *Library of Congress Subject Headings,* there are far fewer for Hispanic Americans. There are headings beginning both HISPANIC AMERICAN and HISPANIC AMERICANS. For example there is a heading HISPANIC AMERICAN BUSINESS ENTERPRISES and also a heading HISPANIC AMERICANS IN BUSINESS.

The term HISPANIC AMERICANS covers works on United States citizens of Latin American descent. Works on citizens of Latin America living in the United States are entered under LATIN AMERICANS–UNITED STATES. In addition to the terms HISPANIC AMERICAN/S there are narrower terms under CHILEAN AMERICANS; CUBAN AMERICANS; MEXICAN AMERICANS; and PUERTO-RICO–UNITED STATES.

There are cross references to terms such as:

COOKERY, MEXICAN AMERICAN
NAMES, MEXICAN AMERICAN
LIBRARIES, UNIVERSITIES AND COLLEGES–SERVICES TO HISPANIC AMERICANS
PUBLIC LIBRARIES–SERVICES TO HISPANIC AMERICANS
TEACHERS OF MEXICAN AMERICANS

Subdivisions such as PARTICIPATION, MEXICAN AMERICAN under the names of individual wars and UNITED STATES ARMED FORCES–HISPANIC AMERICANS also exist.

Headings for literary collections for Hispanic Americans are more complicated than for Afro-Americans because of two different languages in which they may be written. The following are some relevant examples:

For works in English:

AMERICAN DRAMA–MEXICAN AMERICAN AUTHORS
AMERICAN LITERATURE–HISPANIC AMERICAN AUTHORS
AMERICAN LITERATURE–MEXICAN AMERICAN AUTHORS
AMERICAN POETRY–HISPANIC AMERICAN AUTHORS
AMERICAN POETRY–MEXICAN AMERICAN AUTHORS
SHORT STORIES–MEXICAN AMERICAN AUTHORS

For works in Spanish:

CHRISTIAN POETRY, CUBAN AMERICAN (SPANISH)
CUBAN AMERICAN LITERATURE (SPANISH)
CUBAN AMERICAN POETRY (SPANISH)
DECIMAS, CUBAN AMERICAN (SPANISH)
HISPANIC AMERICAN LITERATURE (SPANISH)
MEXICAN AMERICAN DRAMA (SPANISH)
MEXICAN AMERICAN FICTION (SPANISH)
MEXICAN AMERICAN POETRY (SPANISH)
SHORT STORIES, MEXICAN AMERICAN (SPANISH)

HEADINGS FOR HISPANIC AMERICANS IN PERIODICAL INDEXES

Although the subject heading MEXICANS IN THE UNITED STATES was used in the *Readers' Guide* as long ago as a hundred years, the term MEXICAN AMERICANS was not given until the 1947/49 edition. In 1963 a cross reference is made from MEXICANS to MEXICAN AMERICANS, and a little later a see also reference is given from MEXICAN AMERICAN STUDENTS IN THE UNITED STATES to SPANISH SPEAKING STUDENTS. About the same time MEXICAN AMERICAN LITERATURE becomes a heading. In 1969/70 the term CHICANO STUDENTS appears with a see reference to MEXICAN AMERICAN STUDENTS. Since then, cross references are included from CHICANOS to MEXICAN AMERICANS, but HISPANIC AMERICANS is also a heading, so one needs to remember to look in both places. This seems to carry over for other Wilson indexes as well.

Thesaurus of ERIC Descriptors has used HISPANIC AMER-ICANS since 1980 for residents of the United States who are of Hispanic heritage, with MEXICAN AMERICANS or SPANISH AMERICANS as narrower terms. Related terms include LATIN AMERICAN; SPANISH SPEAKING; ETHNIC GROUPS; and MINORITY GROUPS.

Psychological Abstracts has used MEXICAN AMERICANS since 1973 for populations of Mexican descent residing permanently in the United States. There is a see reference from CHICANOS to MEXI-CAN AMERICANS. A broader heading HISPANICS is for popula-tions of Spanish, Portuguese or Latin American descent residing in countries other than the country of their origin. To confuse the issue further, SPANISH AMERICANS was used for accessing references from 1978-81.

Both *Current Law Index* and *Music Index* have headings HIS-PANIC AMERICANS and MEXICAN AMERICANS.

HEADINGS FOR INDIANS OF NORTH AMERICA

There are numerous headings beginning INDIANS OF NORTH AMERICA in the *Library of Congress Subject Headings*. It is im-portant to know that we can find headings also under groups of Indians such as ALGONQUIAN; ATHAPASCAN; and SHOSHO-NI as well as headings under names of individual Indian tribes. For example the term ALGONQUIAN INDIANS lists approximately fifty tribes that have headings. To find references to the names of specific reservations the user needs to look either under the heading INDIANS OF NORTH AMERICA–[state or region] or under the name of a specific tribe. INDIANS OF NORTH AMERICA does not include Indians of Mexico.

In addition to the broad headings under INDIANS OF NORTH AMERICA and the narrower headings under groups and tribes, there is a heading INDIANS which pertains to works on the aborigi-nal people of the Western Hemisphere. This may lead to useful material, also. Other headings include:

ARTS, MODERN–INDIAN INFLUENCE
LIBRARIES AND INDIANS

PALEO-INDIANS
COOKERY, INDIAN

INDIANS as a subdivision can be found under UNITED STATES. NAVY and UNITED STATES. ARMY. The subdivision PARTICIPATION, INDIAN can be found under the name of individual wars. The heading LAW, [name of tribe] is used for works on native law of Indian tribes; however, U.S. laws governing Indians of individual regions or tribes are entered under INDIANS OF NORTH AMERICA–[state]–LEGAL STATUTES, LAWS, ETC.

Literary works by Indians of North America can be found using the same patterns for Afro-Americans and Mexican-Americans, i.e., AMERICAN LITERATURE–INDIAN AUTHORS. Narrow headings such as DAKOTA POETRY; NAVAJO POETRY; or FOLK-SONGS, DAKOTA exist, but, there are not cross references from INDIANS OF NORTH AMERICA–LITERATURE or POETRY to indicate these narrow headings.

HEADINGS FOR AMERICAN INDIANS IN PERIODICAL INDEXES

INDIANS OF NORTH AMERICA has been used consistently throughout the years in the Wilson indexes. *Readers' Guide* has articles listed under specific tribes as well, such as HOPI INDIANS; NAVAJO INDIANS; or DAKOTA INDIANS, but there are no cross reference to them from the broader heading. If articles are given on individuals, there is no way of finding them except by looking under their names. In more recent years, see also references refer to additional specific terms, such as INDIANS (AMERICAN) IN ART, and INDIANS (AMERICAN) IN TELEVISION.

Psychological Abstracts refers users from INDIANS (AMERICAN) and NATIVE AMERICANS to AMERICAN INDIANS. It also has broader headings of ETHNIC GROUPS and MINORITY GROUPS.

In *ERIC,* the term INDIANS is defined as natives of India or of the East Indies, while AMERICAN INDIANS refers to both North and South American Indians. Narrower terms are NONRESERVATION AMERICAN INDIANS and RESERVATION AMERICAN

INDIANS. Related headings include AMERICAN INDIAN EDU-
CATION and AMERICAN INDIAN LANGUAGES.

Current Law Index uses INDIANS OF NORTH AMERICA and
INDIANS, TREATMENT OF. It does provide cross references to
tribes, such as OJIBWA INDIANS or SEMINOLE INDIANS when
articles on them are indexed.

Music Index has INDIAN MUSIC, AMERICAN as its major
entry with INDIAN MUSIC, NORTH AMERICAN as a broader
heading.

GAYS AND LESBIANS

We also looked at access for gays and lesbians. There are headings in the *Library of Congress Subject Headings* under HOMO-
PHOBIA; HOMOSEXUALITY; GAY or GAYS and LESBIAN or
LESBIANS. Headings beginning GAY or GAYS also may encom-
pass lesbian materials. For example, GAY COUPLES is a broader
term that includes both lesbian couples and gay male couples.

Literary works do not follow the pattern for ethnic groups. There
are headings for GAYS' WRITINGS, AMERICAN and LES-
BIANS' WRITINGS, AMERICAN.

In addition to the headings under GAY or GAYS and LESBIAN
or LESBIANS there are cross references to:

AFRO-AMERICAN GAYS
AGED GAY MEN
CATHOLIC GAYS
CHURCH WORK WITH GAYS
JEWISH GAYS
LIBRARIES AND GAYS
SEX INSTRUCTION FOR GAY MEN
SOCIAL WORK WITH GAYS
ABUSED LESBIANS
AFRO-AMERICAN LESBIANS
AGED LESBIANS
MIDDLE AGED LESBIANS
SEX INSTRUCTION FOR LESBIANS
SOCIAL WORK WITH LESBIANS

GAY is also a subdivision under individual military services, e.g., UNITED STATES–ARMED FORCES–GAYS.

GAYS AND LESBIANS IN PERIODICAL INDEXES

HOMOSEXUALITY and LESBIANISM appeared as subject headings in the *Readers' Guide* in the late 1950's and these terms continue to the present. Additional headings, such as HOMO-SEXUALITY AND CHRISTIANITY and ORDINATION OF HO-MOSEXUALS, have been added since these topics have come into more prominence. GAY BASHING and BISEXUALITY are now in the most current years. One of the Wilson indexes, *Social Sciences Index,* has several more headings. We can look under ATTITUDES TOWARD HOMOSEXUALITY; LESBIAN COU-PLES; GAYS; GAY MEN; and HOMOSEXUALITY AND MASS MEDIA.

Psychological Abstracts has been using HOMOSEXUALITY for many years. Its narrower terms are BISEXUALITY; LESBIAN-ISM; and MALE HOMOSEXUALITY; while related terms are TRANSSEXUALISM and TRANSVESTISM.

ERIC uses HOMOSEXUALITY as a major heading with LES-BIANISM given as a narrower term and SEXUALITY as a broader term.

Current Law Index uses several subject headings including GAYS; GAY COUPLES; GAY FATHERS; GAY MILITARY PER-SONNEL; GAY PARENTS; LESBIANS; LESBIAN COUPLES; LESBIAN MOTHERS; DISCRIMINATION AGAINST GAYS as well as HOMOSEXUALITY and HOMOPHOBIA.

HOMOSEXUALITY seems to be the most consistent term used in *Music Index.*

CONCLUSION

Librarians or assistants helping patrons who are requesting in-formation on any of these ethnic or minority groups must be aware of the complexities of the question. What seems to be a simple request might require some explanation rather than a quick answer. Appropriate thesauri should be consulted, and users reminded of different headings or keywords, both general and specific, whether they are using print or online services. We need to remember that one bad library experience for a user can have long-lasting effects, and we can avoid such by providing better informed responses.

REFERENCES

1. Garcia, Joseph, "Black Contributors Invisible in Library" *Tucson Citizen* February 17, 1990, page 1, col. 4.

2. Reichel, Mary. "Letter to the Editor" *Tucson Citizen* March 23, 1990.

3. Jenkins, Edward S. et al., *American Black Scientists and Inventors* (Washington: National Science Teachers Association, 1975).

4. Dickstein, Ruth; Mills, Victoria A.; and Ellen J. Waite, *Women in LC's Terms: A Thesaurus of Library of Congress Subject Headings Relating to Women* (Phoenix, Ariz.: Oryx Press, 1988).

5. Capek, Mary Ellen S., *A Women's Thesaurus: an Index of Language used to describe and locate Information by and about Women* (New York: Harper & Row, 1987).

6. Library of Congress. Office for Subject Cataloging Policy. Collections Services, *Library of Congress Subject Headings* 14th ed. (Washington: Cataloging Distribution Service, 1991).

7. Chan, Lois Mai, *Library of Congress Subject Headings: Principles and Application* 2nd ed. (Littleton, Colo.: Libraries Unlimited, 1986).

8. Walker, Alvin, *Thesaurus of Psychological Index Terms* 6th ed. (Arlington, Virginia: American Psychological Association, 1991).

9. Houston, James E., *Thesaurus of ERIC Descriptors* 12th ed. (Phoenix, Arizona: Oryx Press, 1990).

Creating Signs for Multicultural Patrons

Debra R. Boyd

SUMMARY. The increasing complexity and size of public libraries in North America make them daunting for users of multicultural backgrounds. Based on experience and research at the Ottawa Public Library, specific problems of library directional signs for patrons of this kind are highlighted. Suggestions are given for adjustments which can be made to improve communication with English as a Second Language and Literacy patrons via library sign systems. A complete bibliography is included.

Public libraries are becoming increasingly complex and intimidating as the size and variety of their collections and services expand. Without sufficient guidance, patrons can feel that libraries contain "a wealth of information that is impossible to find."[1] Magnify this frustration and disorientation when considering the needs of library users with differing linguistic and cultural backgrounds. Special consideration should be given to the signs in libraries frequented by these patrons in order to provide the best possible visual guidance system. Properly-designed, multiculturally-sensitive signage is an effective tool for increasing access,

Debra R. Boyd is Library Assistant Specialist, Children's Department, Alta Vista Branch, Ottawa Public Library, 145 Foxfield Drive, Nepean, Ontario, Canada K2G 2J1.

[Haworth co-indexing entry note]: "Creating Signs for Multicultural Patrons," Boyd, Debra R. Co-published simultaneously in *The Acquisitions Librarian* (The Haworth Press, Inc.) No. 9/10, 1993, pp. 61-66; and: *Multicultural Acquisitions* (ed: Karen Parrish and Bill Katz) The Haworth Press, Inc., 1993, pp. 61-66. Multiple copies of this article/chapter may be purchased from The Haworth Document Delivery Center. Call 1-800-3-HAWORTH (1-800-342-9678) between 9:00 - 5:00 (EST) and ask for DOCUMENT DELIVERY CENTER.

meeting user needs and making the voice of the library more welcoming.

While researching general guidelines for the evaluation and revision of the Ottawa Public Library's sign system, the dearth of material on the topic of multicultural signs became apparent. As the largest public library system in Canada's capital region, the Ottawa Public Library/Bibliotheque Publique d'Ottawa serves a richly diverse group of patrons. Canada's multicultural policies, as well as the number of international embassy personnel and new immigrants in the city, have resulted in a sizable collection of foreign language materials in the local library. The Main branch houses books and newspapers printed in forty-four dialects, ranging from Arabic to Yiddish. The Ottawa Library system simultaneously provides facilities for English as a Second Language and Literacy groups. The challenge of providing access and services for so many dissimilar patrons prompted a study of the "friendliness" and effectiveness of the signs of the library. Any public libraries with significant numbers of ethnic patrons will benefit from the results of Ottawa's self-evaluation.

Library signs are an important, non-verbal aid to patrons. Directional signs guide users to the materials and the facilities they desire. Identification signs help library users recognize the achievement of their goals. Instructional signs provide necessary information for the use of items and services. These three types of signs work together to create a system which is an informal type of bibliographic instruction. Good sign systems are an invaluable aid for guiding and informing library patrons, while poor systems can be "visual noise"[2] which confuse and bewilder users. Several books and articles have been written to help libraries develop signs that are of maximum benefit to all users. The book, *Sign Systems for Libraries,* edited by Dorothy Pollett and Peter C. Haskell (R.R. Bowker Co., New York, 1979, ISBN 0-8352-1149-5) and the articles, "Wayfinding in the Library: book searches and route uncertainty" by Gale Eaton (Reference Quarterly, 30:519-527, Summ 91.) and "Lost in the Information Supermarket" by Andrew Yeaman (Wilson Library Bulletin 64:42-46, Dec 89.) are comprehensive and helpful. They provide general guidelines for library signs, but they do not address multicultural signage. Therefore, additional concepts, based on common sense and experience, should be applied to these principles to provide signs that will communicate best to all patrons.

The terminology used on any sign affects its ability to deliver its message. Although English is currently the dominant language of North America, bilingual signs are being used with greater frequency in areas where the population warrants it. Many libraries have wisely followed suit by installing bilingual signs in their buildings. Unfortunately, "library lingo" is still preferred on signs in library buildings. Terms such as "periodicals" and "circulation" mean very little to patrons without North American backgrounds. Guidelines for the use of simplified English and French, known as "simple text," are available from the Canadian government.[3] In order to be more effective for multicultural patrons, the terms used on signs should be revised so that they meet with these recommended standards.

Symbols are a distinctive and useful means of communication on signs. They allow "language limitations to become less important as the need to ask for directions and understanding the responses diminishes."[4] Naturally, the designs need to be carefully chosen to represent the facilities or collections desired. The graphics should quickly and clearly communicate the desired message to the patron. Some interesting options for consideration are found in *A Sign System for Libraries* by Mary S. Mallory and Ralph E. DeVore (American Library Association, Chicago, 1982). Mounted replicas of the chosen design should be used to test people's comprehension before permanent signs are installed.

Consistency of image, placement and use is essential with symbolic signs. Once determined, identical symbols must be repeated on all relevant signs, directories and public relations material to reinforce their meaning among patrons. Unfortunately, the use of symbols alone can be counter-productive "because of conceptual problems, suggesting conflicting or ambiguous meanings."[5] Except for the internationally recognized washroom and elevator symbols, signs with only graphics and no text should be avoided.

When graphics are integrated with simple text, the resulting signs are optimally communicative. Haber's study, "How We Remember What We See," shows that human memory works best if words and symbols are combined.[6] Therefore, the best signs for libraries would consistently use both "simple text" terms in one or more languages, and a carefully selected graphic representation of that term. Be aware that the meaning of both text and symbols can change significantly over time. Evaluate all signs periodically to determine if their messages correspond to currently accepted usage.

An arrow is a universally recognized symbol and, as such, is an extremely useful device for multicultural directional signs. Once again, however, its use must be consistent to avoid misunderstanding. Arrows must always be accompanied by text. The side of the text upon which the arrow appears should be repeated on all signs. Take care that all arrows point only in the direction of the area being identified by the text. Diagonal arrows can be confusing in certain situations. If stairs must be ascended to reach the destined goal, the arrow should indicate this very carefully. Testing of patron responses is recommended before expensive permanent signs are mounted.

Multi-level buildings are an interesting directional problem for library patrons from Europe, Africa and Asia. Some cultures label the street level floor, the "Main floor," and the floor above it, the "first floor." Others perceive the street level floor to be the first floor, and so on. Understandably, this can cause confusion with the numbering of floors in the entire building. Providing clear indications of each floor level at major decision points such as doorways, stairs and escalators is all that is necessary. Frustratingly, there is a lack of awareness of this basic cultural difference. These essential signs are often neglected in library buildings with several stories.

The measures needed to adjust library signs so that they can communicate effectively to patrons of all languages and cultures are easily made. First, determine if bilingual signs are necessary. Second, simplify the terms currently used to clarify the communication. Third, consider the addition of appropriate symbols. By using temporary mock-ups to test patron responses, minimal time and money should be expended in the initial stages and the results will be more effective. Most final adjustments for the libraries' diverse patron groups can be determined and produced in-house.

The Ottawa Public Library is no longer unique in the diversity of patrons it serves. Many public libraries are providing services for increased numbers of users with different language and cultural backgrounds. Revising the sign system is one way of breaking down barriers and enhancing library use for these patrons. Immigrants, especially those from developing countries, regard using a library as a privilege. These new individuals and families are likely to become favorite borrowers as they use the library to learn and become a part of North American society. Not only will the library benefit from increased use by multicultural patrons, but good signs will aid all users in their pursuit of "the right book for the right person at the right time."

REFERENCES

1. Talar, S.A. "Library Signage: decoration and education," *New Jersey Libraries,* Spring 1990, p. 17.
2. Yeaman, Andrew R.J. "Vital Signs: cures for confusion," *School Library Journal,* Volume 23, November 1989, p. 26.
3. *Plain Language: clear and simple,* Multiculturalism and Citizenship Canada, Minister of Supply and Services Canada, Canada Communication Group, Ottawa, 1991. *Pour un style claire et simple,* Multiculturalisme et Citotyennete Canada, Ministre des Approvisionnements et Services Canada, Groupe Communication Canada, Ottawa, 1991.
4. Dalton, Phyllis I., *Library Service to the Deaf and Hearing Impaired,* Oryx Press, Phoenix, Arizona, 1985, p. 204.
5. Wilt, Lawrence J.M. and Gary Kushner, "Symbol Signs for Libraries" *Sign Systems for Libraries,* edited by Dorothy Pollett and Peter C. Haskell, R.R. Bowker, New York, 1979.
6. Haber, Ralph Norman, "How We Remember What We See" *Scientific American,* Volume 222, No. 5, May 1970, p. 104-112.

BIBLIOGRAPHY

Cadoret, Richard, "Signage Tells You Where to Go," *Canadian Interiors,* Volume 23, No. 5, May/June 1986, p. 20-21.
Cohen, Aaron and Elaine Cohen, *Designing and Space Planning for Libraries,* New York: R.R. Bowker, 1979.
Courchesne, Germaine, "Comment construire une bibliotheque selon vos besoins?," *Argus,* Volume 15, No. 3, September 1986, p. 69-71.
Dalton, Phyllis J., *Library Service to the Deaf and Hearing Impaired,* Phoenix, Arizona: Oryx Press, 1985.
Eaton, E.G., "Wayfinding in the Library" *Reference Quarterly,* Volume 30, Summer 1991, p. 519-527.

Haber, Ralph Norman, "How We Remember What We See," *Scientific American,* Volume 222, No. 5, May 1970, p. 104-112.

Henderson, Jenny, *T.L. Robertson Library Sign Manual,* Perth: Western Australian Institute of Technology, 1982.

Kirby, John, *Creating the Library Identity: a manual of design,* Brookfield, Vermont: Gower Publishing Co., Ltd, 1985.

Kupersmith, John, "Don't Do This! Don't Do That!" *Research Strategies,* Volume 2, No. 4, Fall 1984, p. 185.

Mallery, Mary S. and Ralph E. DeVore, *A Sign System for Libraries,* Chicago: American Library Association, 1982.

Murphy, Steven, "Maoritanga at Paraparaumu Public Library" *New Zealand Libraries,* Volume 42, No. 2, October 1979, p. 43-46.

"New York Graphics Seminar: signs for better access" *Library Journal,* Volume 104, No. 3, February 1, 1979, p. 343-344.

Plain Language: clear and simple, Multiculturalism and Citizenship Canada, Minister of Supply and Services Canada, Ottawa: Canada Communication Group, 1991.

Pour un style claire et simple, Multiculturalisme et Citoyennete Canada, Ministre des Approvisionnements et Services Canada, Ottawa: Groupe Communication Canada, 1991.

Reynolds, Linda and Steven Barrett, *Signs and Guiding for Libraries,* London: Clive Bingley Ltd., 1981.

Sign Systems for Libraries: solving the wayfinding problem, edited by Dorothy Pollett and Peter C. Haskell, New York: R.R. Bowker, 1979.

Talar, S.A., "Library Signage: decoration and education" *New Jersey Libraries,* Volume 23, Spring 1990, p. 17-20.

Van Allen, Peter R. Sr., "A Good Library Sign System: is it possible?" *Reference Services Review,* Volume 12, No. 2, Summer 1984, p. 102-106.

Yeaman, Andrew R.J., "Lost in the Information Supermarket" *Wilson Library Bulletin,* Volume 64, December 1989, p. 42-46.

Yeaman, Andrew R.J., "Vital Signs: cures for confusion" *School Library Journal,* Volume 23, November 1989, p. 23-27.

Expanding the Librarians' Role
in Facilitating Multicultural Learning

Nancy D. Padak
Timothy V. Rasinski

SUMMARY. To capitalize on the power of literature to promote intercultural and multicultural appreciation, librarians need to consider how literature will be used as well as what literature should be made available. In this article, we present a framework that school and public librarians can apply to promote multicultural learning through children's literature. We first describe four models for considering the use of children's literature in dealing with cultural differences. We then focus specifically on librarians' roles in helping children de-

Nancy D. Padak is Director of the Reading & Writing Center and Timothy V. Rasinski is Associate Professor in Education at Kent State University, 402 White Hall, Kent OH 44242.

[Haworth co-indexing entry note]: "Expanding the Librarians' Role in Facilitating Multicultural Learning," Padak, Nancy D. and Timothy V. Rasinski. Co-published simultaneously in *The Acquisitions Librarian* (The Haworth Press, Inc.) No. 9/10, 1993, pp. 67-75; and: *Multicultural Acquisitions* (ed: Karen Parrish and Bill Katz) The Haworth Press, Inc., 1993, pp. 67-75. Multiple copies of this article/chapter may be purchased from The Haworth Document Delivery Center. Call 1-800-3-HAWORTH (1-800-342-9678) between 9:00 - 5:00 (EST) and ask for DOCUMENT DELIVERY CENTER.

67

velop, explore, and act upon their cultural values and beliefs. Finally, we provide an example of the framework by summarizing the experiences of a group of elementary school children.

INTRODUCTION

For most of its history, the United States has been recognized as a home, indeed a refuge, for people from many cultures. The traditional assumption that the dominant culture was the best culture led us to encourage immigrants' quick and complete acculturation into the dominant culture. Today, however, our orientations toward cultural diversity are changing. No longer is forced enculturation so widely advocated. Instead, we acknowledge that, although a dominant culture does exist in certain contexts, native cultures should also be fostered and accorded profound appreciation.

This enlightened vision of the country's multicultural heritage has had an impact on schools, which are now charged with helping students learn about other cultures and appreciate a variety of cultural heritages. The intent is for children to understand the principle of cultural diversity and to develop culturally pluralistic attitudes. Schools are viewed as places where tolerance, patience, appreciation, and friendship among children of different backgrounds and cultures are fostered.

We believe that children's literature can be a powerful means to achieve these goals. As they read about new worlds, new ideas, and new options, children can learn about and learn to appreciate other cultures. Moreover, teachers and librarians can help to create environments that promote interpersonal caring and the development of prosocial attitudes and behaviors. In such contexts, children can use literature to explore and act upon their cultural values and beliefs.

School librarians play as important a role as teachers and other educators in achieving this educational goal. As Barron and Bergen (1992) note, "the school library media specialist should be a master teacher, able to work with classroom teachers to integrate information management skills into their curriculum and classes" (p. 523). We would argue that the same is true of public librarians, especially those with responsibilities for children's or young adult literature collections.

In this article, we present a framework that school and public librarians can apply to promote multicultural learning through children's literature. We first describe four models for considering the use of children's literature in dealing with cultural differences. We then focus specifically on librarians' roles in helping children develop, explore, and act upon their cultural values and beliefs. Finally, we provide an example of the framework by summarizing the experiences of a group of elementary school children.

CULTURAL AWARENESS AND APPRECIATION THROUGH CHILDREN'S LITERATURE

To capitalize on the power of literature to promote intercultural and multicultural appreciation, librarians need to consider how literature will be used as well as what literature should be made available. Banks (1989) describes four models, which form a hierarchy for integrating ethnic or multicultural content into school curricula. With some adaptation, the models can provide the basis for making decisions about the use of literature in library activities.

At the lowest level of Banks' hierarchy is the "contributions approach," which isolates a particular culture and focuses on its highlights, heroes, or holidays. Narratives set within the context of important holidays or biographies of important people within a culture lend themselves to this way of using literature. In classrooms, teachers might read a biography of Martin Luther King, Jr. during January or Singer's (1980) *The Power of Light: Eight Stories for Hanukkah* during December, for example, to note the contributions and traditions of African American and Jewish cultures. Book displays or read-aloud sessions in libraries might serve the same function.

Unlike the "contributions approach," which isolates a particular culture, the next model in Banks' hierarchy, the "additive approach," adds content, concepts, and themes from other cultures to the set curriculum. Examples might include supplementing an in-place literature curriculum with stories, folktales, or legends from other cultures or adding a book such as *Journey to Topaz* (Uchida, 1971) to the study of twentieth century American history. Activities based on this model add information from or about other cultures to the curriculum, but do not weave such information through it.

Although the contributions and additive models represent the lower levels of Banks' (1989) hierarchy, these types of multicultural explorations still have merit. Since activities reflecting these models are easy to design and implement, they may represent a good first step toward the goal of using literature to foster multicultural awareness and appreciation. Moreover, left on their own, children tend to drift toward the familiar, selecting stories and books that represent their own cultures (Rudman, 1976). Librarians and teachers can begin the promotion of multicultural understanding, then, by exposing children to stories of other cultures, a process that begins with stocking libraries with books about a variety of peoples, cultures, lifestyles, and points of view (Rudman, 1976).

Providing exposure to multi-ethnic or multicultural literature is not enough, however. In fact, mere exposure might be perceived as a form of tokenism. As we have said elsewhere, "Superficial treatment of different cultures can lead to a reinforcement of stereotypes and misconceptions, including the notion that ethnic cultures are not integral parts of the dominant culture" (Rasinski & Padak, 1990, p. 577). The two higher levels of Banks' hierarchy mitigate these potential problems.

In the "transformation approach," students view abstract themes, concepts, or problems from the perspectives of different cultural groups. In an American history class, for example, students might explore westward expansion from the perspectives of Native Americans, the entrepreneurs who wished to benefit from their exploitation, white settlers, and government officials. Activities based on the transformation model can foster the realization that ethnic groups and the dominant culture are interconnected. In addition, this sort of perspective-taking can actually serve to empower victimized or exploited cultural groups (Banks, 1989).

The highest level of Banks' hierarchy is the "decision-making and social action approach," where children identify problems related to cultural or ethnic differences, engage in inquiry to learn about the problems, make decisions about their resolution, and take actions based on their decisions. Children may decide to focus on discrimination within their schools or communities, for example.

Learning about the problems that they have identified may involve reading literary or factual accounts of other types of discrimination and distilling potential resolutions from these, which might then be applied to the original problem. In other words, literature can provide a springboard for the analysis of hypothetical cases, and children can use episodes from literature as the basis for their own plans of action.

Within these two higher-level models, children use their cognitive abilities to decenter or consider alternative points of view and to solve problems. They identify, analyze, and act upon problems and issues related to living in a multicultural society. And reading literature, which provides unmistakable and realistic contrasts in perspective, can help children realize their own cultural values and beliefs and appreciate various cultural groups' contributions to our heritage and history.

LIBRARIANS' ROLES IN FOSTERING MULTICULTURAL LEARNING

Fortunately, librarians who wish to encourage the use of literature in this way need not be cultural historians or sociologists. They do, however, need "a broad knowledge of books, an understanding of important issues of the past and present facing various cultural groups, and a willingness to entertain and be a part of diverse explorations and calls for social action" (Rasinski & Padak, 1990, p. 578).

One critical aspect of the librarian's role in implementing Banks' model relates to the nature of library holdings. A variety of good books by and about people from many cultures should be available, as should books about multicultural issues, representing all genres of literature and non-fiction. Newspaper and magazine holdings and CD-ROM resources are also valuable assets for exploring multicultural issues. The cataloging system for all these resources, whether on cards in files, in books, or electronic, should be easy for children to use. Toward this end, directions for use can be written for children and posted near the resources. A well-stocked library that is accessible to children can support multicultural explorations.

Promoting the library as a "hub" for activity is another facet of the librarian's role in fostering multicultural learning. By encouraging communication among children, as well as between teachers and children, librarians can promote the discussion and interaction necessary to clarify issues and values related to multicultural understanding. Areas for small group discussions can be created; a special area of the library designed to house books and materials that reflect multicultural themes and that allow for student research can be developed; storage space for "works in progress" can be provided. Bulletin boards or computer files can be established and maintained for children's use. Although these modifications may seem minor, they help children come to view libraries as resources for assembling, synthesizing, and sharing information, rather than simply places to check out books.

Finally, librarians can support children's multicultural explorations by maintaining close contact with classroom teachers. Librarians who know what children are studying in school can assemble print and non-print (e.g., audiovisual) resource materials for children's use in libraries. They can also survey the community for other possible resources, such as people to interview or museums or other community agencies with information related to children's interests. And, of course, they can supplement classroom instruction through library read alouds and by suggesting related extension activities utilizing library resources.

Implicit in all this advice is the need for librarians to forge partnerships with others in the school community (Montgomery, 1992; Thomas & Goldsmith, 1992). In defining the librarian's role in educational reform, Barron and Bergen (1992) assert that "the most important and critical role that the modern school library media specialist has to play is that of partner to the other members of the instructional team" (p. 524). This team extends beyond school libraries into public libraries. Humphrey (1992), writing in response to concerns about illiteracy, describes a plan that involves "surrounding our students with appropriate books at school, helping them make positive connections with public libraries, and encouraging parents and teachers to be involved . . . " (p. 538). This advice applies equally well to the goal of promoting multicultural learning.

CHILDREN'S INVOLVEMENT
IN MULTICULTURAL LEARNING:
AN EXAMPLE

To conclude, we offer an example of the type of multicultural learning opportunity described in this article. The activities, designed by elementary school teachers, school librarians, and public librarians, focus on the internment of Japanese Americans during World War II. In the example, children use libraries to explore issues related to the treatment of this cultural group at an earlier time, as well as to examine current attitudes and opinions.

In classrooms, teachers introduced the problems of Japanese American internment and the differential treatment of Asian Americans in contemporary society. They read the book, *Journey to Topaz* by Yoshiko Uchida (1971), which is a fictional account of a Japanese American family's evacuation and internment in concentration camps during World War II. Together with their teachers, children talked about the issues raised in the book: What could the family have done about the actions taken against it? Was it fair to arrest the father and relocate the family? Was the U.S. government justified in taking these actions?

Next, children identified related concepts and issues of interest to them. Some wanted to read other books about this problem, for example, and others wanted to read newspaper and magazine accounts of these events. Some children wanted to find out if anything had happened to redress the grievances, and still others wondered if something similar could happen today. As soon as children's interests were determined, teachers and librarians met to decide how they could support children's inquiries.

Children's curiosity about this problem took them to their school and public libraries purposefully. They knew what interested them; they knew what they wanted to find out. Some surveyed library holdings to locate fiction related to World War II and the plight of Japanese Americans and other cultural subgroups. They read these books and developed a computerized data base to record bibliographic information and their reactions to what they had read. Others used microfiche to locate and read newspaper accounts about these same events. Still others searched resources using CD-ROM databases. Children also read newspaper and magazine accounts of

recent reparations for survivors of the Japanese American internment. Some students even interviewed grandparents and others in
their neighborhoods who could remember World War II events.

Children used the results of their inquiries in a variety of ways.
Creative drama/role playing from the perspectives of key participants
at the time and from the present was one choice. Others decided to
write letters to elected representatives or newspaper editors sharing
what they had learned and expressing their opinions. One class sponsored a school-wide "Freedom Day," to celebrate progress and highlight enduring problems related to freedom and equality for all citizens. Some responded through art, poetry, or prose and created
displays for their classrooms or school or public libraries.

Librarians' and teachers' roles varied according to the nature of
children's interests. In general, however, librarians provided access
to fiction and nonfiction resources, teachers worked to integrate
children's inquiries with curricular goals. Both assisted children in
locating and, when necessary, recording information. Everyone
helped children clarify their thinking, develop opinions and values,
make sense of what they had learned.

Activities involving children's literature can help students view
important societal events from the points of view of groups not a
part of the dominant culture. Moreover, literature can provide the
catalyst for defining, analyzing, and acting upon problems related to
various ethnic groups in society: "Because it tells the stories of
human events and the human condition and not simply the facts,
literature does more than change people's minds; it changes their
hearts. And people with changed hearts are people who can move
the world" (Rasinski & Padak, 1990, p. 580). By forging partnerships, librarians and teachers can provide opportunities for children
to develop multicultural awareness and values and to act and react
with understanding of and sensitivity to multicultural diversity.

REFERENCES

Banks, J. (1989). Integrating the curriculum with ethnic content: Approaches and
    guidelines. In J. Banks, & C. Banks (Eds.), *Multicultural education: Issues and
    perspectives* (pp. 189-207). Boston: Allyn & Bacon.
Barron, D. & Bergen, T. (1992). Information power: The restructured school
    library for the nineties. *Phi Delta Kappan, 73*, 521-525.

Goodman, K. (1986). *What's whole in whole language?* Portsmouth, NH: Heine-mann.

Humphrey, J. (1992). The glitzy labyrinth of nonprint media is winning the battle with books. *Phi Delta Kappan, 73,* 538.

Montgomery, P. Integrating library, media, research, and information skills. *Phi Delta Kappan, 73,* 529-532.

Rasinski, T., & Padak, N. (1990). Multicultural learning through children's literature. *Language Arts, 67,* 576-580.

Rudman, M. (1976). *Children's literature: An issues approach* (2nd. ed.). New York: Longman.

Singer, I. (1980). *The power of light: Eight stories for Hanukkah.* New York: Farrar, Straus, & Giroux.

Thomas, J. & Goldsmith, A. (1992). A necessary partnership: The early childhood educator and the school librarian. *Phi Delta Kappan, 73,* 533-536.

Uchida, Y. (1971). *Journey to Topaz.* New York: Scribner.

Cultivating Global Consciousness: Programs and Materials for Creating Multi-Cultural Awareness

Lorna C. Vogt

SUMMARY. A high school librarian discusses programs and materials designed to present new dimensions and added depth to the development of cultural awareness. The article explores the utilization of satellite dish receivers, cable television, computerized news services, video tapes, slides, laser discs, art reproductions, recordings, periodicals, newspapers, books, realia, lectures and artistic performances to reflect cultural diversity in today's global society.

INTRODUCTION

Life in a midwestern community influenced by a large University and the world headquarters of the DeKalb Genetic Corporation is comfortable, but may be considered bland in contrast to life in metropolitan communities abounding with multi-cultural activities. It was this setting which created the challenge to develop a library

---

Lorna C. Vogt is Librarian, Sycamore High School, Spartan Trail, Sycamore, IL 60178.

[Haworth co-indexing entry note]: "Cultivating Global Consciousness: Programs and Materials for Creating Multi-Cultural Awareness," Vogt, Lorna C. Co-published simultaneously in *The Acquisitions Librarian* (The Haworth Press, Inc.) No. 9/10, 1993, pp. 77-90; and: *Multicultural Acquisitions* (ed: Karen Parrish and Bill Katz) The Haworth Press, Inc., 1993, pp. 77-90. Multiple copies of this article/chapter may be purchased from The Haworth Document Delivery Center. Call 1-800-3-HAWORTH (1-800-342-9678) between 9:00 - 5:00 (EST) and ask for DOCUMENT DELIVERY CENTER.

77

collection aimed towards expanding the cultural awareness of patrons who have limited contacts with cultural diversity. Through the eyes of a teenager from another culture, who lived in our home while she prepared for admission to the nearby university, I first saw the need for increasing the depth of multicultural opportunities within the schools of a culturally nondiversified community.

Recognizing that all libraries should reflect cultural diversity even if the communities served do not, it was time to begin the quest for a variety of multicultural materials designed to prepare patrons for the possibility of eventually residing in a more diversified environment. Drawing upon my professional training, I followed the writings of professional reviewers who attempted to keep abreast of a rapidly expanding market for quality multicultural materials. Library conference exhibits, use of interlibrary loans, and visits to other libraries allowed me to screen materials designed to satisfy enquiring minds and to provide a background for students who are preparing to take their places in a variety of global communities as they move beyond their present environments.

Multicultural library collections should introduce patrons to the customs, attitudes, language, music, art, religion, work and play of peoples from around the world. Some of the quality materials observed at national conferences were not necessarily appropriate for midwestern needs, while those shunned by coastal librarians were often the most suitable for midwestern libraries. Many of the recommended materials and methods are applicable to a variety of libraries ranging from those serving the secondary level to those aimed towards a more sophisticated and advanced curriculum at the university level.

VIDEOTAPES

Videotape catalogs list an abundance of materials related to nearly every culture in the world. As selectors of these materials, librarians are often forced to rely on reviewing journals to cull through the large quantity of videotapes, which may or may not fit their institution's multicultural curricula. *School Library Journal,* for example, published a series of annotated video lists during 1992. These bibliographies aimed to assist librarians with the selection of "visual documentation of our multicultural diversity."[1] Librarians who have time to preview such materials can best determine whether or not a given production will match the needs of their patrons. Tapes should be screened to determine the quality of their overall cultural presentation. Does the soundtrack tell the patron something about the presented culture or is it merely incidental music with an accompanying generic script? Will the commentary or dialogue hold the viewer's attention? Is the content accurate and unbiased? Was the material scripted to be a videotape or was it transformed from another format? To be effective, is it necessary to use the entire tape or is it possible to select clips to enhance the curriculum?

Educational videotape series such as *French in Action* and *Destinos* offered by The Annenberg/CPB Collection make excellent major purchases for either secondary or university level libraries. They would also be valuable additions to the collections of film cooperatives, which are economical avenues available to many of the smaller libraries. Developed from pooled funds, co-operatives provide access to a variety of materials that are too costly for limited individual budgets.

Not all videotapes need to be purchased. Rental services are a frugal choice for special programs which may not be repeated for several years. Rented videotapes were utilized in the Sycamore, IL, High School library for a recent interdisciplinary introduction to the culture of France. Shown simultaneously at five "viewing sites" within the library, these tapes successfully introduced students to French technology, transportation and the fashion industry.

With the ever increasing popularity of home video production equipment, segments of videotapes produced by amateurs can often be utilized at a fraction of the cost of professionally produced materials. During a recent cross-cultural communication project between students from the same high school and those enrolled at the Bayswater High School in Australia, a videotape produced by the Australian students gave the Americans a first hand look at education within another culture. A more sophisticated approach to this global exchange of ideas is offered by CNN NEWSROOM. Students are encouraged to prepare video reports with the possibility that their stories will be selected by the editorial staff for sharing with students from other countries.

Many videotapes are filmed as continuing education materials for educators who are currently working in the field. These materials should not be overlooked when developing a professional learning materials collection at either the secondary or university level. The constant search for new teaching tactics can best be met with tapes featuring presentations of practical ideas by leading educators. With the tightening of travel budgets, videotaped and/or recorded conference sessions become practical substitutes as they can usually be purchased for a nominal fee. A quality example of such taping was produced for the Music Educators National Conference during the 1990 Symposium on Multicultural Approaches to Music Education, sponsored by the Music Educators National Conference, Smithsonian Institution's Office of Folklife Programs, the Society for Ethnomusicology, and the MENC Society for General Music. Accompanied by a book, *Teaching Music with a Multicultural Approach,* there are four videotapes: *Teaching the Music of African Americans, Teaching the Music of Hispanic Americans, Teaching the Music of the American Indian,* and *Teaching the Music of Asian Americans.* Materials such as these tapes serve not only to help with the training of teachers but to expand the continuing educational opportunities a school can offer to individual classroom teachers. Not only can they be viewed individually but can constitute the basis for departmental in-service meetings.

SATELLITE DISH RECEIVERS

Through the utilization of a Satellite Dish Receiver, it is possible to take advantage of educational programming uplinked from distant locations. Even though many of the satellite signals are scrambled, the "backyard dish" can capture numerous teleconferences, foreign newscasts, and other cultural telecasts on several of the clear channels. Those residing in rural areas with no connections to cable television services should note that the available descramblers are relatively inexpensive and provide access to numerous educational signals.

Among the clear channels is CBC's French station [A-1, 15, now A-E, 15] in Montreal, Canada, which affords the possibility of instruction by immersion into the French language via the air waves.

Satellite Telecommunications for Learning [SCOLA, S-2, 23] offers an exposure to over 25 world cultures on a daily basis. Approximately 20 hours of Italian-language programming is presented each week by Italy's Radiotelevisione Italiana [RAI, F-3, 24.] Dish owners in the southern states can access a wide range of Spanish programming on the Morelos Satellites [M-1 and M-2.] Clips from the GalaVision [G-1, 20 and Univision [F-3, 7] Spanish programs make valuable cultural enrichment materials. Foreign language teachers appreciate commercials that have been clipped from the commercial programming. These clips offer a brief exposure to a sampling of the influence of televised advertising on another culture's way of life and its economy. The Monitor Channel [F-4, 20] provides an analytical look at the news and can be utilized to introduce viewers to the multicultural impact of world news.

CABLE TELEVISION

Newton M. Minow claims that "The most important educational institution in America is television"[2] and from the moment the sound of Archie Bunker flushing his toilet was heard in thousands of American homes, the educational value of television was introduced to viewers, who in many cases were unaware of their introduction to multicultural attitudes. Educators who had been utilizing the many diversified cultural offerings on some of the channels geared towards a more specialized audience were now offered the possibility of culling multicultural information from the weekly programming offered by the major network channels.

Weekly television guides provide an overview of quality programming, which in many cases consciously or unconsciously concentrates on cultural enrichment. Offered by the leaders in the field of educational broadcasting, these programs are aimed towards the general public; however, creative librarians and classroom teachers recognize their educational value. Among the leading channels to watch are Arts and Entertainment, Bravo, The Learning Channel, The Discovery Channel, PBS, and C-Span.

Cable in the Classroom, a monthly publication, organizes many educational program listings by subject matter and directs educators toward commercial-free programming. In addition to tips for the utilization of cable programs within the classroom, sources of available study guides and support materials are identified.

COMPUTERIZED NEWS SERVICES

Many local cable television companies offer expanded learning tools such as the X-Press Information Services. Accessed through a software program, "X-Press, X-Change" is designed to provide the user with access to the news within minutes of its release by informational sources such as Associated Press, TASS, Xinhua, Kyodo News International, Agence France Presse, Copley News Service and CNN. It also provides the patron with a wealth of cultural information as well as lesson plans for *CNN Newsroom* and *Assignment Discover.* Other instructional aids include *Global Library Project* support materials to accompany the *Mind Extension University* broadcasts.

NEWSPAPERS, PERIODICALS
AND OTHER SERIAL PUBLICATIONS

A major breakthrough in the field of multicultural serial publications was the introduction of the *MultiCultural Review* in January, 1992. In addition to the feature articles aimed towards fostering discussions based on ethnic, racial and religious diversity, this quarterly publication will provide a comprehensive introduction to sources of multicultural materials. Librarians and other educators will find quality reviews published for the purposes of improving collections of materials aimed towards supporting multicultural instruction. In the premier issue, "Continuing Diversity: A Column of Periodical Reviews," edited by Richard R. Centing of the Ohio State University Libraries, explored several interesting titles among which can be found another Haworth Press publication, *Journal of Multicultural Social Work.*

Ethnic NewsWatch, a full text CD ROM database, provides electronic access to large quantities of multicultural information taken from the ethnic and minority newspapers and magazines published in America. This database brings together a wealth of ethnic information collected to reflect the many multicultural changes which have occurred within America. Designed to enhance both school and academic collections, *Ethnic NewsWatch* includes two complete databases, full text and directory information, presented in a user friendly bilingual format searchable in both English and Spanish.

Statistical information regarding the countries and their respective cultures can be gleaned from the old standards available in nearly all libraries–*The Statesman's Year-Book, World Factbook*, and the *World Almanac*. Quanta Press, a compact disc publishing company, offers *The CIA WORLD* which serves well as a good introductory tool for the study of cultural backgrounds related to 249 countries. Another easy to use favorite is the Culturgrams for the 90's, a series of brief pamphlets designed to introduce the culture of nearly a hundred different countries. Each *Culturgram* covers the "Customs and Courtesies" including greetings, visiting habits, eating habits, and gestures; the "People and their Attitudes" covering personal appearance, population, language, and religion; the "Life-style" depicting the diet, business habits, recreation and holidays; and finally the "Nation" touching upon the Government, economy, education, and other items of interest.

BOOKS

Educators expect to find books in multicultural library collections while jobbers anticipate orders designed to fulfill the purposes of the individual institutions where these collections are being developed. To aid in the selection of materials, recent conference exhibits have included more and more bibliographical catalogs prepared by publishers who are vying for position in the promotion and sale of materials for the development of multicultural collections. Among the better of these bibliographies are *Cultural Diversity* by Bantam Doubleday Dell and *Many Voices, Many Books. . . Strength Through Diversity: A Multicultural Catalog* published by Baker and Taylor Books with assistance from the Before Columbus

Foundation. The latter, which is well annotated, covers both fiction and nonfiction titles about the African American, Asian American, Hispanic, Latino, Chicano, and American Indian cultures.

The Wisconsin Department of Public Instruction offers an annotated bibliography compiled by Ginny Moore Kruse and Kathleen T. Horning entitled *Multicultural Literature for Children and Young Adults.* First published in 1988, the 78 page booklet is already in its third edition and offers a variety of titles "by and about African-Americans, American Indians, Asian-Americans, and Hispanic-Americans."[3]

The Multicolored Mirror: Cultural Substance in Literature for Children and Young Adults edited by Merri V. Lindgren for the Madison, WI, based Cooperative Children's Book Center can be obtained from Highsmith. The work includes an annotated bibliography of recent multicultural children's titles.

Another Wisconsin based company, Demco Media, offers two bibliographies of interest. The first *Turtleback Books by Demco Media: Cultural Diversity* is an annotated bibliography of children's and young adult books. The bibliography contains over 100 titles, of which nearly one third are considered suitable for the secondary level. The second nonannotated list, *Demco Media Turtleback Books: Spanish Language and Bilingual Books,* adds a few titles of interest to librarians who serve bilingual patrons and/or support Spanish language instruction.

One only needs to pick up a professional magazine or visit a conference to observe the abundance of materials in today's market. The old reliable publishers such as Gale Research and Facts on File are among the many quality publishers who are keeping abreast with the increased interest in multicultural publications. To select the best available materials the standard professional journals should be consulted for their reviews of the more timely publications. As the market becomes saturated with multicultural materials, these reviewing journals will help professionals as they struggle to select only those materials worthy of being added to a collection developed to meet a quality library's high standard of excellence.

LECTURES, ARTISTIC PERFORMANCES AND REALIA

Multicultural experiences can not and should not all come from within the confines of the printed page or from the limits of a television or computer screen. To broaden the horizons of the students at the Sycamore, IL, High School, annual lectures and interdisciplinary festivals are developed around the theme of a cultural group which evolves from some aspect of the school's curriculum.

Based on an Australian and American cross cultural communication project, the first of these festivals coincided with the 200th anniversary of the founding of Australia. In honor of this major event, the Illinois Secretary of State was offering an exchange between our state and Australia and it was possible to add the school's name to the list of host schools for the Australian authors. One of the authors, Rodney Hall, captivated the student body with stories of life in Australia and helped the students understand differences and similarities between the two cultural groups. To further enhance the lectures, posters, book marks, stuffed Australian animals, flags, eucalyptus branches and other realia surrounded the students as they listened to their guest. As a follow-up activity, contacts were made with a potential sister school in Bayswater, Australia, and shortly thereafter, letters arrived from the newly adopted school. These letters told about the adolescent culture from down under and encouraged the recipients to seek further information. Books and videotapes about Australia were in demand and the students were permitted to browse through the new acquisitions during their leisure time.

The success of this first celebration provided the necessary impetus for the continuation of cultural enrichment programming to enhance the curriculum. A request for information pertaining to Spanish art spawned the next event which involved numerous departments of the school. As the plans for the Spanish Fiesta developed, student interest grew in accord with the excitement generated by the faculty and library staff. Pinatas were designed and hung from the library ceiling to spark student interest in the forthcoming fiesta. Plans for this program developed rapidly and included Spanish music, Spanish dancing, an art lecture and slide show on Picasso, an art exhibit, Spanish poetry reading, and a look at bullfighting and life in Spain through the works of Ernest Hemingway.

The students liked the programming and showed an interest in our continuing the annual cultural extravaganzas. To meet their expectations, the faculty grouped together for a third time to develop an interdisciplinary introduction to the culture of France. Through the co-operation of the classroom teachers in the fields of history, geography, English, economics, science, and other related courses, cultural information was spread throughout the curriculum. Once again cultural displays were constructed in the library and the programming was expanded to cover the entire day. Speakers were engaged for the morning hours. Phil Wells, a former art professor and former Dean of Fine Arts at Northern Illinois University, introduced the students to the French Impressionists. A Northern Illinois University graduate student from France talked with the students about the culture of her homeland and fielded questions regarding adolescent activities. During the afternoon, students had an opportunity to view videotapes depicting the culture of modern day France.

ART PRINTS, POSTERS, SLIDES, VIDEODISCS

During our school's cultural festivals, the speaker's podium was surrounded with framed art reproductions. Serving as a backdrop for the art lectures by Phil Wells, the collection of Gaylord prints, which we had borrowed from the Northern Illinois Library System's audiovisual collection, brought back fond memories to Mr. Wells. He spoke highly of the reproductions, which are no longer available, and told of a collection of prints he had purchased to loan to his high school students during the earliest years of his educational career. Wells mused that the inevitable nicks which marred the frames were overlooked in deference to the advancement of culture within the students' homes.

It was Professor Wells endorsement of reproductions as an medium for introducing students to one aspect of a country's culture, which encouraged the searching for prints to fill the gap created by Gaylord when they discontinued their print collection. Many fine prints can be obtained from art supply dealers. Many of these prints are not framed, but are useful for the creation of interesting bulletin board displays. Calendars, which often feature the works of the masters, provide another source of prints for bulletin board displays designed to introduce the students to a country's artistic heritage.

An interesting series of posters related to cultures can be obtained from the American Library Association. Embassies and travel agencies can often supply attractive posters depicting a variety of cultural activities.

Slides are an excellent means for introducing not only the artistic masterpieces of a culture, but provide the opportunity to assist with the visualization of numerous facets of a particular culture. When selecting slides, care should be given to the framing of the picture, the accuracy of color and the clarity of detail within the transparent image which must maintain its quality even when greatly magnified for viewing on the silver screen.

Videodiscs provide a clarity of artistic reproduction which can not be equaled by other forms of technology. In spite of their "projected quality," they are not as flexible for lecturing as the individual slides which can easily be arranged to fit the lecturer's outline; however, this should not deter librarians from developing videodisc collections which have a multitude of other educational possibilities.

Quanta Press offers an excellent CD-ROM, *Coates Art Review: Impressionism,* which includes a satisfactory digital/visual representation of each of the impressionistic masterpieces selected for inclusion on the disc. If their future discs are as good as the disc devoted to the Impressionists, the world of CD-ROMs may play a significant role in the utilization of art as an introduction to a specific culture.

CONCLUSION

To be truly effective, collection development policies and interdisciplinary cultural programming must expand beyond stressing a particular cultural group. Quality library collections must branch into the exploration of the pluralistic society which prevails within America. Educational librarians should adopt a goal to cultivate global consciousness within all students by affording them the opportunity to explore a global society through the utilization of programs and materials aimed towards the development of a multi-cultural awareness.

SOURCE DIRECTORY

1. *Cable in the Classroom*
IDG/Peterborough
80 Elm St.
Peterborough, NH 03458
2. *Coates Art Review: Impressionism* and *CIA World*
Quanta Press, Incorporated
1313 Fifth St. SE, Suite 208C
Minneapolis, MN 55414
3. CNN NEWSROOM hotline
1-800-344-6219
4. *Cultural Diversity; a Bibliography of Young Adult & Adult Books Reflecting the Heritage and Experience of American Cultures*
Bantam Doubleday Dell Publishing Group Inc.
666 Fifth Avenue
New York, NY 10103
5. Culturgrams for the 90's
Brigham Young University
David M. Kennedy Center for International Studies
Publication Services
280 HRCB
Provo, UT 84602
(801) 378-6528
6. *Demco Media Turtleback . . . bilingual books*
Demco Media
P. O. Box 14260
Madison, WI 53707
7. Destinos Series
The Annenber/CPB Collection
1-800-LEARNER
8. *Ethnic Newswatch*
Softline Information Inc.
PO Box 16845
Stamford, CT 06905

9. French in Action Series
The Annenberg/CPB Collection
1-800-LEARNER
10. Kruse, Ginny Moore and Kathleen T. Horning
Multicultural Literature for Children and Young Adults
Publication Sales
Wisconsin Department of Public Instruction
P. O. Box 7841
Madison, WI 53707-7841
(800) 243-8782
11. Lindgren, Merri V., editor
Multicolored Mirror: Cultural Substance in Literature for Children and Young Adults
Highsmith Co., Inc.
W5527 Highway 106
P. O. Box 800
Fort Atkinson, WI 53538-0800
12. *Many Voices, Many Books . . . Strength Through Diversity: A Multicultural Catalog*
Baker and Taylor Books
Commerce Service Center
Mt. Olive Church Road
Commerce, GA 30599
13. *Multicultural Review*
Greenwood Publishing Group, Inc.
88 Post Road West, Box 5007
Westport, CT 06881-5007
800-225-5800
14. Posters–Culture Series
American Library Association Graphics
50 East Huron Street
Chicago, IL 60611
15. Teaching Music with a Multicultural Approach
Music Educators National Conference
1902 Association Drive
Reston, Virginia 22091
16. *Turtleback Books . . . Cultural Diversity*
Demco Media

P. O. Box 14260
Madison, WI 53707
17. *X-Press X-Change*
X-Press Information Services
Regency Plaza One
4643 S. Ulster St., Suite 340
Denver, Colorado 80237
(800) 7PC-NEWS

REFERENCES

1. Mandell, Phyllis Levy. "Cultural Diversity Videos, Part I, African-Americans." *School Library Journal.* Jan. 1992: 49.

2. Minow, Newton N., *How Vast the Wasteland Now?*, New York: Gannett Foundation Media Center, 1991. p. 13.

3. Kruse, Ginny Moore and others. *Multicultural Literature for Children and Young Adults; a Selected Listing of Books 1980-1990 by and About People of Color.* Madison, WI: Cooperative Children's Book Center, University of Wisconsin-Madison, and Wisconsin Department of Public Instruction, 1991. iii.

Surviving, Multiculturally, in Hard Times

Lyn Miller-Lachmann

SUMMARY. While demographic changes point to the need for more multicultural children's books, the recent recession threatens to destroy the progress that has been made in this area. The threat comes from three sources–the decline in school and library purchasing power, the loss of library professionals trained to evaluate and to select multicultural books, and the contraction of mainstream presses. The example of the early 1980's, when a recession and cutbacks in Federal programs sharply reduced the number and variety of multicultural titles, does not bode well for multicultural publishing today; however, demographic changes, the whole language movement, and the existence of mandated multicultural curricula present a more hopeful picture, as does the emergence of alternative presses. Because of the long lead time required in publishing books, the consequences of the recession are likely to endure through the middle of the 1990's, and librarians must be proactive in ensuring the continued supply of multicultural books for children and young adults.

INTRODUCTION

The recent unrest in Los Angeles and elsewhere has once again focussed the nation's attention on the plight of inner cities and their

Lyn Miller-Lachmann is Adjunct Librarian, Siena College Library, 515 Loudon Road, Loudonville, NY 12211.

[Haworth co-indexing entry note]: "Surviving, Multiculturally, in Hard Times," Miller-Lachmann, Lyn. Co-published simultaneously in *The Acquisitions Librarian* (The Haworth Press, Inc.) No. 9/10, 1993, pp. 91-100; and: *Multicultural Acquisitions* (ed: Karen Parrish and Bill Katz) The Haworth Press, Inc., 1993, pp. 91-100. Multiple copies of this article/chapter may be purchased from The Haworth Document Delivery Center. Call 1-800-3-HAWORTH (1-800-342-9678) between 9:00 - 5:00 (EST) and ask for DOCUMENT DELIVERY CENTER.

91

predominantly minority residents. The unrest followed the acquittal of four white policemen who were videotaped in the process of beating a black motorist, Rodney King. Underlying the precipitating event, however, were twelve years of diminished hopes and a declining standard of living among urban African Americans. The violence also raised the nation's awareness of other ethnic and racial conflicts–between African-American residents and Korean-American storekeepers, between Latino immigrants, newcomers to the neighborhoods, and the African Americans who had lived there for generations, and between older and more recent immigrants from Asia and Latin America.

The urban unrest in the spring of 1992 came on the heels of an economic recession that most analysts believe began almost two years earlier. Unemployment, already high among urban and minority teenagers, rose to over 40% in some areas of Los Angeles during the recession.[1] Young people of diverse ethnic and racial groups competed for the few remaining jobs, further exacerbating tensions.

At the same time as urban youths from diverse backgrounds scramble for scarce opportunities, the minority population of the United States continues to grow. In many urban school districts, more than half of the students are African American, Asian American, Latino, or American Indian. By the middle of the decade, more than a third of all youngsters in school will belong to these groups.[2]

As educators have become aware of the demographic changes, a call has gone out for more books that present the experiences of youngsters who are not white and middle class. Minority children, it is argued, need to see themselves portrayed positively in books, while white children need to see, in non-stereotypical ways, the people with whom they will be working and living in the twenty-first century. In the late 1980's, publishers began to produce children's and young adult books that reflect the diversity of the population. While some of those books have perpetuated misconceptions and stereotypes, many others are honest and complex portraits of young people and their communities. Writers of color have found new audiences for their stories and perspectives; dozens of African-American, Asian-American, American Indian, and Latino authors were published for the first time between 1986 and 1991. Articles in professional journals and bibliographies have appeared to publicize and to evaluate the explosion in books. Suddenly, multicultur-alism is the "hot topic" among authors, publishers, teachers, and librarians.

While the changing U.S. population points to the need for even more multicultural materials in schools and public libraries, the same recession that has worsened racial and ethnic conflicts also threatens to destroy the progress that has been made in making multicultural materials available to young people. The threat comes from three sources. The first is the decline in the purchasing power of schools and public libraries as state and local budgets across the nation feel the brunt of the recession. The second, also a conse-quence of the state and local budget crisis, is a loss of library personnel trained to evaluate and to select multicultural materials. The third is the contraction of the publishing industry. This is the most damaging in the long run, because even though budgets may increase and librarians may be rehired when the recession ends, the books may not be there when libraries are ready to buy. As the experience of the early 1980's suggests, publishers hurt by the sudden loss of a major market will be reluctant to publish for that market again, particularly if their commitment to multicultural pub-lishing was rather tenuous to begin with.[3] If fewer books are being produced overall, and fewer editors are available to search out new writers of color, this too will decrease the number and variety of multicultural books that libraries can buy. All of these factors point to the need for librarians to be aware of the recession's impact and to support those books that present the diversity of the American experience.

THE DECLINE IN LIBRARY PURCHASING POWER

As tax-supported institutions, schools and public libraries felt the consequences within months of the recession's onset. In many areas of the country, particularly the Northeast and California, real estate values plummeted, eroding the tax base. Tax revolts occurred across the nation as incomes failed to keep pace with inflation and many lost their jobs or feared they would be next.

According to a nationwide survey conducted by *Library Journal,* 1991 was the first year in which libraries in almost all areas of the country felt the full impact of the recession.[4] Frozen book budgets, cuts in staff, and shortened hours resulted. While the *LJ* survey focussed on public libraries, school libraries also experienced hard times, with some having to close in the absence of state mandates forcing them to stay open. Some of the public libraries hit the hardest were in large, culturally diverse cities such as New York, Boston, and Baltimore.

As yet, there is little research on the impact of reduced school and library spending on the purchases of multicultural children's books in the past few years. However, at the beginning of the 1980's, the curtailment of many Federal antipoverty programs, along with the 1981-82 recession, sharply reduced school and library purchases of multicultural books.[5] In general, such books have tended to sell better to schools and libraries than to bookstore buyers; only the most well-known authors have enjoyed substantial success in bookstores.[6] Many books considered multicultural are works of nonfiction that support the elementary and secondary curriculum. With the rise of the whole language movement in the late 1980's, multicultural books received a boost, as teachers integrated into their language arts and social studies curricula high-quality fiction and nonfiction representing diverse cultures. In many states, a multicultural approach to the curriculum was mandated in the last several years. Before the recession, therefore, multicultural books represented a major growth area for publishers, though the number of titles still remains relatively small.[7]

Hard economic times threaten the gains. While it is unlikely that strapped school districts will move back to basal readers and anthologies, the number and variety of books in the classroom will be adversely affected by cuts in materials budgets. For example, rather than buying new titles, teachers will make do with the previous year's dog-eared books. Faced with frozen or reduced budgets, school and public libraries will not be able to supplement the curriculum in as much depth and breadth. Librarians will continue to order multicultural books, but they will order fewer titles and fewer copies of each title. Smaller budgets and fewer orders translate into a loss of power for school and public librarians when they approach publishers to request more multicultural titles. In discussions and at professional conferences, many librarians have expressed the fear that the more well-publicized the budget cuts and freezes are, the more difficult it will be for librarians to convince publishers of their need for additional materials.

REDUCTIONS IN PROFESSIONAL LIBRARY PERSONNEL

Cutbacks in library budgets have affected professional staff as well as book purchases. According to a survey conducted by the American Library Association, more than 40% of library personnel managers had to reduce staff in 1991.[8] School libraries have suffered similar reductions. In many districts throughout the country, layoffs have forced the remaining librarians to cover two or more elementary schools. Larger schools have had to make do with one credentialed librarian instead of two or three. In some states, the most well-documented being California, the absence of properly certified librarians in schools is endemic.[9]

More research needs to be done on how materials selection differs when the selecting is done by credentialed librarians, teachers, or library aides. Observers of the situation in California, where the lack of school library standards and school librarians has existed for more than a decade, suggest several problems. Often teachers and district staff do not have access to review journals and bibliographies in the library field. Review journals such as *Booklist, School Library Journal, Wilson Library Bulletin, Horn Book,* the *Bulletin for the Center of Children's Books, Voice of Youth Advocates, Multicultural Review,* and the *Interracial Books for Children Bulletin* provide a variety of perspectives upon new and forthcoming works of multicultural literature for children and young adults. Given that most of those selecting books–be they librarians, teachers, or library aides–are not members of the group in question, professional library publications are essential in the evaluation of books for accuracy, authenticity, and cultural sensitivity. And while the field of education can boast several excellent works dealing with the methodology of multicultural education, those works do not analyze materials in great depth, and most of the materials recommended are older "classics" rather than current publications. Those not in the library profession are less likely to be aware of the frequently-updated multicultural bibliographies published by the Cooperative

Children's Book Center or other less well-publicized selection tools.

Another issue that may arise when administrators rather than librarians select books is one of intellectual freedom. A California school librarian writing in *School Library Journal* reported one district administrator telling him "you don't put books for seventh and eighth graders in a middle school" because "sixth graders may read them."[10] Multicultural books tend to raise controversial issues of cultural conflict, prejudice, and urban problems and are therefore likely to be banned by those who do not have an awareness of the importance of intellectual freedom or training in how to respond to challenges.

Finally, cutbacks in professional staff in schools and public libraries mean that less time can be spent in the complex process of book selection. A public librarian in a small, culturally diverse city in upstate New York once told me that, due to a steep budget cut, he delayed hiring a replacement children's librarian and ordered his children's books directly from *School Library Journal*'s best books list. While *SLJ* is certainly a legitimate source, it presents only one of many points of view. Furthermore, the *SLJ* list is a general one. It does not give special attention to the kind of multicultural books that better represent the population in his community, and it does not include books that are not outstanding stylistically but may present a unique and authentic perspective.

"DOWNSIZING" IN THE PUBLISHING INDUSTRY

Unlike schools and public libraries, which have a mission of serving their users, the mission of publishers is to make a profit for their stockholders. Advertising copy notwithstanding, multicultural books do not get published because they benefit society but because there is a market for them. Lists are developed one to three years in advance, and while some first-time authors break into the field, most of the published fiction and nonfiction has been written by established authors.

In the last major recession, which coincided with the Reagan Administration's gutting of many Federal antipoverty programs, multicultural publishing suffered tremendously. Many previously established authors of color had trouble finding publishers for their manuscripts, and almost no new ones broke into print in the early 1980's. Less than 1% of all children's books published in 1985 or 1986 were written or illustrated by African Americans; the numbers were even more dismal for Latino, American Indian, and Asian-American authors.[11] Editors told authors of multicultural stories that there was no market for their work or even that it was "too controversial" to be published. At the same time as minority authors and authors of multicultural books found it increasingly harder to find mainstream publishers, the overall output of major presses increased during the early and mid 1980's. Most of those new books were series romances sold primarily in bookstores; their characters were almost uniformly white, suburban, and middle class.

Historical parallels between the most recent recession and the one of the early 1980's are easy to draw. Both have been accompanied by sharp reductions in spending for libraries and schools. The conservative backlash of the late 1970's and early 1980's wiped out many gains in race relations and opportunities for Americans of color, and in the early 1990's the country continued to be polarized by race and class. Moves toward a multicultural curriculum in schools and colleges have been opposed by conservatives who claim that traditional Western values are the only ones worthy of teaching as well as by those who want the curriculum reduced to those "basic skills" seen as necessary for competing with the Japanese.

However, there are some differences between the current situation in the publishing industry and that of ten years ago. Some of those differences bode ill for the future of multicultural publishing; others offer a more hopeful picture.

First the bad news. In contrast to the situation in the 1980's, the publishing industry is not expanding overall in the 1990's. Leveraged buyouts have saddled publishers with huge debts as the number of independent big presses continues to decrease. Across the economy, "downsizing" is the word of the 1990's as overpaid executives attribute their companies' losses to too many goods and too many workers. The fate of several publishers, the most notable being Macmillan, has been thrown into doubt as a result of the bankruptcy filings of their parent companies. Many in the library field fear that both book sales and the output of new children's titles peaked in 1990.[12] With the reduction in the number of titles published comes a reduction in the number of editors hired to find authors and guide manuscripts to production. In the past few years, many editors at mainstream presses have complained of the difficulty of finding authors of color. Staff reductions will further stymie their efforts and lead them to concentrate on established authors and less innovative manuscripts that require less editorial intervention. Because of the long lead time required in publishing a list, the effects of the recession of the early 1990's will continue through the middle of the decade.

Librarians have already seen the effects upon multicultural publishing of the general downsizing in the publishing industry. The highly-regarded revision of Harper and Row's Land and People series, renamed Portraits of the Nations and published by Harper-Collins, was cancelled after the third year due to disappointing sales. Many in the new crop of multicultural authors who broke into print in the late 1980's have had books delayed or cancelled for economic reasons. However, this has happened to authors across the board; unlike in the early 1980's, there is little evidence that multicultural authors have been singled out.

SOURCES OF HOPE FOR MULTICULTURAL BOOKS

Another significant change from the early 1980's, and a reason to remain hopeful about the future of publishing multicultural books, is the existence of mandated curricula in this area. In response to the nation's growing diversity and interdependence with the rest of the world, many states and local school districts have mandated some form of global curricula. Along with more extensive treatment of Asia, Africa, Latin America, and people of color in the United States has come an emphasis upon materials that present Third World perspectives and interpretations. In times of cutbacks, programs that are mandated receive highest priority. As a newly-mandated program, multicultural education requires the acquisition of materials for the first time. Both new titles and older classics stand to benefit.

Finally, while textbooks often occupied the center of the book-banning battlefield in the late 1970's and early 1980's, more and more classrooms are abandoning textbooks and embracing trade books as a means of teaching a variety of subjects. Language arts, social studies, and even science classes are reading currently-published fiction and nonfiction as part of the movement toward whole language. The whole language movement began in the late 1980's, and despite the difficulties of keeping up with the literature in a time of budget shortfalls, it shows no sign of fading.

Given the economic imperatives facing the publishing industry, school and public librarians have to be proactive rather than reactive in ensuring the continued supply and variety of multicultural books. Publishers tend to follow fads—one year the hot genre is romance, the next, mystery, and so on. While genres such as romance and mystery rise and fall in popularity, the trend toward the increasing diversity of the U.S. population is not likely to change, and books that reflect that diversity should not be thought of by librarians or publishers as a passing fad.

Although librarians must support efforts by mainstream presses to publish more and better multicultural titles for children, the works of small presses should not be ignored. During the dark years of the 1980's, small alternative presses filled the multicultural void, keeping the hopes and careers of many authors alive. These presses flourished, and some, like Children's Book Press, became quite large. Besides filling an important need, the small presses, by virtue of their success and the attention they received, helped to prod the major houses to publish more multicultural books. Today, small presses continue to introduce new authors to the field, and they are the only publishing houses where a significant proportion of the owners and editors are themselves people of color. Interviews with multicultural small press publishers in spring 1992 indicate that they are managing to prosper in spite of hard times precisely because they continue to fill a niche.

Economic difficulties frequently pit the diverse groups of a society against each other, and this has certainly been the case during the most recent recession in the U.S. By giving highest priority in the acquisition budget to children's books written from the perspective of the growing minority population in the U.S., librarians not only ensure the continued supply of those books; they give all

American youngsters the tools to work together in order to survive
hard times and to build a better future.

NOTES

1. Richard W. Stevenson: "Rebuilders Face Deep Faults in South-Central
Area." *New York Times*, May 6, 1992: A23.

2. Nancy F. Chavkin: "Joining Forces: Education for a Changing Population." *Educational Horizons* 68 (Summer 1990): 190.

3. Walter Dean Myers: "The Black Experience in Children's Books: One
Step Forward, Two Steps Back." In *The Black American in Books for Children:
Readings in Racism,* 2nd ed. (ed. by Donnarae McCann and Gloria Woodard).
Metuchen, N.J.: Scarecrow Press (1985): 224.

4. Judy Quinn and Michael Rogers: "Library Budgets Survey '91: Hard
Times Continue." *Library Journal* 114 (January 1992): 14.

5. Myers: "The Black Experience in Children's Books": 224.

6. "Multicultural Publishers Confab: Attendance Down, Optimism Up."
Publishers Weekly (November 8, 1991): 15.

7. Heather Vogel Frederick: "Needed: Stories That Reflect Many Cultures."
The Christian Science Monitor, May 1, 1992: 15.

8. Quinn and Rogers: "Library Budgets Survey '91": 14.

9. Richard K. Moore: "A Tale of Two School Systems." *School Library
Journal* 36 (October 1990): 54.

10. ibid.: 54.

11. Kathleen T. Horning and Ginny Moore Kruse: *CCBC Choices 1986*. Madison, Wisc.: Cooperative Children's Book Center (1987), 2.

12. Kathleen T. Horning and Ginny Moore Kruse: *CCBC Choices 1991*. Madison, Wisc.: Cooperative Children's Book Center (1992), 1.

Is There Diversity in Suburbia?

Karen Parrish

SUMMARY. Multiculturalism seems to be the buzz-word of the '90s. The New York State Education Department has mandated diversity requirements at all levels. As librarians, it is our responsibility to reinforce these programs by providing quality multi-ethnic literature to our patrons. To support this trend, it is necessary for public libraries to incorporate these materials into their collections. The following is an informal survey of three local suburban libraries (names changed–I shall call them Suburbville, Burg, and Gotham) to determine if, in fact, they are addressing this issue in their children's and young adult collections.

INTRODUCTION

Give me Your tired, your poor,
Your huddled masses yearning to
breathe free,
The wretched refuse of your teeming
shore.
Send these, the homeless, the tem-

Karen Parrish is employed by Washington-Warren BOCES in upstate New York. She is Elementary Librarian in the Fort Edward, New York school district and K-12 Librarian in the Indian Lake, New York school district.

[Haworth co-indexing entry note]: "Is There Diversity in Suburbia?," Parrish, Karen. Co-published simultaneously in *The Acquisitions Librarian* (The Haworth Press, Inc.) No. 9/10, 1993, pp. 101-114; and: *Multicultural Acquisitions* (ed: Karen Parrish and Bill Katz) The Haworth Press, Inc., 1993, pp. 101-114. Multiple copies of this article/chapter may be purchased from The Haworth Document Delivery Center. Call 1-800-3-HAWORTH (1-800-342-9678) between 9:00 - 5:00 (EST) and ask for DOCUMENT DELIVERY CENTER.

101

pest-tost to me,
I lift my lamp beside the golden
door!

–Emma Lazarus (Goley, p. 93)

America, land of the free, home to the immigrant, here we are.
But, if you aren't like us (white, Anglo-Saxon, Protestant), are you
welcome? Are you respected for your native culture or shunned for
being different? Do the words freedom and equality have the same
meaning for all Americans or are some of us second and even third
class citizens? People come to this country for a variety of reasons
but the bottom line is, they seek something that was denied them in
their native land. They are starved for political and religious freedom and the right to speak their mind. Many come here to escape
terror and starvation. All are looking for a better life for themselves
and their children, as were our forefathers so many years ago. All
who reside here have roots elsewhere. Even our Native-American
brothers, it is believed, came across the Bering Straits; but they
were the first. What has reduced these proud people to a substan-
dard existence in a land they founded? I think it is the same arro-
gance that has given Americans the "ugly American" label echoed
world wide. What other country would send ambassadors to countries without requiring them to speak the language? I find this an
absurd assumption on our part that all others should have to con-
verse in English.

From 1969-1971, I lived in a small city, Kenitra, Morocco. I
saw, first hand, the manner in which we impose ourselves on
others. The US Navy was a guest in this Arab country and yet
time and again I witnessed an attitude which sickens me to this
day. Most Americans seldom left the confines of the base.
When they did, they were quick to criticize the culture and the
Arab people. Words like "rag-head" and "MoRab" were often
heard. No respect was shown for their religion or their coun-
try. Morocco is a poor country led by a King who is trying to
bring his nation into the 20th century. He carefully introduces
the new in a careful balance with old traditions. I personally
found this to be a beautiful, unique country with warm, gener-

ous, proud people. The difference in attitude lies in not trying to expect them to conform to our standards. I accepted them for who they were and they reciprocated in kind. We got along fine and I enjoyed a wonderful experience.

When people arrive in the United States, they must learn many new things in order to survive. Language is the major obstacle, but simple everyday tasks such as shopping and doing laundry may be overwhelming. They need their heritage to fall back on for security in trying times. They shouldn't be expected to leave their culture on the dock when they arrive. As Timothy V. Rasinski and Nancy D. Padak observed, "the traditional orientation toward the cultural diversity of the country, however, has been characterized by the implicit assumption that the dominant culture is the best culture. New arrivals were encouraged to adopt the dominant Anglo-Saxon, Protestant culture" (Rasinski p. 576). What will happen in the next decade when this dominant culture becomes the minority? Will things automatically change and roles reverse? And, if this were to happen, would that be any more just than what is being practiced now? Maybe the time has come to initiate some changes. We have the opportunity to make things right in our own society and hopefully, in the process, better prepare all of our populace for dealing with the coming global economy.

In 1986, U.N. Secretary-General Javier de Cuellar stated, "Youth constitutes a global resource of the first magnitude" (de Cuellar p. 197). One way to initiate change begins with our children. If they grow up without bias, things could be better for future generations. An excellent way to address this is through children's readings. "Educators and literary authorities are increasingly recognizing the role of children's literature in shaping attitudes and in stimulating children's language and cognitive development" (Norton p. 103). Rasinski and Padak say, ". . . we believe that children's literature can be a powerful way for children to learn about and appreciate other cultures" (Rasinski p. 576). They go on to state, "Literature has long been seen as a vehicle for fostering cultural awareness and appreciation. Because it tells the stories of human events and the human condition, and not simply the facts, literature does more than change minds; it changes people's hearts" (Rasinski p. 577).

All of this is well and good but where do we, as librarians, go from here? What do we look for in children's offerings? What comprises "good" multicultural literature? One of my favorite books, as a child was *Little Black Sambo*. It was the one obvious exception to the norm of white protagonists in children's literature. As Jean Marzollo notes, "The problem of *Little Black Sambo* was not the story, though. It was the racist characterization of the people in the story" (Marzollo p. n/a). As collection compilers, we need to be aware that everything available is not necessarily good. We have to beware of falling into the trap of tokenism.

BACKGROUND-PURPOSE

In 1991 while I was taking a three week children's literature course and because of the brevity of the session, the professor divided the class into groups which in turn were required to teach their designated chapter from the text. My partner and I chose "Multicultural Literature." I was unfamiliar with the term and anxious to learn more about it. Armed with a bibliography, I descended on my local public library (Suburbville) and to my chagrin found a very poor representation of literature for, by, or about other cultures. The nonfiction section had a series of books which ranged from Arabs . . . to Zulus in America or a close facsimile thereof. The fiction representation was limited to award winners. When I questioned the Children's librarian about this, her response was, "Nobody ever requests it. We have few foreigner's in town." As I thought about this, I became less satisfied with her answer. To me, it seemed these works should be inclusive; it's not something children would ask for.

This brought up the query; do predominately white, affluent, suburban libraries need diversity in their collections? In a recent article in *Newsweek,* author Julius Lester commented on the change in children's letters he has received, " . . . in the '60s and '70s (they) were from black kids. Now the letters are almost all from white kids in the Midwest who say, 'There are no black kids in our area and this is my only experience in knowing about slavery' " (speaking of his book *Too Be A Slave*) (Jones p. 65). Children need to understand racial and ethnic cultures in order to respect them.

In reading the local library's mission statement, I found the following, " . . . shall provide informational, educational, cultural and recreational reading resources, services and programs for the people of the area the Library is chartered to serve" (Suburbville 1965 p. 1). I have to conclude, after investigating this library's attitudes and collection, that the word cultural in this instance, refers to the arts. Their Book Selection Policy also proved interesting, "Library materials to be included in the Library must satisfy acceptable standards of quality and fill a need. In evaluating quality both of fiction and non-fiction, the following factors are considered: authority and competence of the author, clarity and accuracy, literary style, significance of subject usefulness and format." It goes on to state, "The Library will also select the best new children's books and appropriately replace worn copies. The Library will maintain a collection that should be broad enough to provide meaningful materials for children of all ages, levels of ability and cultural background" (Suburbville 1986 p. 1).

After our presentation, a classmate told me the situation at Suburbville would soon change. She worked at Suburbville part-time and was assigned the task of using their jobber's catalog and ordering all the children's books listed that were not among the present holdings. This added to my frustration because no effort was being made to insure that the selections were of "quality" books. Marzollo notes, " . . . characterizations don't mean negative characterizations; a writer certainly should be free in a story to create an unpleasant minority group character, but a writer must respect that character–must understand why the character does the things he or she does. Other multicultural books have respectful characterizations but bad stories. And there are those that are just plain boring or too preachy to entertain. But many multicultural picture books are magnificent, and these are the ones children should be exposed to" (Marzollo p. n/a). "Superficial treatment of different cultures can lead to a reinforcement of stereotypes and misconceptions, including the notion that ethnic cultures are not integral parts of the dominant culture" (Rasinski p. 577).

We have returned to the question of what comprises "quality" multicultural literature. The following criteria related to literature that represents Black Americans, Native Americans, Hispanic Americans, and Asian Americans reflect the recommendations of the Children's Literature Review Board, Anna Lee Stensland, and the Council on Interracial Books for Children. There are seventeen points elaborated on which take up two full pages. For the sake of brevity, I will only paraphrase the main points. It is important that minority groups be depicted in an accurate, non-stereotypical way. The settings should be realistic and authentic. Language used should not be offensive or degrading. Positive role models should be provided for the reader and the characters should appear as individuals, not part of a stereotypical group. Actually, they are the same things anyone would want to see as a depiction of themselves (Norton 1991 p. 534-536).

To explore how effective suburban libraries have been in addressing the issue of multicultural literature, I visited three local facilities which I will call Suburbville, Burg, and Gotham where I conducted an informal survey. All are demographically similar and are often grouped in studies. Due to time and space restraints, I created a select fiction bibliography limiting myself to ten entries each for children's and young adult titles within the four accepted ethnic classifications (Black or African Americans, Hispanic, Native Americans, and Asian)(see Survey). I attempted to incorporate several lesser known titles which would reflect depth in a collection. Four sources were used in selecting the titles: *(1) Many Voices, Many Books . . . Strength Through Diversity–The Multicultural Catalog* from Baker and Taylor Books; *(2) Multicultural Literature for Children and Young Adults* from the Cooperative Children's Book Center; *(3) Comics to Classics* by Arthea J. S. Reed; *(4) Multicultural Literature* (a bibliography) created by Sharon Waagner and Karen Parrish.

SURVEY CONCLUSIONS

Having completed this research and survey, I found myself left with even more questions. Burg has the best representation of multicultural books but their budget could account for this. It is about $1 million more than the other two. I wasn't able to determine how selective each was in their acquisitions but all three children's specialists said they relied solely on jobber lists for purchases. I was surprised at the completeness at Suburbville but couldn't help but

THE SURVEY

BLACK (AFRICAN AMERICAN)- YOUNG ADULT

TITLE	SUBURBVILLE	BURG	GOTHAM
ANNIE JOHN		X	X
BLUE TIGHTS	X		
FALLEN ANGELS	X		X
THE FRIENDS	X	X	X
LET THE CIRCLE BE UNBROKEN	X	X	X
RAINBOW JORDAN	X	X	X
SWEET WHISPERS, BROTHER RUSH	X	X	
WAITING FOR THE RAIN	X	X	X
WHICH WAY FREEDOM?	X		X
WORDS BY HEART	X	X	

BLACK (AFRICAN AMERICAN)- CHILDREN'S

TITLE	SUBURBVILLE	BURG	GOTHAM
ABIYOYO	X		X
AT THE CROSSROADS		X	X
BROTHER TO THE WIND	X	X	X
THE DRINKING GOURD	X	X	
THE FRIENDSHIP	X	X	X
ME, MOP, AND THE MOONDANCE KID	X	X	X
MIRANDY, AND BROTHER WIND	X	X	X
THE MYSTERY OF DREAR HOUSE	X		X
THE PATCHWORK QUILT	X	X	X
THE SHIMMERSHINE QUEENS	X		X

SURVEY (continued)

HISPANIC- YOUNG ADULT

TITLE	SUBURBVILLE	BERG	GOTHAM
A SHROUD IN THE FAMILY			
BASEBALL IN APRIL & OTHER STORIES			
CRAZY LOVE			
FAMOUS ALL OVER TOWN	X	X	X
THE HONORABLE PRISON	X		
HOW THE GARCIA GIRLS LOST THEIR ACCENT	X	X	
IN NUEVA YORK			
INTAGLIO: A NOVEL IN SIX STORIES			
MACHO			
POCHO			

HISPANIC- CHILDREN'S

TITLE	SUBURBVILLE	BURG	GOTHAM
AMIGO MEANS FRIEND			
CLASS PRESIDENT	X	X	X
DANZA		X	
FELITA		X	
FIESTA			
GILBERTO AND THE WIND		X	X
THE KING'S FIFTH		X	
ROSA'S SPECIAL GARDEN	X	X	
SANTIAGO	X	X	
STRINGBEAN'S TRIP TO THE SHIN- ING SEA	X	X	X

SURVEY (continued)

ASIAN- YOUNG ADULT

TITLE	SUBURBVILLE	BURG	GOTHAM
CHILD OF THE OWL	X	X	X
CHILDREN OF THE RIVER		X	X
THE HAPPIEST ENDING		X	
HOMEBASE			
IN THE EYE OF WAR			
THE JOY LUCK CLUB	X	X	X
KIM-KIMI	X		
REBELS OF THE HEAVENLY KINGDOM		X	
RICE WITHOUT RAIN		X	
SO FAR FROM BAMBOO GROVE			

ASIAN- CHILDREN'S

TITLE	SUBURBVILLE	BURG	GOTHAM
ELAINE, MARY LEWIS AND THE FROGS		X	
EL CHINO	X	X	
THE HAPPY FUNERAL	X	X	
HIROSHIMA NO PIKA	X	X	
HOW MY PARENTS LEARNED TO EAT		X	X
IN THE YEAR OF THE BOAR AND JACKIE ROBINSON	X	X	X
PARK'S QUEST	X		X
SACHIKO MEANS HAPPINESS	X	X	
TALES FROM GOLD MOUNTAIN	X	X	
TIKKI TIKKI TEMBO	X	X	X

SURVEY (continued)

NATIVE AMERICAN- YOUNG ADULT

TITLE	SUBURBVILLE	BURG	GOTHAM
A WOMAN OF THE TRIBE		X	
THE BEET QUEEN	X	X	X
CANYONS	X	X	
THE EARTHSHAPERS			
MOHAWK TRAIL		X	
THE MOCCASIN MAKER			
THE NIGHT THE WHITE DEER DIED		X	
SWEETGRASS	X	X	X
TRACKS	X	X	X
WHEN THE LEGENDS DIE		X	

NATIVE AMERICAN- CHILDREN'S

TITLE	SUBURBVILLE	BURG	GOTHAM
CORN IS MAIZE	X		X
DANCING TEEPEE		X	X
DEATH OF THE IRON HORSE			X
DR. COYOTE			
I WEAR THE MORNING STAR		X	X
THE LEGEND OF THE INDIAN PAINT BRUSH	X	X	X
RACING THE SUN			
THE SIGN OF THE BEAVER	X	X	
SING DOWN THE MOON	X	X	
THE STORY OF THE JUMPING MOUSE	X	X	X

wonder if it wasn't accidental, considering the earlier statement made by my fellow student. There appears to be no consistency throughout the collections except for the fact that Hispanic and Native Americans were poorly represented.

I found it rather difficult to find any one complete list of books. It appears that not all fiction is classified by ethnic group. Even annotated bibliographies fail to identify culture if the main theme is suicide, for example. This can be a burden for those trying to develop a diverse collection. One would have to use many sources, including literature texts, to do a proper job. Even the recently released, *Our Family, Our Friends, Our World* does not critically analyze its 1038 entries. Author Lyn Miller-Lachmann states, "This is not supposed to be a list of the Best of Multicultural Literature. . . . We tried to be inclusive rather than completely comprehensive" (Grondahl p. D1).

I found inconsistencies again in the texts being used at the academic level, in both the reading department and library school. They cannot decide how to broach this subject. Norton devotes a complete chapter to multicultural literature and divides it into four basic groups as our survey represented. Cullinan added a short section on Jewish Americans, the Holocaust, and the nuclear threat. Donelson's *Literature for Today's Young Adults* does not even acknowledge the term, multiculturalism, and the only related term to be found is "ethnic" which can be located on a total of five pages. This does not seem to be a good message to be sending to future book selectors. The Cooperative Children's Book Center sticks to the basic four as does the bulk of the Baker and Taylor multicultural catalog. The latter does, however, include a short insert called "multicultural" which is every thing not in the big four. I see this as a future problem. I have the disturbing feeling we may be creating a new segregation.

In regard to this issue, I contacted Susan Roman, Executive Director for Children's Services at ALA. She acknowledged that she too had concerns about this and had brought it up at a recent White House Conference on Library and Information Services. She said that many neglect to see the potential danger as they rush around trying to get multicultural books on the shelves. Ms. Roman also felt that there was a need for a good annotated bibliography which is more inclusive as well as being critical (Roman 1991). What then is multiculturalism?

CONCLUSIONS

I have to conclude that the meaning of multiculturalism is dependent on the context in which it is being applied. If we were considering it in regard to the United States, I would have to respond: Native American, Hispanic, Asian, and Black or African American. However, I have seen bibliographies include Hawaiian, Jewish, and Eskimo cultures. It supposedly refers to cultures other than the dominate one. I see a need for more "quality" multicultural children's books. It would be refreshing to see more picture books depicting various ethnic groups interacting in a positive way.

If we are considering this in a more universal sense, I would say the term would have to relate to all cultures. In this regard, it would be more to my liking to use the term Globalism. This would mean learning about, appreciating, and respecting the uniqueness of mores other than our own, no matter who the "we" is.

Overall, I find that in this country, the term is used in various ways, depending on the special interest group who is trying to incorporate it in its agenda–it is trendy to be Multicultural. In some instances, it has even been expanded to include women, AIDS, and the gay community.

The value of offering good multicultural literature in our libraries? As Norton states in her introduction to the chapter on literature diversity, "Through multicultural literature, children who are members of racial or ethnic minority groups realize that they have a cultural heritage of which they can be proud, and that their culture has made important contributions to the United States and to the world. Pride in their heritage helps children who are members of minority groups improve their self-concepts and develop cultural identity. Learning about other cultures allows children to understand that people who belong to racial or ethnic groups other than theirs are real people, with feelings, emotions, and needs similar to their own–individual human beings, not stereotypes. Through multicultural literature, children discover that while not all people may share their personal beliefs and values, individuals can and must learn to live in harmony" (Norton 1991 p. 531).

Roberta Long asserts, "If black children or Native Americans or Asians don't see themselves in books, they won't see themselves important people. And we will be sending that message to white children, too" (Jones p. 64). Bernice E. Cullinan, author of *Literature and the Child*, tells us, "It is important to have multicultural literature in schools and libraries because stories do shape readers' views of their world and of themselves. School children learn that their multiethnic friends all share the same needs and feelings, and multicultural literature echoes these common bonds" (Cullinan p. 575-577).

I think that in order to eliminate bias and discrimination, a more universal approach is desirable. When I discussed the lack of total diversity in what is being taught in colleges with Vic Sgambato, activist in the "A World of Difference" movement sponsored by the Anti-Defamation League of B'nai B'rith, he was appalled. Vic has been using a program in his Fort Plain Elementary School called "Standing in Someone Else's Shoes" which he imposes prejudices on all of the class at various times and allows biases to fester for a couple days, then turns the tables. It is a tough but effective teaching tool (Sgambato p. 13-16). I like the editor's comments in the initial issue of *Multicultural Review*, "Simple acts of human kindness: respect, courtesy, and dignity. People touching, reaching one another. Ultimately, multiculturalism is a state of mind rather than a personal or political agenda." All people should be represented both in our literature and on our library shelves. We must take care not to inadvertently become censors by neglecting to order those works important to, and about, all aspects of our very diverse society. "Our library collections can and should reflect this cultural diversity even if our own communities do not" (Camarata p. 190). Only through understanding and mutual respect can we ever achieve global peace and harmony—only through our children and their literature can we help pave the way for a better future. The powers this places in our hands, as librarians, is awesome. Let's not blow it!

REFERENCES

1. Camarata, Corinne. "Makin Connections: Introducing Multicultural Books." *School Library Journal.* 37 (Sept. 1991): 190-91.

2. Cullinan, Bernice E. *Literature and the Child.* New York: Harcourt Brace Javanovich, 1989.

3. de Cuellar, Javier. *U.N. Chronicle.* New York: Jan. 1986. cited in "Kids Need Libraries: Schools and Public Libraries Preparing the Youth for the World of Tomorrow." *Journal of Youth Services in Libraries* (Spring 1990): 197.

4. Donelson, Kenneth L. and Alleen Pace Nilsen. *Literature for Today's Young Adult.* New York: Harper Collins, 1989.

5. Goley, Elaine P. "Developing Library Collections to Serve New Immigrants." *School Library Journal.* (Oct. 1985): 93-97.

6. Grondahl, Paul. "Of Many Cultures." *The Times Union* (Albany] 28 March 1992, sec. D:1,3.

7. Jones, Malcolm J. "Its' A Not So Small World." *Newsweek* (Sept 9, 1991) 64-65.

8. Kruse, Ginny Moore and Kathleen T. Horning. *Multicultural Literature for Children and Young Adults.* Madison, Wisconsin: Cooperative Children's Book Center, 1991.

9. *Many Voices, Many Books* ... *Strength Through Diversity: The MultiCultural Catalog.* Somerville, N.J.: Baker and Taylor, 1991.

10. Marzollo, Jean. "Multiculture Books for Every Classroom." *Instructor* (Feb 1991): n/a.

11. Mitchell-Powell, Brenda. "From the Editor." *Multicultural Review.* 1 (January 1992): 3.

12. Norton, Donna E. "Language and Cognitive Development Through Multicultural Literature." *Childhood Education* 62 (Nov/Dec 1985): 103-08. *Through the Eyes of a Child.* New York: MacMillan, 1991.

13. Rasinski, Timothy and Nancy D. Padak. "Multicultural Learning Through Children's Literature." *Language Arts* 67 (Oct 1990): 576-80.

14. Reed, Arthea J.S. *Comics to Classics.* Newark, DE.: International Reading Assoc., 1988.

15. Roman, Susan. personal interview. Nov. 1991.

16. Sgambato, Vic. "Standing in Someone Else's Shoes." *Education and Society.* (Winter 1989): 13-16.

17. Suburbville Children's Librarian. personal interview. Aug.1991.

18. Suburbville Library. "Policy 10" *Book Selection Policy.* Mar. 13, 1985, revised May 22, 1986. "Policy 9" *Mission Statement* Mar. 13, 1985, revised May 22, 1985.

AT THE ACADEMIC LEVEL

The Diversity Research Guide Program: The University of Arizona Library's Experience

Louise Greenfield
Atifa Rawan
Camille O'Neill

SUMMARY. The University of Arizona Library's Diversity Research Guide Program was implemented in the Spring of 1991 with a grant from the University's Office of Undergraduate Academic

Louise Greenfield is Head Library Instruction Librarian, University of Arizona, Library Instruction Department, Main Library, Tucson, AZ 85721. Atifa Rawan is Government Documents Librarian, University of Arizona, Government Documents Department, Main Library, Tucson, AZ 85721. Camille O'Neill is Library Instruction Librarian, University of Arizona, Library Instruction Department, Main Library, Tucson, AZ 85721.

[Haworth co-indexing entry note]: "The Diversity Research Guide Program: The University of Arizona Library's Experience," Greenfield, Louise, Atifa Rawan, and Camille O'Neill. Co-published simultaneously in *The Acquisitions Librarian* (The Haworth Press, Inc.) No. 9/10, 1993, pp. 115-129; and: *Multicultural Acquisitions* (ed: Karen Parrish and Bill Katz) The Haworth Press, Inc., 1993, pp. 115-129. Multiple copies of this article/chapter may be purchased from The Haworth Document Delivery Center. Call 1-800-3-HAWORTH (1-800-342-9678) between 9:00 - 5:00 (EST) and ask for DOCUMENT DELIVERY CENTER.

115

Affairs. The program's goal was to develop a series of library guides that would increase undergraduate students' awareness of resources existing within the U of A Library that support diverse viewpoints. The guides were designed as teaching tools to introduce undergraduate students to library resources and research methods. The four graduate students hired to develop eight guides participated in a comprehensive training program, which emphasized instruction on bibliography preparation. As a result of the Diversity Research Guide Program, the graduate student participants were exposed to current issues in academic libraries and to the profession of librarianship. The guides were widely disseminated, and are being used by the University's students, staff, and faculty, and by people from institutions and organizations within the Tucson community.

INTRODUCTION

The University of Arizona is a Research I institution, a category reserved for universities with high levels of research activity, coupled with comprehensive academic programs at the undergraduate, masters, and doctoral levels. The University of Arizona (U of A) has an enrollment of over 35,000 full-time and part-time students. Almost 27,000 of these students are undergraduates.[1]

The University is located in the city of Tucson, a Sonoran high-desert community with a metropolitan-area population of 732,372 (Pima County). The ethnic demographics of Arizona and the rest of the Southwest are changing. The percentages of Hispanics and American Indians within Arizona's population have increased in the last few years.[2]

In recent years, the University has committed itself to strengthening the undergraduate experience for its increasingly diverse student body. Special efforts have been made to attract and retain minority students. In fact, one of the University's objectives is to improve ethnic minority education, and to assure equal access, achievement, retention, and graduation of under-represented ethnic minority and socioeconomic groups. In addition, the University of Arizona has more than 2,000 international students enrolled, and ranks among the top 20 universities in the United States in number of foreign students. Students come from most states in the U.S., and from more than 110 other countries around the world.[3]

Because of its proximity to the international border with Mexico, the University has provided educational opportunities for students not only in Latin American studies, Spanish and Portuguese languages and literature, but also in related areas within the disciplines of agriculture, anthropology, architecture, economics, education, fine arts, history, law, medicine, and sociology.

The University of Arizona is committed to providing equal educational opportunity for all, and has strong affirmative action and diversity action plans and programs. The University's definition of diversity encompasses differences in age, color, ethnicity, gender, national origin, physical or mental ability, race, religion, sexual orientation, socioeconomic background, Vietnam era veteran status, or unique individual style.[4]

THE UNIVERSITY OF ARIZONA LIBRARY

The goal of the University of Arizona Library is to encourage and promote a pluralistic environment in which people of all backgrounds feel comfortable expressing their unique heritage. In concert with the University's goal to attain a diverse work force by the year 2000, the Library is committed to recruiting, hiring, and promoting under-represented group members.[5] Diversity within the Library staff will enable the Library to better serve the diverse faculty, staff, and students of this University, and will ensure a culturally enriched work force.[6]

Through its collections and services, the Library seeks to be a model of and a model for this intellectual and social diversity. The Library's vision for diversity represents a new effort to move beyond statements of concern to plans for action that will encourage diversity among our patrons and staff, and in our collections and services. The Library, through its activities, provides various programs to serve the needs of students, faculty, staff and other library users.[7]

The University of Arizona Library provides a comprehensive research collection supporting undergraduate education, as well as graduate programs in more than 100 departments and fields. The collection includes more than 3,043,217 volumes and 3,447,731 microforms: a total of almost 6.5 million items. Current periodical subscriptions number 21,621. The University of Arizona Library is a member of the Association of Research Libraries and is ranked 23rd in volumes held. The acquisitions budget is approximately $4.4 million.

While the research collection of the University of Arizona Library is very strong, students often find the information difficult to access. Materials are available in a variety of formats, and are housed in many buildings, departments, and branches. Because the University of Arizona Library has not yet fully implemented the integrated online system, library users must consult many types of reference sources in order to find information on their topics. This process becomes even more complicated when students are doing research on topics related to diverse groups. Subject headings used for various minority and ethnic groups, for example, are often outdated and may vary from source to source. During recent years, informal surveys of freshmen's initial reactions to research and to the University of Arizona Library have revealed that students feel overwhelmed, confused, and nervous about approaching research and using the Library. The guides were designed to help undergraduate students understand the types of sources available and how to use them successfully.

THE DIVERSITY RESEARCH GUIDE PROGRAM

The Diversity Research Guide Program successfully reached its goal of developing a series of research guides designed to increase undergraduate students' awareness of the resources within the U of A Libraries that support diverse viewpoints. The program was implemented in the Spring of 1991 with a $4,000 grant from the Office of Undergraduate Academic Affairs. The program had the support of the University Library Administration, and was coordinated by Louise Greenfield, Head Library Instruction Librarian, Camille O'Neill, Library Instruction Librarian, and Atifa Rawan, Government Documents Librarian. In addition, many library staff members contributed their expertise.

The coordinating team wanted to hire graduate students from a variety of academic backgrounds, and preferably, students who did not represent the majority cultures on campus. Job announcements, posted at such campus locations as the Student Placement Center, the Office of Minority Student Affairs, the Black Studies Department, and the Center for Disability Related Resources, included background information about the project, and a list of qualifications for applicants. Students were sought who had an interest in diversity-related issues, strong interpersonal skills, and the ability to work independently. Other preferred qualifications included experience with library computerized databases, word processing skills, and some experience in developing subject bibliographies.

From the seven candidates interviewed, four were selected. They were: Elizabeth Abraham, M.A. Candidate, Department of Economics; Charles Dymond, M.F.A. Candidate in Creative Writing, Department of English; Andrea R. Johnson, M.L.S. Candidate, Graduate Library School; and Reed Scull, Ph.D. Candidate, College of Education.

The Program was intended to span Spring semester 1991. The majority of grant funding went to student salaries, with a small portion covering the materials cost of guide reproduction. Computer equipment in the coordinators' offices was made available for word processing. The resulting eight guides, which were produced and distributed through the Library Instruction Department, were:

1. *Guide to Research Materials Treating Native American Affairs, 1973-1991*, by Andrea Johnson.
2. *Research Guide to Materials in the U. of A. Libraries: African-Americans in Higher Education*, by Reed Scull.
3. *Disability-Related Resources: A Guide to Practical Materials in the U. of A. Libraries*, by Charles Dymond.
4. *Guide to Research Material on Women in the Business Community*, by Elizabeth Abraham.
5. *Politics, Current Events, and Minority Issues*, by Andrea Johnson.
6. *Guide to Research Material on Women and Religion*, by Elizabeth Abraham.
7. *Participation in the Political Process*, by Reed Scull.
8. *Gays and Lesbians: Breaking the Stereotype*, by Charles Dymond.

PROJECT METHODOLOGY AND IMPLEMENTATION

Our approach toward the project was one of collaboration and team work, and we hoped that we would all learn from each other. The group met biweekly for two hours during the first few months of the project. The four graduate students discussed their understanding of undergraduate students' library research needs, and their own library experiences. They presented their areas of interest, ideas for topics, and their expectations for this project.

Throughout the process, the coordinators provided the four students with encouragement, assistance, and direction. Their work was critiqued as it progressed. We encouraged them to share with each other their own experiences and discoveries. One student volunteered to do a training session for her peers on Pro-Cite, a bibliographic management package, and spent hours of her own time helping students individually.

Training

The students participated in a comprehensive training program that introduced them to library resources and research methods. While all four students were avid library users, and one a Graduate Library School student, they were eager to have an introduction to the resources of areas of study with which they were unfamiliar. Because much of their experience in this and other libraries was based on the special focus of their graduate programs, they welcomed the training opportunity. Training sessions were conducted while the students began exploring topic ideas.

Each session was given by a library subject specialist. The coordinators informed each librarian of the research guide project's purpose. We discussed content and focus, and described the types of topics students were considering. While the subject content of the training sessions varied, all sessions covered the library's collections in the particular area, subject approaches, access tools, special collections, and reference materials. The sessions were informal, with much student interaction and questioning. We encouraged students, with the full cooperation of our staff, to view the librarian/instructors as resource people to whom they could refer for individual help and assistance as they produced their own research guides.

Training sessions covered women's studies, ethnic studies, political science, the media collection, the Science-Engineering Library, Special Collections, and Government Documents Departments. Each session was about an hour in length and presenters provided handouts for each student. The time that students spent in the training was considered part of their working time, for which they were paid in full. The students' strong interest in the sessions was demonstrated by their consistent attendance.

GUIDE FORMATS

The research guides were to be designed as teaching tools for an undergraduate audience. For that reason, in addition to listing sources and their locations, they needed to teach students how to begin researching a topic, and how to use reference and access tools effectively. It was very important that the guides be inviting and relevant to the undergraduates for whom they were being prepared. Four meetings were devoted to discussing guide formats, deciding which elements were important to include, and deciding what approaches might be successful. The students and coordinating team discussed the essential elements of a bibliography, including: subject headings, call number locations, annotations, online services, non-book formats, foreign language materials, formats and graphics, number of pages, personal statements, introductions, lists of related U of A Library bibliographies available, lists of campus resource centers and names of individuals for information and referral. We discussed the need for guidelines to ensure consistency and standardization, while at the same time allowing for sufficient flexibility to incorporate innovative ideas and new approaches. Students examined a variety of samples of bibliographies prepared by our own staff or from other libraries.

As a result of these meetings, we decided that each guide should include a stated introduction and purpose. The following is an excerpt from Chuck Dymond's guide on *Gays and Lesbians: Breaking the Stereotype.*

This guide will introduce you to some of the materials available in the U of A library system which deal with homosexuality. Although this guide is only an introduction and therefore incomplete, its scope and purpose are twofold. First it will examine some materials which directly address the issue of homophobia, its roots and its effects, as well as some strategies for dealing with it. Second it will try to broaden your perceptions of what it means to be homosexual by looking at a number of books, journal articles, films and other materials about gays and lesbians and the diversity which exists within their community.

Foreign language materials were not included because of the emphasis on undergraduate research. The availability of nonprint materials in the library, such as videos and slide/tape programs, was emphasized. Although we originally decided on a five page limit to make the bibliographies appear as inviting as possible, we soon discovered this was not realistic. It was more important to us to have a highly readable and uncrowded format, and to allow more room for explaining specific sources and how to use them effectively. Each guide listed other relevant U of A Library guides, subject specialists within and outside of the library, and appropriate resource centers.

While ensuring a certain level of consistency, the program allowed for individual ideas and approaches. One guide includes a section on browsing, directing students to browse the stacks in a number of call number ranges to get a sense of the different subject treatments of particular topics. Two guides identify national organizations which might be helpful in obtaining current literature on minority-related issues and the political process. The students decided that the eight guides should be produced as a series, and that it would be helpful to have an identifiable logo. They also recommended that the back page of each guide include a directory of library services and departments, as well as library hours and information about library services to disabled users.

TOPIC SELECTION

Much time was spent on topic selection. Since the research guides were designed to increase undergraduate students' awareness of the resources within the University of Arizona Libraries that support diverse viewpoints, topic selection was based on the graduate students' own ideas and interests, undergraduate students' opinions, the needs which reference staff had identified, and faculty responses.

The U of A Library has an active bibliography program with over 1000 pathfinders, guides, and bibliographies on file in the Library Instruction Department. The Library staff produces approximately 40 per year. In order to assist with their topic selection, the graduate students reviewed the topics already addressed by existing guides. In addition, students attended campus and community meetings and forums on diversity related issues. They talked to undergraduate students about the project, and solicited their suggestions and ideas. The forums helped the graduate students obtain information on issues of concern to undergraduates on this campus, and provided them with an opportunity to talk about the research guide project. These meetings assisted the graduate students in selecting and directing their topics toward areas where there were identified needs. Students' decisions were also informed by discussions with library staff. The reference staffs were especially helpful in identifying topics often requested by undergraduates for which the library has no current bibliographies or guides. Faculty in a variety of departments and heads of campus resource centers, such as the Native American Resource Center and the Center for Disability Related Resources, were also contacted, and they provided valuable insight and ideas. Each of the guides addresses unique aspects of several diverse groups on campus. The research guide, *Gays and Lesbians: Breaking the Stereotype,* is the first U of A Library bibliography produced on the topic of homosexuality.

STUDENTS' PERSONAL STATEMENTS

Each guide contains a personal statement by its compiler, stating why they chose the topic and why they believe it is important. Four of these statements are presented below.

Guide to Research Materials Treating Native American Affairs, 1973-1991, by Andrea Johnson.

"There has been a resurgence of emphasis in the colleges and universities around the country for greater sensitivity to and understanding about the diverse backgrounds in our communities. There has also been a great deal of discussion about the language used and propagated within society. These issues must raise questions in the minds of everyone, of all ethnicities, genders, physical capabilities, and sexual preferences. Information is available to help us better understand these complex issues, but finding that information can often be difficult. I hope that the sources I have presented here will give students and researchers a way to pose their questions and find the answers. For, how can sensitivity and understanding grow without solid information and knowledge?"

Disability-Related Resources: A Guide to Practical Materials in the U. of A. Libraries, by Charles Dymond.

"As a result of having polio in 1957, I have a natural interest in the challenges facing persons with disabilities in their struggle to become free and independent. I believe that struggle will fail unless the community of disabled people becomes more skillful in dealing with the problems they encounter in their daily lives. I also believe that, by banding together with other disenfranchised groups in their common fight to become a part of society as a whole, we can become a pivotal force in making the world a place where all people can live together in peace and prosperity."

Guide to Research Material on Women in the Business Community, by Elizabeth Abraham.

"As a person who firmly believes in the equality of women, and one who was born in a country where a majority of the women have never heard of women's rights, equality, etc., I was curious to know if American women fared better than their Indian counterparts. Women seem to have broken loose most of their shackles and have managed to succeed in almost all the fields into which they have decided to venture. This pathfinder is a small tribute to all the trailblazers and all the women, who, in the years gone by, have in their own way contributed to make life easier for us women born in the modern era."

Participation in the Political Process, by Reed Scull.

"It is perhaps inevitable that in order to effect change in society, people must become engaged in a greater participation in and understanding of the political process. One step towards active participation is to find organizations involved in issues of voter registration, political organizing, or civil rights. Just as important as active participation is an understanding of the political system. Such understanding should enable the individual to take a reasoned, critical view of his or her own part in the process. This guide is purposed toward achieving both the goals of understanding and action."

FOLLOW-UP

A follow-up questionnaire was sent to the students who participated in the project. They were asked to comment on strengths, weaknesses, potential improvements to the program, what they learned from the program, and the quality of the training sessions. Participants were asked if their understanding of issues of diversity were changed by the experience.

Students' responses to the questionnaires indicated a great deal of enthusiasm for the project. Several commented that the open, collegial atmosphere gave them the freedom and encouragement to develop their own ideas, and to express their individuality in the guides.

Some of the participants mentioned they had developed a greater respect for, and interest in, libraries and the profession of librarianship. One student enrolled in graduate library school after completing the Diversity Research Guide Program, another began part-time work as a student assistant in the University of Arizona Library. The student who was already enrolled in graduate library school is seeking a permanent position as an instruction librarian. She commented that she would like to develop a library instruction program, in which "diversity and learning about other cultures and lifestyles is fully integrated into the library's services." The fourth student expressed enthusiasm for the opportunities presented by the project for making professional contacts.

Student participants assessed both strengths and weaknesses of the project. Strengths of the program included the training sessions, and the supportive atmosphere in which students worked. Andrea Johnson mentioned experiencing "some difficulty with ongoing communication" due to students' busy and frequently conflicting schedules. One student suggested that the training program could have been further strengthened by including more in-depth training in searching CD-ROMs.

Participants felt they were able to provide helpful feedback, and to both teach and learn from each other. Reed Scull stated he learned a great deal about minority group issues focused upon by other student participants. Elizabeth Abraham stated, "It was an interesting mixture of students. Some of them were familiar with the library and there were others like me who didn't know the difference between an index and a bibliography." She continued, "Students shared their ideas during the brainstorming sessions and helped broaden our ideas and knowledge especially in their areas of research."

Students also felt they learned a great deal about library research and library resources. Wrote Elizabeth Abraham, "I think that this project, especially the training, will be of immense help if we [the participants] are ever to do any serious research in the future."

Students expressed an increased understanding of other minority groups, including those they researched personally, and those researched by other project participants. Charles Dymond stated, "I think my understanding of my own experiences is always changing–broadening and deepening; but doing the bibliography on gays and lesbians made me uncomfortable, which increased my awareness of my own prejudices." Andrea Johnson commented, "I learned how much distance and frustration can separate groups from the library when they feel there is nothing available to them. But I also learned that this situation is easily changed when the library makes the information it holds truly accessible."

Students identified some collection weaknesses relating to their topics. They expressed frustration when the library collection did not support vital areas appropriate for their bibliographies. A weakness mentioned by several respondents was that the program had to come to an end. They expressed a desire for the program to become permanent.

Because this was a new project, we as the coordinators approached it with openness and with the expectation of learning from it. The ongoing semester-long relationship with the four graduate students provided us with a new perspective on library education. Through our supervision of the project, we gained a greater understanding of students' issues concerning the library. For example, government publications provided much relevant information for the students' projects. As a result, the students received in depth instruction in this area.

We enjoyed the continuing warm relationship with these students, and felt that we could introduce them to the profession of librarianship in a very personal way. We found our roles as teachers, librarians, and mentors rewarding. The program gave us an opportunity to work together as a team, and to learn to value each others' strengths.

The project provided us with a purpose for reaching out to the campus organizations and resource centers. The students were an additional link to the student population. We learned a great deal about the issues and groups researched by the graduate students.

We also encountered some of our own frustrations. The coordinators would have liked to have more time and funding to continue this successful project. We wanted to have the ability to hire more students to work on the project. We would like to have a follow up survey to attempt to determine how the guides are being used by members of the campus community. We felt frustration with the difficulties encountered in accommodating our handicapped student. Our office equipment was not always suitable to his needs. High shelving in the stacks were difficult for him to reach.

CONCLUSION

The guides produced as a result of our work on the Diversity Research Guide Program have been widely disseminated. A list of diversity-related resource centers and organizations on campus and within the Tucson community was developed, and guides were sent to these groups. In addition, the guides are included in many of the orientation and instruction sessions presented to students, staff, and faculty at the University of Arizona. The research guides have been made available for library staff to use with their own departments and constituencies. They were also made available to educational institutions in the Tucson area. The Library's Diversity Training Committee coordinated a discussion meeting for library staff and several members of the University Diversity Action Council members at which time students spoke about their work with the program. This helped to inform library staff of the outcome of the program, introduced them to the four graduate students, and assisted the coordinators in identifying additional opportunities for distribution of the guides and further ways that they might be used. The coordinators mounted an exhibit in the library to publicize the eight guides, as well as other sources which provide access to our diverse collections. Such efforts have increased the University community's awareness of the types of resources available on our campus which reflect diverse perspectives. This is an ongoing effort which has not ended with the production of these eight guides. The program helped to sensitize library staff to the need to assess our collection strengths in relation to the representation of educational resources which support differing viewpoints. Faculty members have requested the guides for use with their classes, and the stand where copies of the guides are available must be restocked weekly. The coordinators are planning a faculty seminar to discuss the library's role in strengthening the integration of diversity-related resources into the curriculum and the classroom. The Library's Diversity Action Committee has sponsored a diversity film series to introduce the campus community to Library owned films which present opinions, ideas, and controversies in a variety of diversity related issues. The Library is being recognized throughout the campus for its commitment to diversity education.[8]

REFERENCES

1. University of Arizona. Office of Institutional Research. Personal Communication.

2. Arizona Dept. of Economic Security. Labor Market Information, *Affirmative Action Planning Information* Phoenix, (Spring 1991), 26.

3. University of Arizona, International Student Center, personal communication.

4. University of Arizona, *Diversity Action Plan* (Tucson, May 1990), 9.

5. University of Arizona. Library, *The University of Arizona Strategic Plan: Vision Statement for the Year 2000* (Tucson, 1992).

6. University of Arizona. Library, *Affirmative Action Plan* (Tucson, 1991).

7. University of Arizona. Library, *The University of Arizona Library Diversity Action Plan* (Tucson, July 1991), 3.

8. Copies of the Diversity Research Guides are available upon request from Louise Greenfield at the University of Arizona Library. Sample guides available on request from the authors.

Education
for Multicultural Librarianship:
The State of the Art
and Recommendations
for the Future

Monica Foderingham-Brown

SUMMARY. This article discusses the current state of education for multicultural librarianship, examining the manner in which minority students and faculty are recruited and retained in library schools, and to determine whether individual curriculums are being adapted to fit this imperative. Catalogs of individual library schools were examined and the professional literature searched to see how, if at all, diversity issues are being addressed. More sustained effort is needed to bring multiculturalism into the mainstream of library education, and this paper makes recommendations to achieve this goal.

Monica Foderingham-Brown is a MLS student at SUNY Albany. She worked with New York Public Library-Epiphany Branch, and at the New York City Police Department-Policy Academy Library prior to attending Library school at SUNY Albany.

[Haworth co-indexing entry note]: "Education for Multicultural Librarianship: The State of the Art and Recommendations for the Future," Foderingham-Brown, Monica. Co-published simultaneously in *The Acquisitions Librarian* (The Haworth Press, Inc.) No. 9/10, 1993, pp. 131-148; and: *Multicultural Acquisitions* (ed: Karen Parrish and Bill Katz) The Haworth Press, Inc., 1993, pp. 131-148. Multiple copies of this article/chapter may be purchased from The Haworth Document Delivery Center. Call 1-800-3-HAWORTH (1-800-342-9678) between 9:00 - 5:00 (EST) and ask for DOCUMENT DELIVERY CENTER.

131

INTRODUCTION

It is an inescapable fact that the United States of America is the most multiethnic and multicultural society in the world. Whether this coming together of diverse peoples in search of the American dream is viewed as a melting pot or a bubbling, boiling cauldron, the quality of life for all members of society can only be maintained and/or improved if equality of access and opportunity exists for everyone regardless of their race or socioeconomic status. This is especially important in light of the fact that recent demographic projections indicate that by the year 2000, one in three Americans will belong to a minority ethnic group, and that there are important changes in birth rate within most ethnic groups. H.L. Hodgkinson has said that the child to female ratio must be about 2.1 for a group to sustain itself.[1] In 1985 the ratio for African-Americans was 2.4, and for Mexican-Americans it was 2.9. Conversely, the ratio for Whites was 1.7.

As the twentieth century draws to a close and we prepare to enter the twenty first century, access to information will become an even more powerful determinant of each individual's quality of life. Librarians hold the keys to unlocking these vast stores of information in a variety of formats in a way that no other profession does. Are library schools sensitizing their students to the multicultural and multiethnic nature of the public with which they will have to interact when they go out into their various library situations? Are students being made aware of the important role they will have to play in ensuring equality of access for all sectors of the population? Yes, technological advances–computers, databases, CD ROMS etc.–have revolutionized the study of librarianship and they have to be addressed. But are library schools downplaying or ignoring the human factors, e.g., multicultural issues, to place more emphasis on technology?

It is my firm belief that in order for library schools to remain relevant and vital institutions, the questions raised in the previous paragraph must be addressed by library school deans, faculty and others in policy-making positions. It is for this reason therefore that the implications of multicultural librarianship for schools of library and information science, is the central topic of this paper.

POTENTIAL CONTRIBUTION OF MINORITIES
TO THE FIELD OF LIBRARY
AND INFORMATION SCIENCE

Information leads to knowledge and knowledge is power, and here I do not mean 'power' in the Machiavellian context. The individual's need for access to information ranges from basic facts for daily survival, to the ability to fully realize and fulfil one's intellectual potential. Questions such as how to get a job, where to live, where to go to school, what to buy, what to base an opinion on, who to vote for, where to obtain health and legal information and how to cope with a crisis all require information for decision making.

In the broader context, equal access to information is vital to a democratic society. Information gives people choices, and true freedom is impossible unless individuals first know their range of choices and actions available and then act on them. Mary Lenox believes that hopelessness results from a perception of a lack of choices, and that as professionals and concerned human beings we must participate in the development of public policies and practices designed to guarantee access to the poorest and wealthiest among us.[2] Our world is approaching the stage where those persons with mastery over the technology of accessing information (librarians), can use it to greatly enhance the quality of life for their users. This is even more crucial as it relates to those members of minority groups in this country who face countless socioeconomic obstacles to realizing their American dream. There is an urgent need for minority librarians who are from similar backgrounds to the clients they serve, and are therefore able to be positive role models for children and young adults who they encounter in school and public libraries, who can understand the informational needs of their adult clients in public libraries and so tailor library services accordingly–Information and Referral (I&R) services, job information, immigration and citizenship information, literacy programs, and English as a second language (ESL) classes. Librarians are also needed who can collect, document and disseminate information on our history to help minorities better understand their proud and triumphant history, therefore providing them with the empowerment and motivation to rise above institutionalized barriers to educational success. In academic libraries, minority academic librarians can adapt library instruction programs to meet the unique needs of minority students who are insufficiently prepared for higher education because of pervasive inequities in the American educational system. It is for these reasons therefore that a concerted effort to recruit minority students for higher education in library and information science assumes a new sense of urgency.

CURRENT STEPS BEING TAKEN BY LIBRARY SCHOOLS TO INCREASE MINORITY RECRUITMENT

University at Albany–State University of New York

(a) The Miles Program–The Multicultural Internship/Library Education Scholarship (MILES) is a program sponsored jointly by the libraries at the University at Albany and the School of Information Science and Policy. MILES offers underrepresented minority students interested in a career in librarianship and information systems paid internship and graduate scholarship opportunities. Students accepted into the program will receive a paid pre-professional internship in the university libraries during the last year of their undergraduate studies. Students who successfully complete the internship program may apply to the library school, and if accepted they will receive a full tuition scholarship.

(b) Rockefeller College Diversity Committee–The Rockefeller College of Public Affairs and Policy includes the School of Information Science and Policy, and the diversity committee represents the college of diversity issues. One of the points on its action plan is improve student recruitment initiatives through:

    (i) Recruitment from the undergraduate population;

    (ii) Developing a recruitment plan for minority undergraduate students;

    (iii) Encouraging departments to visit Southern colleges on recruitment trips;

    (iv) Hosting career fairs to attract people from the community.

(c) SUNYA also has a variety of minority fellowships and assistantships with annual stipends up to $12,000 for the former, and $13,000 for the latter.

State University of New York at Buffalo

"There is a special need for individuals with strong ethnic and bilingual backgrounds (especially those who are African-American, Hispanic, Native American Indian, and of Asian and Pacific background) who can help improve social services in the nation's cities."[9]

This statement displays the commitment on the part of the University at Buffalo to furthering multicultural librarianship, and their Special Programs Division coordinates university-wide efforts to provide an academic and social environment that is supportive of minority students. The number of minority fellowships awarded by the University has quadrupled since 1984, along with the total amount of such awards. These

> SUNY under-represented minority graduate fellowships offer complete support to qualified students. They are recruited at career information fairs and graduate school information events for minority students. A Minority Student Recruitment Task Force composed of library professionals, faculty and local library professionals analyzed several recruitment techniques: brochures were found to be least effective, and personal contact the most effective method of attracting students of color to the profession . . . The Task Force is contemplating creating a new minority recruitment position. The job of the recruiter would be to make personal contacts, reaching students at undergraduate institutions and working with minority agencies.[10]

University of California–Los Angeles

(a) The Graduate Advancement Program (GAP) makes awards based on need as demonstrated by standard university financial aid criteria.

(b) The Graduate Opportunity Fellowship Program (GOFP) provides fellowships to students from groups traditionally underrepresented in graduate programs.

(c) LCSA Multiethnic Recruitment Scholarship Program–California State University administers a multiethnic Recruitment Scholarship Program funded through the federal library services and Construction Act. Scholarships are available annually and are granted to qualified students through selected public-libraries and graduate library schools in California.

(d) The REFORMA (National Association to Promote Library Service to the Spanish Speaking) UCLA mentor program encourages Latino students to attend the school by providing prospective applicants with individualized guidance from REFORMA members.

(e) A mentoring program for African-American students entering the library school was established in 1990 by the California Librarians Black Caucus–Greater Los Angeles/UCLA to increase the number of African-American information professionals, and provide a more supportive environment during the student's educational experience.

University of Hawaii–Offers $10,000 fellowships in conjunction with ALU LIKE, a community based organization dedicated to Hawaiian affairs, to recruit native Hawaiians into librarianship.

University of Kentucky awards several non-service minority fellowships which vary in amounts up to $7,000 per annum.

University of Southern Mississippi has special funds for minority students assistantships dependent on federal funding under the Higher Education Administration's Title IIB Program. The Audrey Ailer scholarship is also awarded to minority candidates.

Louisiana State University has the Nathaniel Gaither assistantship for minority students who will increase the cultural diversity of the program.

University of Michigan–This library school has merit-based opportunity awards for minority students.

University of Maryland at College Park–Minority students who are Maryland residents, and who will be first time full time graduate students are eligible to apply for grants through the graduate school.

University of Pittsburgh–The school has a three year affirmative action plan focusing on recruiting minority students. Title IIB fellowships provide stipends and tuition grants to women and minority M.L.S. and Ph.D. students. Under the University's Commonwealth Fund, tuition is provided for minority students through the Commonwealth Scholarship award. Eligible students must be Pennsylvania residents and demonstrate scholastic abilities. They are appointed as graduate students assistants.

University of North Carolina–Greensboro

(a) Actively seeks to promote racial integration by recruiting and enrolling a large number of Black students. There is no mention of specific aid for them however.
(b) University of North Carolina–Chapel Hill
(c) Under the Board of Governors General Minority Presence Grant Program, Black students may be eligible for financial assistance if they are North Carolina residents, enrolled for at least three hours of degree credit course work, and demonstrate financial need. These grants are also available for doctoral study, providing up to $9,000 annually to Black residents of North Carolina.

Rutgers University–The Ralph Johnson Bunche Distinguished Graduate Student Award provides $7,000 per academic year to exceptional full-time students with backgrounds of substantial educational and cultural disadvantage.

University of Rhode Island–Recruitment efforts at state and regional library association meetings target minority members who hold library support staff positions. Scholarship grants from the H.W. Wilson company are specifically earmarked for minority students.

Syracuse University–African-American graduate fellowships are awarded by the graduate school on recommendation of a fellowship selection committee. In 1991-1992, the award was $8,775 plus a full tuition scholarship.

Simmons College–School officials contact minority students and ethnic studies departments at universities in Massachusetts. The Massachusetts Black Librarian Network (MBLN) and individual minority librarians, especially alumni, receive information on scholarships and are consulted as sources of potential new recruits. The school is also represented at minority career fairs. Each year Simmons earmarks institutional grant funds to be awarded to minority students.

University of Texas at Austin–A faculty member serves as the minority affairs advisor for the library school, and is available for consultation and assistance on matters of concern to minority students. Each year the school offers a limited number of graduate opportunity fellowships which are awarded based on merit and need to Black-Americans, Mexican-Americans, Native Americans and Puerto Rican students. In the academic year 1989-1990 these awards provided stipends ranging from $3,000 to $8,000 plus tuition and fees for nine months of study.

University of South Florida–Financial assistance includes Graduate Equal Opportunity Grants.

University of Washington–The school has established the Sylvia Finley Multiethnic Fellowship to recruit minorities into the profession. There are also other scholarships all based on financial need.

University of Wisconsin-Milwaukee–This school has the Advanced Opportunity Program (AOP) Fellowship where preference is given to minority students and Wisconsin residents who qualify. There is also a Design for Diversity Plan with affirmative action goals to attract minorities into the profession and it is represented at minority career and recruitment fairs.

Rosary College–The school is working with Chicago Public Library on a grant proposal for a cooperative program providing scholarship support for MLS candidates from minority groups.

Clark Atlanta University–The School of Library and Information Science is allocated a limited number of fellowships which are awarded to students based on the usual scholarship award criteria. More specifically, the Patricia Roberts-Harris fellowship is designated to provide federal financial assistance for fellowship awards to graduate and professional students who demonstrate financial need. The purpose of this fellowship is to increase the representation of minorities at the graduate and professional levels by providing awards and support services to assist them in full-time study.

University of California-Berkeley–In conjunction with the Northern California Library Schools Recruitment Committee, the school takes part in a minority mentoring program designed to bring more students of color into the library field.

RECOMMENDATIONS FOR THE FUTURE

Ann Knight Randall has outlined several recommendations for improving the recruitment of minority students for library schools.[5] Some of these measures are outlined below.

(1) Potential candidates for library and information science programs would be identified considering their educational eligibility, motivation and experience. This can be done by:

    (a) Working with career counsellors, advisors and placement officers at the undergraduate level in four year and community colleges;

    (b) Encouraging library support personnel to consider entering graduate library and information science programs;

    (c) Cooperation between libraries and library schools to develop and/or disseminate information about educational and pre-professional work programs;

    (d) Increasing the numbers of minority faculty who can serve as role models and mentors for students.

(2) Efforts should be made to attract more minority undergraduates into library schools, and contact made with recent graduates about career possibilities in the profession by:

    (a) Identifying financial aid sources and facilitating minority access to financial assistance, resources, programs and information;

    (b) Designing flexible admissions criteria that would broaden the acceptable entrance requirements;

    (c) Increasing the number of fifth and sixth year cooperative degree programs with subject major fields and other graduate subject fields;

    (d) Enriching the curriculum by adding relevant courses and organizing specializations within the degree programs.

(3) Public awareness about the career of librarianship should be increased by:

    (a) Working with community-based programs such as Girl Scouts, Boy Scouts, YMCA, etc., to open experiences with libraries and librarian careers for young adults;

    (b) Using the ALA public relations program in libraries to heighten interest and awareness of what public librarians do;

    (c) Organizing seminars and exhibits during National Library Week and other occasions;

    (d) Designating one or more staff members in libraries to respond to questions about librarianship as a career.

(4) Minority professional opportunities for advancement and retention in librarianship would be increased by:

    (a) Encouraging staff to take advantage of continuing education opportunities, and facilitate it by allowing them time off and giving them full or partial reimbursement of fees;

    (b) Increasing promotional and internal transfer opportunities for qualified minorities;

    (c) Targeting institutional racism practices and unethical or unacceptable actions in libraries and library education through programming and internal review processes.

Finally, the fact that recruiting of minority students is included in the 1992 Standards for Accreditation of library schools speaks volumes of its importance to the vitality of our profession; and it is hoped that this will spur renewed effort on the part of those institutions which have been inactive in this area in the past.

CURRENT STATE
OF MINORITY FACULTY RECRUITMENT

Today, minority faculty represent between 2% and 5% of the nation's higher education faculty, and this is due to several factors. Herman Totten says, "the most basic factor . . . is a low supply and demand for minorities for faculty positions due to barriers to entry;

policies of exclusion; institutionalized preferences; specific values and goals of academic institutions; and the overall organizational character of universities that collectively have systematically kept supply and demand low."[6] Statistics from E.J. Josey's 1989-1990 survey indicate the severity of this situation relating to library schools.[7] Six schools have no minority faculty; 16 have 1; 2 have 3; 2 have 4; 1 has 5; 1 has 6; and twelve institutions did not respond to this question. Of these numbers, African-Americans are the largest group, followed by Asians, then American Indians, and lastly Hispanics.

On the basis of her own perceptions and experiences of White academia, Marcia Sutherland believes that the fit of Black faculty in White academia is an uneasy one due to the pervasive nature of White racism.[8] Affirmative action programs have had limited success over the years because of opposition and lip service by administrators, and the fact that their very nature makes them controversial. There has also been a low turnout of minority doctorate holders over the past twenty years. In the actual recruitment process, the minority candidate will most likely not have any advocates on the search team or receive any patronage from the 'old boy' network.[9] As a result, existing faculty can function as gatekeepers, controlling access to their ranks. So if any progress is to be made, the actions of the faculty must be examined.

So, what actual steps are being taken at present to increase minority faculty recruitment at graduate library schools? Literature on this aspect of multicultural librarianship is very sparse. So the conclusion must be drawn that there is much scope for improvement in this area.

Rutgers University–A minority caucus is being created for doctoral students and faculty members in the library department. A conference scholarship fund will be established to enable broad minority participation in professional conferences; and a survey of Ph.D. students will identify potential candidates for faculty positions. Recruitment of more minority faculty will utilize two pre-existing organizations: a consortium of library school Deans and the Association for Library and Information Science Education (ALISE).

University of Pittsburgh–Efforts to fill three current faculty vacancies have centered on minority candidates.

University of Wisconsin-Milwaukee–The school has a Design for Diversity Plan with affirmative action goals in faculty recruitment and a mandate for multicultural staff policies.

University at Albany-State University of New York–The Rockefeller College Diversity Committee has as one point on its action plan to improve faculty recruitment initiatives.

RECOMMENDATIONS FOR THE FUTURE

Ohio University and Clarion University have recently increased their number of minority faculty due to the successful implementation of some of the following general suggestions.

1. Tapping into minority faculty networks by utilizing minority caucuses within professional associations for example. Within the ALA there are the Black, Hispanic (REFORMA), Asian/Pacific, Chinese and American Indian Caucuses.
2. Bringing young scholars in for lecture series–these series address current professional trends and can be used as a basis for identifying potential faculty members who can function as visiting professors. Through these series minority lecturers can familiarize themselves with the faculty and campus, and the faculty can assess the lecturers' strengths and weaknesses.
3. Using personal contacts.
4. Identifying and contacting fellowship programs–identifying minorities who take part in these programs which support minority Ph.D.'s and creating mentoring relationships with minority scholars can be used to recruit potential faculty members. In the mentoring relationship, a designated minority faculty member makes contact with the various caucuses and organizations that address minority needs.

When a pool of minority candidates has been identified for a position, minority faculty at the institution should be utilized to give an accurate assessment of it, and take an active role in the hiring process.

It is extremely important that aggressive action be taken in this area immediately, because approximately 50% of the nation's faculty will be retiring in the next fifteen years;[10] and 30% of the present kindergarten population belong to minority ethnic groups. It is hoped that by the time they enter college and university the situation will have improved.

Importance of Multicultural Issues to Library and Information Science Curriculums

Previous sections of this paper have dealt with the manner in which the recruitment of minority students and faculty for graduate schools of library and information science can positively impact on the relevance and effectiveness of the institutions. But, the fact that all library school graduates should ideally have a common body of knowledge of multicultural and diversity issues is of extreme importance. All library school students should be able, through library school curriculums, to learn how an ethnic group's history, language, culture, race and socioeconomic conditions influence their information needs. Why? It all comes down to the issue of access. In a society where each individual's access to education, health care and other basics of daily survival is determined by one's ability or inability to pay for them, libraries should continue their historical role of serving all their clients well regardless of their economic situation. As we move into the twenty first century, access to information will become so important that extreme care must be taken not to have a society of information 'haves and have nots.' And we must never lose sight of the fact that librarianship is a service profession. Betty J. Turock, chair of the library and information science program at Rutgers University has said that "currently library education is paying less attention to services and more to technology."[11]

Graduate library schools that address diversity issues in their curriculums will also attract more minority students who will prefer a curriculum that is relevant to their needs. Potential school media specialists and children's librarians in public libraries will want to learn how to choose books that will encourage and empower their young readers; books with fictional characters and real persons who triumphed over obstacles similar to their own. Students will also need to know how best they can serve the needs of members of non-traditional racial and ethnic groups in academic and public libraries.

CURRENT STATE OF MULTICULTURALISM IN LIBRARY SCHOOL CURRICULUMS

E.J. Josey's 1989-1990 survey[12] shows that 32 or 69.5% of library schools surveyed do not offer core courses related to library services to minorities; 13 or 28.3% provide some courses; and one (1) or 2.2% did not answer. Regarding elective courses, 31 or 67.4% did not provide any courses, and 15 or 32.6% did not provide any courses, and 15 or 32.6% said that they provide some references to library services in this field. The following is a summary of library schools that have courses on multiculturalism in their curriculums.

University of Arizona

- Children's literature in Spanish;
- Mexican-American literature.

University of California Los Angeles (UCLA)

- Ethnic groups and their bibliographies;
- Africana bibliography and research methods;
- African-American Bibliography;
- Information services in culturally diverse communities;
- Library service to special population groups;
- Latin American research resources.

Emporia State University

- Information transfer and special population groups.

Kent State University

Houses the Center for the Study of Ethnic Publications and Cultural Institutions in the United States of America. One of its functions is to develop a curriculum for library schools which emphasizes library services to ethnic publications. Their library school curriculum includes the course–Ethnic library services and collections.

University of Iowa

• Libraries in a multicultural society.

Louisiana State University

• Black literature in New Orleans (it utilizes the resources of the Amistad collection in that city).

University of Maryland-College Park

• Library service to the disadvantaged (this includes minority racial and ethnic groups).

North Carolina Central University

• The African-American collection;
• Ethnic materials for children and adolescents.

University of North Texas

• Seminar in information resources and services for special clienteles;
• Seminar in trends and issues in literature for children and young adults.

Faculty research includes information resources and services relating to three of the main minority groups–Black, Hispanic and Native Americans.

University of Pittsburgh

• African-American resources and services;
• World Librarianship;
• Library services to special populations;

- Multicultural materials for children and young adults;
- Librarianship and libraries in society: Behavioral perspectives for the information professions.

Queens College-City University of New York

- Multicultural Librarianship: materials and services;
- Fundamentals of library and information science.

University of Rhode Island

- Plans to introduce a course in multicultural resources in the 1993 academic year.

University of Texas at Austin

- Has a Latin American Library Service specialization which includes four courses:
- Latin American archives;
- Latin American publishing and book trade;
- Seminar in Latin American library studies;
- Information resources on Latin America.

University of South Florida

- Books and related materials of Latin American Countries for children and young people.

Texas Woman's University

- Multicultural Librarianship.

University of Washington

- Services for special groups.

Wayne State University

- Multicultural information services and information;
- Foundations of African-American bibliography and resources.

Clark Atlanta University

- Ethnic materials for children and young people;
- Information resources for Afro-American studies.

University of Hawaii

- Information resources for Hawaiian studies;
- Information resources for Pacific Islands Studies;
- Asian research materials;
- Asian-American materials for youth.

University at Albany-State University of New York

The Rockefeller College Diversity Committee has as one of the points on its 1991-1992 Action Plan to review curricula to identify and develop course content which addresses diversity in all college programs. This would be achieved by making use of course evaluation forms to determine course content on diversity issues.

There are currently no courses which directly address multiculturalism at the library school however.

Indiana University

- Latin American bibliography.

University of Illinois at Urbana-Champaign

- Information needs of particular communities;
- African bibliography.

To shed further light on multiculturalism in library school curriculums, Josey's survey[13] indicated that with reference to lectures offered which related to cultural minorities, 37 schools or 80.5% provided no lectures; 7 schools or 15.2% offered some lectures; and 2 schools or 4.3% gave no response.

Regarding the offering of independent study courses related to minorities, 36 schools or 78.3% said that minorities were not the subject of independent study courses; 7 schools or 15.2% said some are offered; and 3 schools or 6.5% did not respond.

Josey believes that ensuring that minority faculty members in library schools assist in developing the curriculum would ensure that it would be one of inclusion rather than the one of exclusion it has been for many years.[14]

In addition there will not always be minority faculty at each institution so White faculty should be made aware of the information needs and experiences of all the minority groups so that they can then sensitize their students to the issues.

REFERENCES

1. Hodgkinson, H.L. *All one system: demographics and education–kindergarten through graduate school.* (Washington, D.C.: Institute for Educational Leadership, 1985).

2. Lenox, Mary F. "Educating the Black librarian and information professional for leadership in the twenty-first century." *Educating Black Librarians.*

3. University at Buffalo-State University of New York. School of Library and Information Studies 1990-1993 Graduate Catalog.

4. *Bringing us together: a selected resource guide to cultural diversity activities in the library community.* (ALA-Office of Library Personnel Resources, 1992).

5. Randall, Ann Knight. "Minority recruitment in librarianship." *Librarians for the new millennium* (Chicago: ALA-Office of Library Personnel Resources, 1988).

6. Totten, Herman L. "Perspectives on minority recruitment of faculty for schools of library and information science" *Journal of education for library and information science.*

7. Josey, E.J. "Education for library services to cultural minorities."

8. Sutherland, Marcia. "Black faculty in White academia: the fit is an uneasy one" *Western Journal of Black Studies.* Volume 14 Number 1 1990.

9. Moore, W. Jr. "Black faculty in White colleges: a dream deferred." *Educational Record* Volume 68 Number 4 Fall-Winter 1987-1988.

10. Totten, Herman L. "Perspectives on minority recruitment . . . "

11. Josey, E.J. "Education for library services to cultural Minorities."

12. Ibid

13. Ibid.

14. Ibid.

A Comparative Analysis of Libraries in Historically Black Colleges and Universities

Lorene B. Brown

SUMMARY. A grant awarded from the Andrew Mellon Foundation to the Association of College and Research Libraries made possible the compilation and publication of statistics on libraries in historically black colleges and universities. This important and needful document represents the most comprehensive collection of statistics on these libraries in twenty years.

This study presents a comparative analysis of these libraries classified into five types by the control/funding of their parent institutions. The types of libraries in historically black colleges and universities delineated in this study were federal; independent private; independent United Negro College Fund; land-grant and state. The variables selected from the *ACRL/HBCUS Survey* selected to compare the sixty-eight libraries were the collections; expenditures; personnel; enrollment and faculty members. Also, this study compared the collections and expenditures of the universities with the collections and expenditures of 114 non-ARL libraries.

Lorene B. Brown is Associate Professor, School of Library and Information Services at Clark Atlanta University, James P. Brawley Drive at Fair Street, Atlanta, GA 30314.

[Haworth co-indexing entry note]: "A Comparative Analysis of Libraries in Historically Black Colleges and Universities," Brown, Lorene B. Co-published simultaneously in *The Acquisitions Librarian* (The Haworth Press, Inc.) No. 9/10, 1993, pp. 149-182; and: *Multicultural Acquisitions* (ed: Karen Parrish and Bill Katz) The Haworth Press, Inc., 1993, pp. 149-182. Multiple copies of this article/chapter may be purchased from The Haworth Document Delivery Center. Call 1-800-3-HAWORTH (1-800-342-9678) between 9:00 - 5:00 (EST) and ask for DOCUMENT DELIVERY CENTER.

INTRODUCTION

In 1987 the Association of College and Research Libraries appointed an ad hoc Committee on Historically Black Colleges and Universities Project. The primary objective of this Committee was to determine how the Association could render assistance to libraries in historically black colleges and universities. The members of the Committee were Chairperson, Beverly P. Lynch; Lorene B. Brown; Joseph H. Howard, Casper LeRoy Jordon; and Barbara Williams-Jenkins.

A grant from the Andrew Mellon Foundation permitted the Committee to convene a group of 30 librarians from historically black colleges and universities in Atlanta. These librarians requested, as one of their major priorities, the collection of statistics about their libraries by the Association. The Association honored this request and set up the mechanism for the collection of these statistics. The ACRL utilized the same format used for the collection of statistics from the Association of Research Libraries and for its non-ARL University Library Statistics Survey. The questionnaires were mailed to the libraries in historically black colleges and universities in July, 1990. Of the 98 libraries receiving the questionnaires, 68 responded representing 73 historically black colleges and universities.[1]

The Andrew Mellon Foundation supported the compilation of the statistics by Robert E. Molyneux and the issuance of a publication similar to the reports of the ACRL university library statistical projects. This volume, *ACRL/Historically Black Colleges and Universities Library Statistics 1988-89*, published in 1991, will provide the data for this paper.[2]

The *ACRL/HBCUS Survey* represents a significant document as twenty years had passed since statistics were collected on these libraries. In 1970, Casper L. Jordan[3] published an inventory of 51 libraries in historically black colleges and universities. Jessie Carney Smith[4] wrote the most definitive analysis of libraries in historically black colleges and universities in 1977. This landmark volume, funded by the Council on Library Resources, utilized statistical data and information collected from libraries in eighty-five historically black colleges and universities.

PURPOSE AND METHODOLOGY

The purpose of this study is to present statistical data on libraries in historically black colleges and universities characterized by the historical control and financial support of their parent institutions. It is significant to delineate those institutions, and thusly their libraries, as they run the entire gamut of quality within higher education in America today. These libraries are represented with a collection of less then 20,000 volumes to a collection of more than 1,000,000. Their total library expenditures span from a low of $73,124 to a high of more than $11 million. The enrollment of these institutions extend from 288 students to a high of 9,634 and the number of faculty members range from 16 to 482.

The grouping of these institutions posed one of the inherent problems of classification, that is the difficulty of establishing a nomenclature that each of the institutions would fit. For example, Tuskegee University represents an independent United Negro College Fund institution, and it is also a member of the 1890 land-grant institution created by the Morrill Act. While Howard University receives the majority of its funding from the federal government, it was founded and is historically defined as a private institution. Also, Howard University represents the only historically black college and university library holding membership in the Association of Research Libraries. Religious denominations have served and continue to play major roles in the financial support and control of private historically black colleges and universities. The categorization of these institutions by religious denominations was not used, as most of these church supported/affiliated institutions are classified under the independent United Negro College Fund institutions. The five categories representing the classification of the institutions in this study are listed below:

1. Federal: The University of the District of Columbia is the only institution that falls in this category. It is controlled and funded by the federal government.
2. Independent Private: This category includes five institutions that are privately controlled but are non-UNCF members. The funding for these institutions are received from public and private sources.

3. Independent UNCF: This group of accredited privately supported institutions was organized in 1940 as the United Negro College Fund institutions to participate in cooperative fund raising activities. These institutions receive their financial support from private and public sources and are privately controlled.

4. Land-Grant: The Morrill Act of 1890 required that land-grant funds from the Morrill Act of 1862 be made available to black institutions. There are 17 institutions in this category and 16 of these are state institutions. These institutions receive the majority of their financial support from public sources and are state controlled, with the exception of Tuskegee University which is privately controlled.

5. State: These institutions located, for the most part, in southern states receive the majority of their financial support from public sources and are controlled by their state governments.

ANALYSIS OF STATISTICAL DATA

This study will analyze statistics on libraries in historically black colleges libraries by the type of institutions described above, utilizing sixteen variables selected from the *ACRL/HBCUS Survey*. The variables that will be analyzed fall into five major categories:

1. Collections
2. Expenditures
3. Personnel
4. Enrollments
5. Faculty Members.

Collections

The variables selected from the *ACRL/HBCUS Survey* to describe the collections of the 68 libraries reporting in this survey are the number of volumes in library; the number of volumes added (gross); the number of monographs purchased; the number of current serials titles (purchased and not purchased); and the total number of microform units. The following presents a discussion of these variables by the five types of institutions.

Volumes in Library

Table 1 shows that Howard University holds the largest number of volumes (1,729,875) in the library while Mary Holmes College is represented with the smallest number of volumes (17,732). The University of the District of Columbia reported 483,188 volumes in its library. The five independent private institutions held a total of 2,174,876 volumes with a mean of 434,975. The 27 independent United Negro College Fund institutions held a total of 3,059,588 volumes in their libraries with a mean of 113,318. The libraries in the land-grant institutions held 2,952,725 volumes with a mean of 246,060 volumes. The 23 state institutions responding to the survey reported 4,041,178 volumes in their libraries with a mean of 175,703. These figures further validate the fact that historically black colleges and universities may be characterized on a wide spectrum and that their libraries are reflective of these gradations (see Table 1).

Volumes Added (Gross)

The University of the District of Columbia added 12,858 volumes and the five independent institutions increased their holdings with a total sum of 80,776 volumes and a mean of 16,155 volumes. Howard University, in this category, supplied 60,854 volumes of this total. The 27 United Negro College Fund libraries added 65,403 volumes with a mean of 3,515 volumes. The 12 land-grant institutions added 63,706 volumes with a mean of 5,309 and the libraries in the category of state institutions added a total of 92,114 volumes with a mean of 4,005 (see Table 1).

Monographs Purchased

During 1988-89, the University of the District of Columbia purchased 2,787 monographs while the five independent institutions bought a total of 34,407 and a mean of 6,881. For the independent

TABLE 1. Data on Collections of Historically Black Colleges and Universities by Type of Institution, 1988-1989

Type of Institutions	COLLECTIONS				
	Volumes in Library	Volumes Added (Gross)	Monographs Purchased	Current Serials (Total)	Microform Units (Total)
Federal					
University of the District of Columbia	483,188	12,858	2,787	3,246	548,220
Independent Private (IP)					
Hampton University	332,003	16,590	6,792	1,364	475,955
Howard University	1,729,875	60,884	27,167	27,931	2,641,300
Mary Holmes College	17,732	224	NR	100	1,065
Meharry Medical College	69,817	2,420	NR	1,505	1,968
Southwestern Christian College	25,449	640	448	150	1,270
SUM	2,174,876	80,776	34,407	31,050	3,121,558
MEAN	434,975	16,155	6,881	6,210	624,312
Independent United Negro College Fund (UNCF)					
Atlanta University Center	373,084	6,747	6,740	1,385	59,433
Barber Scotia College	69,719	1,345	NR	145	2,627
Benedict College	117,210	1,434	2,248	410	19,831
Bennett College	87,000	NR	NR	NR	NR
Bethune-Cookman College	133,432	4,760	3,920	634	NR
Dillard University	139,600	NR	2,679	619	NR
Fisk University	193,525	3,199	2,544	300	5,523
Huston-Tillotson College	74,491	1,797	NR	320	52,476
Jarvis Christian College	73,090	1,373	1,373	490	NR
Johnson.C. Smith University	111,959	2,651	2,451	795	16,091
Knoxville College	86,700	5,200	4,000	173	NR
Lane College	90,675	1,051	NR	247	9,012
LeMoyne-Owen College	77,367	1,202	NR	275	1,114

TABLE 1 Continued

| | COLLECTIONS | | | | |
Type of Institutions	Volumes in Library	Volumes Added (Gross)	Monographs Purchased	Current Serials (Totals)	Microform Units (Total)
Independent UNCF (continued)					
Morris College..........	86,902	2,512	NR	684	83,785
Oakwood College.........	105,580	2,034	1,100	1,020	12,000
Paine College..........	83,048	1,934	1,427	445	9,745
Saint Paul's College....	56,819	NR	203	225	31,169
Shaw University.........	115,000	8,000	NR	135	8,000
Stillman College........	94,007	1,423	1,423	339	6,518
Talladega College.......	87,964	1,021	876	490	3,050
Texas College..........	82,988	600	1,000	162	24,598
Tougaloo College........	97,353	2,823	2,391	420	7,085
Tuskegee University.....	257,359	6,407	5,896	1,098	1,378
Virginia Union University...	131,852	1,348	1,099	341	30,000
Voorhees College........	100,413	1,542	NR	514	4,565
Wilberforce University....	57,451	NR	722	385	11,350
Wiley College..........	75,000	5,000	3,500	360	11,000
SUM	3,059,588	65,403	45,642	3,246	410,352
MEAN	113,318	3,515	1,755	477	15,783
Land Grant (LG)					
Alabama A&M University...	222,517	3,635	1,735	1,489	459,963
Alcorn State University...	161,232	1,008	917	774	281,269
Delaware State College...	139,847	12,094	10,340	1,385	326,169
Florida A&M University...	449,944	19,101	13,430	5,330	86,575
Fort Valley State College...	186,365	1,982	1,623	1,213	179,487
Lincoln University (MO)...	114,732	3,042	2,825	2,487	21,004
University of Maryland-Eastern Shore......	123,579	3,070	3,936	NR	464,257
North Carolina A&T State University......	348,192	7,619	NR	1,713	448,205

TABLE 1 Continued

| | Volumes in Library | Volumes Added (Gross) | COLLECTIONS | | |
Type of Institution			Monographs Purchased	Current Serials (Total)	Microform Units (Total)
Land Grant continued					
Prairie View A&M University......	234,782	1,499	482	1,629	325,631
South Carolina State College....	256,695	4,595	1,149	1,149	449,082
Southern University-Baton Rouge..	372,252	NR	6,428	1,768	89,135
Tennessee State University......	342,588	6,060	4,937	1,360	643,432
SUM	2,952,725	63,706	47,802	20,313	3,774,209
MEAN	246,060	5,309	3,983	1,693	314,517
State (S)					
Albany State College...........	150,410	8,727	8,982	1,210	500,727
Bluefield State College........	65,320	1,191	1,033	468	360,452
Bowie State University.........	148,733	7,430	NR	1,056	331,738
Central State University.......	149,675	911	NR	1,319	529,613
Cheyney University.............	151,894	2,835	204	NR	33,810
Coahoma Community College......	28,914	2,012	1,967	302	2,322
Coppin State College...........	140,152	1,998	1,818	664	234,391
Elizabeth City State University.	128,260	2,769	2,892	1,549	411,272
Fayetteville State University...	163,575	3,129	2,946	2,388	381,378
Grambling State University.....	254,779	6,270	NR	1,361	93,661
Harris Stowe State College.....	88,690	913	NR	318	4,008
Jackson State University.......	335,599	9,680	3,346	2,709	406,415
Lawson State Community College.	28,574	1,018	1,018	147	9,076
Lincoln University (PA)........	167,438	2,726	524	626	205,796
Mississippi Valley State.......	104,324	1,957	1,444	728	248,159
Morgan State University........	306,664	9,278	8,263	2,310	392,297
Norfolk State University.......	289,948	7,144	9,015	2,252	58,880
North Carolina Central University.....	460,869	4,698	3,142	1,811	139,497
Bishop State Community College...	42,913	988	988	273	2,784

TABLE 1 Continued

Type of Institution	COLLECTIONS				
	Volumes in Library	Volumes Added (Gross)	Monographs Purchased	Current Serials (Total)	Microform Units (Total)
State continued					
Southern University, Shreveport..	43,460	1,546	1,246	381	17,966
Texas Southern University........	450,040	6,558	6,065	2,223	314,846
West Virginia State College......	182,089	1,802	1,415	871	18,778
Winston-Salem State University...	158,858	6,534	6,263	1,397	11,537
SUM	4,041,178	92,114	62,571	26,363	4,709,403
MEAN	175,703	4,005	2,720	1,146	204,757

NR: Not Reported

Source: ACRL/HBCUS Survey

United Negro College Fund institutions; a total of 45,642 monographs were purchased with a mean of 1,755. The land-grant institutions purchased 63,706 monographs with a mean of 5,309 while in 1988-89, the state institutions in this survey bought 62,571 monographs and a mean of 2,720 (see Table 1).

Current Serials (Total)

Table 1 indicates that the University of the District of Columbia held 3,246 current serials and that the five independent private institutions held a total of 34,407 with a mean of 6,881. The 27 independent United Negro College Fund libraries held a total of 3,246 current serials titles and a mean of 477 while the 12 libraries in the land-grant institutions reported a total of 20,313 with a mean of 1,693 current serials. The state institutions contained a total of 26,363 current serials titles with a mean of 1,146 (see Table 1).

Microform Units (Total)

The University of the District of Columbia reported 548,220 microform units in 1988-89 and the five independent private institutions reported a total of 3,121,558 units with a mean of 624,312. The 27 United Negro College Fund libraries held 410,352 microform units with a mean of 15,783. The total number of microform units located in the 12 land-grant institutions was 3,774,209 with a mean of 314,517 and the 23 libraries in the state institutions reported 4,707,403 microform units with a mean of 204,757 (see Table 1).

EXPENDITURES

The expenditures of the 68 reporting libraries represent funds from their institutions' budgets, research grants, special projects, gifts and endowments and fees for services. The expenditures discussed in this section are monographs; current serials; library materials (total); salaries and wages (total); other library expenditures; and total library expenditures.

Monographs

Table 2 indicates that the University of the District of Columbia did not report its expenditures for monographs in this survey. Of the five independent private institutions, three responded to this question with total expenditures of $12,688,133 and a mean of $253,626. The 22 independent United Negro College Fund libraries reporting spent $1,570,550 on monographs with a mean of $60,406. The land-grant institutions reported $1,634,453 in expenditures for monographs with a mean of $136,204 while the 23 libraries in the state institutions spent $1,503,919 and a mean of $65,388 (see Table 2).

Current Serials

The University of the District of Columbia did not respond to the question relating to expenditures for current serials. Four of the independent private libraries reported a total of $2,911,569 with a mean of $582,314. The 23 independent United Negro College Fund libraries spent a total of $803,655 with a mean of $30,910. Eleven of the 12 land-grant libraries participating in the survey spent $2,210,986 with mean of $96,130 and the 23 libraries in state institutions reported a total of $2,094,657 spent on current serials with a mean of $174,555 (see Table 2).

Library Materials (Total)

Of its total library expenditures, the University of the District of Columbia spent $1,022,624 or 31 percent on library materials. The five independent private libraries reported a total of $4,558,299 and a mean of $911,652 on library materials. This represented 33 percent of their total library expenditures. The libraries in the United Negro College Fund institutions reported that $2,967,069 or 39 percent of their total library expenditures was allocated to library materials. The land-grant institutions spent $4,961,397 or 42 percent of their library expenditures on library materials. This represented an average of $413,450 for each of these 12 institutions. Of the 21 libraries in state institutions responding to this question,

TABLE 2. Data on Expenditures of Historically Black Colleges and Universities by Type of Institution, 1988-1989

Types of Institutions	EXPENDITURES					
	Monographs	Current Serials	Library Materials (Total)	Salaries and Wages (Total)	Other Operating Expenditures	Total Library Expenditures
Federal						
University of the District of Columbia	$ NR	$	$1,022,624	$2,146,822	$ 110,593	$ 3,283,039
Independent.Private (IP)						
Hampton University..	234,670	204,681	478,443	462,548	54,018	1,017,056
Howard University...	10,025,380	2,694,799	3,792,169	5,331,431	2,147,235	11,427,835
Mary Holmes College.	NR	4,783	9,255	61,000	1,395	73,124
Meharry Medical College.........	NR	NR	252,931	489,961	89,950	832,842
Southwestern Christian College.	8,083	7,307	25,461	57,210	15,339	98,010
SUM	12,688,133	2,911,569	4,558,259	6,402,150	2,307,937	13,448,867
MEAN	253,626	582,314	911,652	1,280,430	461,587	2,689,773
Independent United Negro College Fund (UNCF)						
Atlanta University Center.........	409,788	211,176	679,076	778,078	527,663	1,991,468
Barber Scotia College.........	NR	NR	NR	NR	NR	NR
Benedict College.....	61,855	22,333	106,227	NR	NR	NR
Bennett College.....	NR	NR	NR	NR	11,182	NR
Bethune-Cookman College.........	159,500	36,000	238,900	232,223	NR	477,723
Dillard University..	23,000	40,000	86,359	188,015	113,560	397,334
Fisk University.....	44,767	NR	44,767	NR	43,896	228,533

TABLE 2 Continued

| | | | EXPENDITURES | | | |
Type of Institutions	Monographs	Current Serials	Library Materials (Total)	Salaries and Wages (Total)	Other Operating Expenditures	Total Library Expenditures
Huston-Tillotson College	11,533	14,752	44,499	98,257.	10,318	153,623
Jarvis Christian College	45,000	18,512	69,381	NR	4,971	NR
Johnson C. Smith College	92,352	28,896	143,068	230,021	24,176	402,265
Knoxville College	100,000	12,000	125,000	NR	NR	252,800
Lane College	10,575	9,536	22,108	124,784	358	148,250
LeMoyne-Owen College	30,000	12,000	48,495	100,596	NR	151,091
Morris College	NR	NR	NR	NR	NR	NR
Oakwood College	34,023	23,148	68,646	210,581	20,435	307,229
Paine College	48,230	42,816	93,406	117,180	5,662	217,248
Saint Paul's College	5,933	8,628	263,312	102,117	60,790	426,219
Shaw University	NR	5,000	9,090	130,673	120,023	259,786
Stillman College	59,000	17,486	80,651	126,425	19,293	230,009
Talladega College	69,000	23,430	92,430	75,500	6,000	175,930
Texas College	8,422	5,138	19,410	NR	NR	NR
Tougaloo College	59,765	23,941	93,673	141,100	1,396	242,169
Tuskegee University	155,000	167,097	340,382	318,053	41,200	715,039
Virginia Union University	30,000	20,000	55,200	117,717	NR	172,917
Voorhees College	NR	25,000	81,500	126,550	15,850	223,900
Wilberforce University	18,260	19,266	40,562	NR	22,867	183,073
Wiley College	94,547	17,500	120,927	111,679	NR	232,606
SUM	1,570,550	803,655	2,967,069	3,329,549	1,049,640	7,589,213
MEAN	60,406	30,910	114,118	128,059	40,371	291,893

TABLE 2 Continued

			EXPENDITURES			
Types of Institutions	Monographs	Current Serials	Library Materials (Total)	Salaries and Wages (Total)	Other Operating Expenditures	Total Library Expenditures
Land Grant (LG)						
Alabama A&M University............	$ 84,575	$ 238,230	$ 347,089	$ 578,403	$ 108,410	$ 1,043,181
Alcorn State University...........	31,644	62,264	107,683	410,419	140,065	659,897
Delaware State College...........	349,208	87,254	528,280	394,721	1,350	924,351
Florida A&M University...........	350,200	652,932	1,277,328	1,241,889	100,000	1,485,889
Ft. Valley State College........	102,473	121,765	285,443	NR	174,381	NR
Lincoln University (MO)...........	17,577	68,332	100,860	249,353	53,242	405,455
U. Maryland-Eastern Shore........	177,745	145,012	465,057	628,189	142,933	1,247,546
North Carolina A&T State University..	347,496	247,474	635,719	1,123,756	176,934	2,076,046
Prairie View A&M University........	25,345	225,000	281,679	625,431	461,867	1,368,977
South Carolina State College........	NR	NR	235,821	401,939	195,682	NR
Southern University Baton Rouge........	NR	131,000	429,138	928,319	NR	1,357,457
Tennessee State University........	148,190	115,395	267,300	765,933	64,990	1,123,223
SUM	1,634,453	2,094,657	4,961,397	7,348,352	1,619,854	11,692,022
MEAN	136,204	174,555	413,450	612,363	134,988	974,335

TABLE 2 Continued

	EXPENDITURES					
Types of Institutions	Monographs	Current Serials	Library Materials (Total)	Salaries and Wages (Total)	Other Operating Expenditures	Total Library Expenditures
State (S)						
Albany State College	$ 25,264	$ 40,316	$ 125,744	$ 257,194	$ 86,613	$ 469,551
Bluefield State College.........	40,500	13,711	85,922	116,256	NR	202,178
Bowie State University.........	NR	86,892	133,540	394,698	45,500	592,416
Central State University.........	1,295	89,468	100,651	307,366	8,818	431,733
Cheyney University..	26,605	67,470	101,475	434,676	21,120	564,471
Coahoma Community College.........	NR	6,000	NR	NR	NR	NR
Coppin State College	64,231	41,436	124,844	NR	27,172	NR
Elizabeth City State University.........	115,657	64,064	NR	397,115	34,062	660,604
Fayetteville State University.........	100,000	129,332	268,332	578,909	93,304	942,545
Grambling State University.........	NR	161,767	195,320	496,237	71,261	765,692
Harris Stowe State College.........	27,401	18,847	46,248	154,190	8,152	208,590
Jackson State University	159,780	66,027	272,505	549,431	431,083	1,262,406
Lawson State Comm. College	16,612	4,131	30,212	109,411	NR	139,623
Lincoln University (PA)	26,563	114,585	192,194	325,244	NR	517,838

TABLE 2 Continued

EXPENDITURES

Types of Institutions	Monographs	Current Serials	Library Materials (Total)	Salaries and Wages (Total)	Other Operating Expenditures	Total Library Expenditures
Mississippi Valley State College.....	$ 52,684	$ 45,316	$ 108,000	$ 303,106	$ 10,000	$ 424,227
Morgan State University.........	236,698	349,672	641,834	791,286	151,428	1,586,659
Norfolk State University........	226,019	129,304	376,389	723,747	100,000	1,215,136
North Carolina Central University	78,115	307,920	413,795	745,440	44,800	1,216,505
Bishop State Comm. College.........	10,000	27,500	46,000	117,291	2,565	170,114
Southern University Shreveport........	7,389	13,000	20,389	204,153	6,089	233,631
Texas Southern University........	152,735	269,147	451,623	733,323	158,338	1,560,917
West Virginia State College.........	17,228	55,081	95,149	217,104	126,749	439,002
Winston-Salem State University........	119,143	110,000	240,773	384,413	116,820	743,006
SUM	1,503,919	2,210,986	4,070,939	8,340,590	1,543,874	14,346,845
MEAN	65,388	96,130	176,997	362,634	67,125	623,776

NR: Not Reported

Source: ACRL/HBCUS Survey

$4,070,939 or 28 percent of their library expenditures was spent on library materials. This represented a mean of $176,977 (see Table 2).

Salaries and Wages (Totals)

These figures represent the salaries and wages of the professionals, non-professionals and students employed in the libraries participating in this survey. Table 2 shows that the University of the District of Columbia spent $2,146,822 or 65 percent of its total library expenditures on salaries and wages. The five private independent libraries reported that $6,402,150 or a mean of $1,280,430 was expended on salaries and wages. This represented 20 percent of the total library expenditures for the five institutions. The libraries in the United Negro College Fund institutions reported that their salaries and wages for 1988-89 amounted to $3,329,549 or 43 percent of their total library expenditures, and the mean was $128,059. Of the $11,692,022 reported by the land grant institutions for their total library expenditures, $7,348,352 or 62 percent was spent on salaries and wages, a mean of $612,363. The libraries in the state institutions reported that their salaries and wages amounted to $8,340,590 or 58 percent of the total library expenditures. This represented a mean of $362,634 for salaries and wages for these institutions (see Table 2).

Other Operating Expenditures

The University of the District of Columbia spent $110,593 on other operating expenditures. The five independent private institutions reported a total of $2,307,937 and a mean of $461,587. The libraries in the United Negro College Fund institutions reported a total of $1,049,640 and an average of $40,371 for other operating expenditures. The land-grant libraries spent a total of $1,619,854 with a mean of $134,988 while the libraries in the state institutions reported that their other operating expenditures amounted to $1,543,874 with a mean of $67,125 (see Table 2).

Total Library Expenditures

Table 2 shows that the total library expenditures for the University of the District of Columbia was $3,283,037. The five independent private institutions reported $13,448,867 with a mean of $2,689,773. The libraries in the United Negro College Fund institutions reported $7,589,213 and a mean of $291,893 for total library expenditures for 1988-89. The land-grant institutions reported that their total library expenditures were $11,692,022 with a mean of $974,335 while the libraries in the state institutions reported total library expenditures of $14,346,845 and a mean of $623,776 (see Table 2).

PERSONNEL

The categories of library personnel included the professional staff members, the non-professional staff members and the student assistants. Table 3 shows that the University of the District of Columbia employed a total of 71 persons. The five independent private institutions reported a total of 301 persons with a mean of 60. The United Negro College Fund institutions reported 477 persons working in the library with a mean of 18, and the libraries in the land-grant colleges and universities reported 462 library personnel with a mean of 38. The state institutions reported that 719 persons were employed in their libraries during 1988-89 with a mean of 31. The number of personnel by each category is illustrated in Table 3.

ENROLLMENT

The enrollment includes both graduate and undergraduate for 1988-89. Table 4 shows that the University of the District of Columbia enrolled 3,634 graduate and undergraduate students. Three of the five independent private institutions participating in the survey enrolled graduate and undergraduate students and the total enrollment for these institutions was 16,294 with a mean of 3,259. There were 30,961 students with a mean of 1,191, attending the 25 United Negro College Fund institutions that responded to this question. Four of these institutions reported that their libraries served graduate and undergraduate students. The libraries in the 12 land-grant institutions reported an enrollment of 39,725 with a mean of

3,310 and all of these institutions enrolled graduate and undergraduate students. Of the 22 state institutions responding to this question, 12 reported that their libraries served graduate and undergraduate students. This group of institutions enrolled 59,164 students with a mean of 2,572 during 1988-89 (see Table 4).

FACULTY MEMBERS

The 64 libraries responding to this question reported a total of 10,966 faculty members. The University of the District of Columbia reported 482 faculty members and the independent private institutions reported 1,510. There were 2,209 faculty members with a mean of 85, employed in the independent United Negro College Fund institutions. The land-grant institutions retained 3,176 faculty members with a mean of 265; while the state institutions reported that 3,589 faculty members with a mean of 156 were employed at their institutions. Table 3 gives the sum and mean of faculty members at each institution participating in the survey by type of institution (see Table 4).

CONCLUSIONS

The *ACRL/HBCUS Survey* represents the most comprehensive collection of statistical data on libraries in historically black colleges and universities in twenty years. Variables were selected from *ACRL/HBCUS Survey* for analysis and grouped by the five types of institutions delineated in the study. It was anticipated that the statistics collected in the *ACRL/HBCUS Survey* could be utilized for comparison with the earlier studies and for comparison with the statistical projects of the Association of College and Research Libraries.

Jordan concluded, when comparing libraries in the privately and publicly supported historically black colleges and universities that:

The situation is about even between the privately and publicly supported institutions.[5]

TABLE 3. Number of Personnel in Historically Black Colleges and University Libraries by Type of Institutions

Type of Institution	Professional Staff	Non-Professional Staff	Student Assistants	Total
Federal				
University of the District of Columbia ..	24	41	6	71
Independent Private				
Hampton University.......	9	25	NR	NR
Howard University........	83	126	25	234
Mary Holmes College......	1	2	20	23
Meharry Medical College-.	9	22	0	31
Southwestern Christian College.....	3	0	10	13
SUM	105	175	56	301
MEAN	21	35	11	60
Independent United Negro College Fund (UNCF)				
Atlanta University Center	19	20	10	49
Barber Scotia College....	2	2	15	19
Benedict College.........	5	7	NR	NR
Bennette College.........	3	2	NR	NR
Bethune-Cookman College..	5	6	9	20
Dillard University.......	5	1	0	6
Fisk University..........	6	3	4	13
Huston-Tillotson College.	4	1	1	6
Jarvis Christian College.	4	1	24	29
Johnson C. Smith University.......	6	5	25	36

				NR	NR
Knoxville College	3	5		15	20
Lane College	3	2		7	13
LeMoyne-Owen College	3	3		33	42
Morris College	1	8		15	25
Oakwood College	4	6		11	17
Paine College	3	3		6	13
Saint Paul's College	4	1		2	7
Shaw University	4	7		5	15
Stillman College	3	2		17	21
Talladega College	2	1		10	14
Texas College	3	6		6	16
Tougaloo College	4	10		21	43
Tuskegee University	12	3		10	17
Virginia Union University	4	4		13	20
Voorhees College	3	5		NR	NR
Wilberforce University	2	2		10	16
Wiley College	4				
SUM	120	117		269	477
MEAN	4	4		11	18

169

TABLE 3 Continued

Type of Institution	Professional Staff	Non-Professional Staff	Student Assistants	Total
Land Grant				
Alabama A&M University...	12	14	6	32
Alcorn State University..	6	12	19	37
Delaware State College...	10	13	3	26
Florida A&M University...	19	36	12	67
Fort Valley State College...	5	8	5	18
Lincoln University (MO)...	7	8	6	21
University of Maryland–Eastern Shore...	11	12	23	46
North Carolina A&T State University...	17	25	17	59
Prairie View A&M University...	16	15	16	47
South Carolina State College...	8	8	26	41
Southern University–Baton Rouge...	18	19	NR	NR
Tennessee State University...	16	25	29	69
SUM	144	194	161	462
MEAN	12	16	18	38
State				
Albany State College....	5	6	6	17
Bluefield State College..	3	4	2	8
Bowie State University...	6	11	11	28
Central State University	4	7.	6	17
Cheyney University......	6	6	4	16

Institution				
Coahoma Community College	2	3	12	17
Coppin State College	9	16	15	40
Elizabeth City State University	7	8	3	18
Fayetteville State University	12	14	20	46
Grambling State University	8	12	31	51
Harris Stowe State College	4	3	2	9
Jackson State University	11	20	50	81
Lawson State Community College	2	2	8	12
Lincoln University (PA)	7	8	7	22
Mississippi Valley State College	8	9	15	32

TABLE 3 Continued

Type of Institution	Professional Staff	Non-Professional Staff	Student Assistants	Total
State continued				
Morgan State University..	14	20	50	84
Norfolk State University.	9	24	35	68
North Carolina Central-..	18	16	4	38
Bishop State Community College..........	2	3	1	6
Southern University- Shreveport..........	5	1	0	6
Texas Southern University	14	26	18	58
West Virginia State College..........	5	9	10	24
Winston-Salem State University..........	6	9	7	22
SUM	164	236	316	719
MEAN	7	10	14	31

Source: ACRL/HBCUS Survey

172

The Smith study indicated that with respect to the number of volumes in their library collections, public supported institutions while showing deficiencies, ranked higher than libraries in private supported institutions.[6] Also, this study revealed that "total library budgets were generally higher in the publicly supported institutions than in the private supported ones."[7]

The dissimilarity in the format of the questionnaires that were utilized to collect the data in the *ACRL/HBCUS Survey* and the studies described above, coupled with the differentiation of the types of libraries provided barriers for a stringent comparative analysis. However, these statistics can be very useful for individual libraries that are listed in the earlier studies and the *ACRL/HBCUS Survey*, to compare and trace their growth and developmental patterns over the last twenty years.

The statistics collected from the non-ARL libraries by the Association of Colleges and Research Libraries provide for a more exacting comparison with the statistics in the *ACRL/HBCUS Survey* as the formats for collecting the statistics are the same. These 114 libraries represented in the *ACRL University Library Statistics 1988-89*[8] were designated as Research Institutions I and II and Doctorate Granting Colleges and Universities I and II in the 1987 Carnegie classification and to 7 Canadian university libraries with similar scope and mission. While all of these non-ARL libraries served graduate students, it should be noted that 32 or 47 percent of the institutions in the *ACRL/HBCUS Survey* enrolled graduate students (see Table 4). Individual institutions in the *ACRL/HBCUS Survey* may compare their libraries with similar institutions represented by these non-ARL libraries.

Table 5 presents the means of selected variables in the categories of collections and expenditures for the libraries participating in the *ACRL/HBCUS Survey* and the 114 non-ARL libraries reporting in the ACRL 1988-89 Survey. A discussion of these comparisons are presented below and represent the conclusions for this study:

Sixty-eight libraries representing 73 institutions, responded to the *ACRL/HBCUS Survey*. Of these sixty-eight libraries 27 were located in independent United Negro College Fund institutions, 23 were state controlled libraries; the land-grant institutions were rep-

TABLE 4. Enrollment and Number of Faculty Members in Historically Black Colleges and Universities, 1988-1989

Type of Institutions	Enrollment	Number of Faculty Members
Federal		
University of the District of Columbia..........	3,634*	482
Independent Private		
Hampton University..........	5,305*	289
Howard University..........	9,634*	1,174
Mary Holmes College..........	454	23
Meharry Medical College..........	613*	NR
Southwestern Christian College ...	288	16
SUM	16,294	1,511
MEAN	3,259	375
Independent United Negro College Fund		
Atlanta University Center........	8,038	564
Barber Scotia College..........	420	38
Benedict College..........	1,409	118
Bennett College..........	NR	NR
Bethune-Cookman College..........	1,807	111
Dillard University..........	1,400	104
Fisk University..........	743*	63
Huston-Tillotson College..........	465	49
Jarvis Christian College..........	478	47
Johnson C. Smith University.......	1,173	79
Knoxville College..........	1,000	75
Lane College..........	530	48

College		
LeMoyne-Owen College	981	NR
Morris College	NR	NR
Oakwood College	1,159	81
Paine College	530	50
Saint Paul's College	499	43
Shaw University	1,606	80
Stillman College	717	50
Talladega College	490	36
Texas College	450	30
Tougaloo College	848	60
Tuskegee University	3,269*	289
Virginia Union University	1,101*	78
Voorhees College	580	29
Wilberforce University	785	55
Wiley College	483	32
SUM	30,961	2,209
MEAN	1,191	85

TABLE 4 Continued

Type of Institutions	Enrollment	Number of Faculty Members
Land Grant		
Alabama A&M University	2,861*	258
Alcorn State University	2,207*	147
Delaware State College	1,720*	140
Florida A&M University	6,152*	540
Fort Valley State College	1,867*	146
Lincoln University (MO)	1,611*	142
University of Maryland- Eastern Shore	1,576*	91
North Carolina A&T State University	5,070*	419
Prairie View A&M University	4,855*	231
South Carolina State College	3,344*	202
Southern University, Baton Rouge	3,854*	475
Tennessee State University	4,608*	385
SUM	39,725	3,176
MEAN	3,310	265
State		
Albany State College	2,104*	133
Bluefield State College	1,429	146
Bowie State University	1,661*	119
Central State University	2,729	117
Cheyney University	1,216*	112
Coahoma Community College	1,475	56
Coppin State College	NR	108
Elizabeth City State University	1,568	103
Fayetteville State University	1,904*	163
Grambling State University	5,285*	264

Harris Stowe State College........	550	37
Jackson State University..........	6,777*	286
Lawson State Community College....	933	60
Lincoln University (PA)...........	1,027*	73
Mississippi Valley State..........	1,554*	103
Morgan State University...........	2,960*	205
Norfolk State University..........	6,294*	451
North Carolina Central University	3,176*	282
Bishop State Community College....	705	49
Southern University, Shreveport..	751	73
Texas Southern University........	8,620*	356
West Virginia State College......	4,509	138
Winston-Salem State University...	1,937	155
SUM	59,164	3,589
MEAN	2,572	156

*Graduate and Undergraduate Enrollment

Source: ACRL/HBCUS Survey

TABLE 5. The Means of Variables Selected from the ACRL/HBCUS Survey
and the ACRL University Library Statistics 1988-89

Institutions	COLLECTIONS				
	Volums in Library	Volumes Added (Gross)	Monographs Purchased	Current Serials (Total)	Microform Units (Total)
Federal................	483,188	12,858	2,787	3,246	548,220
Independent Private......	434,975	16,155	6,881	6,210	624,312
Independent United Negro College Fund..........	113,318	3,515	1,755	477	15,783
Land Grant..............	246,060	5,309	3,983	1,693	314,517
State..................	175,703	4,005	2,720	1,146	204,757
All HBCUs Libraries......	186,935	4,998	3,371	1,415	196,308
Non-Association of Research Libraries.....	812,591	23,286	14,277	6,775	909,708

resented with 12 libraries; five of the reporting libraries were located in independent private institutions; and one was a federal controlled library.

Only one library reported holdings of more than 1,000,000 volumes and this was an independent private institution. The federal controlled library contained 483,188 volumes and the five independent private libraries reported the largest average number of holdings with 434,975 volumes. An average of 234,975 volumes was reported by the 12 land-grant institutions; and the libraries in the state institutions reported 175,703 as the mean for the number of volumes held in the 23 participating libraries. The United Negro College Fund institutions reported an average of 113,378 volumes held in their libraries. The total average for the libraries participating in the *ACRL/HBCUS Survey* was 186,935 volumes while the

TABLE 5 (continued)

		EXPENDITURES			
Monographics	Current Serials	Library Materials (Total)	Salaries and Wages (Total)	Other Operating Expenditures	Total Library Expenditures
NR	NR	$1,022,624	$2,146,822	$110,593	$3,283,039
$253,626	$582,314	911,652	1,280,430	461,587	2,689,773
60,406	30,910	114,118	128,059	40,371	291,893
136,204	144,555	413,450	612,363	134,988	974,335
65,388	96,130	176,997	362,634	67,125	623,776
103,053	131,490	279,052	492,276	106,966	878,276
491,902	800,364	1,388,673	1,723,657	395,703	3,517,674

NR: Not Reporting
Sources : *ACRL/HBCUS Survey* and the *ACRL University Library Statistics 1988-89*

average number of volumes held in the non-ARL libraries was 812,591 (see Table 5).

With respect to the average number of volumes (gross) added during 1988-89; the five independent private institutions added an average of 16,155 volumes and the University of the District of Columbia added 12,858 volumes. The land-grant libraries added an average of 5,309 volumes; the state institutions increased their holdings with an average of 4,005 and the 27 United Negro College Fund institutions reported a mean of 3,515 volumes added to their libraries (see Table 5).

The five independent private libraries reported 6,881, the largest number of monographs purchased and the land-grant institutions purchased an average of 3,983 monographs. The federal controlled library purchased 2,787 monographs while the libraries in the state institutions purchased an average of 2,720 monographs. An average of 1,755 monographs were purchased by the United Negro College Fund institutions. The average for the libraries discussed above was 3,371 and for the non-ARL libraries, the average was 14,277 volumes (see Table 5).

The libraries in the five independent private institutions held 6,210 current serials titles, the largest average number reporting; while the federal controlled library owned 2,787. The libraries in the land-grant institutions held an average of 1,693 current serial titles in their collections and the libraries in the state institutions reported an average of 1,146. The United Negro College Fund institutions held an average of 477 current titles in their libraries. The average for all of the libraries participating in the *ACRL/ HBCUS Survey* was 1,415 and the non-ARL libraries reported an average of 6,775 current serials (see Table 5).

The five independent private institutions ranked the highest with an average number of 624,312 microform units. The federal controlled library owned 548,220 microform units. The libraries in the land-grant institutions owned an average of 314,517 microform units; libraries located in state controlled institutions held an average of 204,757 microform units while the libraries serving the United Negro College Fund institutions reported an average of 15,783 microform units. The libraries representing all of the historically black colleges and universities reported an average of 196,308 microform units while the non-ARL libraries held an average of 909,708 (see Table 5).

The libraries in the independent private institutions reported an average of $253,626 spent on monographs. The land-grant institutions expended an average of $136,204 for monographs in libraries and the libraries in the state institutions spent an average of $65,388. The libraries representing the United Negro College Fund institutions spent an average of $60,406 for monographs and the federal supported library did not respond to this question. The libraries in the *ACRL/HBCUS Survey* reported an average of $103,053 expended on monographs while the non-ARL libraries reported an average of $491,902 (see Table 5).

The highest average expenditure for current serials was reported by the independent private institutions at $582,314. The libraries in the land-grant institutions spent an average of $174,555 while the libraries in the state institutions reported an average of $96,130. The libraries serving the United Negro College Fund institutions spent an average of $30,910 for current serials and the federal controlled library did not respond to this question. All of the libraries in the *ACRL/HBCUS Survey* reported an average of $131,490 for current serials and the non-ARL libraries spent an average of $800,364 in this category (see Table 5).

The independent private institutions reported the largest average amount for library materials at $911,652. Libraries located in land-grant colleges and universities reported an average $413,450. The state institutions spent an average of $176,997 on library materials and the libraries representing the United Negro College Fund institutions expended an average of $114,118. The federal controlled library participating in this survey expended $1,022,624 for library materials. The average amount for library materials spent by the libraries in the *ACRL/HBCUS Survey* was $279,052 while the non-ARL libraries expended $1,388,673 (see Table 5).

For total salaries and wages, the five independent private institutions expended an average of $1,280,430. The land-grant libraries used an average of $612,363 of their budgets for salaries and wages and the state institutions spent an average of $362,634. The libraries serving the United Negro College Fund institutions spent an average of $128,059 for salaries and wages and the federal controlled library expended $2,146,822. For the libraries participating in the *ACRL/HBCUS Survey*, the average spent on total salaries and wages was $492,276 and the average for non-ARL libraries during the same period was $1,723,657 (see Table 5).

Libraries representing the five independent private institutions reported an average of $461,587 expended for other operating expenditures. The land-grant institutions expended an average of $134,988 while the libraries in state institutions spent an average of $67,125 on other operating expenditures. The libraries in the United Negro College Fund institutions expended an average of $40,371 for other operating expenditures and the one library controlled and supported by the federal government spent $110,593 in this category. For other operating expenditures, the average amount expended by the libraries responding to the *ACRL/HBCUS Survey* was $106,966 and $395,703 for the non-ARL libraries (see Table 5).

The average total library expenditures was the highest in the five independent private institutions at $2,689,773. The land-grant institutions spent an average of $974,335 on library expenditures and the state institutions expended an average of $623,776. The libraries serving the United Negro College Fund institutions spent an average of $291,983 for library expenditures and the one federal controlled library spent a total of $3,283,039 in this category. The average total library expenditures for the institutions reporting in the *ACRL/HBCUS Survey* was $878,276 and the non-ARL institutions expended an average of $3,517,674 (see Table 5).

REFERENCES

1. Five institutions, Clark Atlanta University, the Interdenominational Theological Seminary, Morehouse College, Morris Brown College, and Spelman College are served by the Atlanta University Center.

2. American Library Association. Association of College and Research Libraries *ACRL/Historically Black Colleges and Universities Library Statistics 1988-89*. Compiled by Robert E. Molyneux. Chicago: The Association, 1991. Hereafter in this paper, this document will be referred to as the *ACRL/HBCUS Survey*.

3. Jordan, Casper LeRoy. "Black Academic Libraries: An Inventory," *Occasional Papers No. 1*, Atlanta: Atlanta University, November 1970.

4. Smith, Jessie Carney. *Black Academic Libraries and Research Collections: An Historical Survey*. Westport, Connecticut: Greenwood Press, 1977.

5. Jordan, p. 30.

6. Smith, p. 147.

7. Ibid., p. 153.

8. American Library Association. Association of College and Research Libraries. *ACRL University Library Statistics 1988-89*. Compiled by Denise Bedford. Chicago: The Association, 1990.

THE GOVERNMENT

U.S. Government Publications in Ethnic Studies: An Often Overlooked Source

Linda Bowles-Adarkwa
LaVonne Jacobsen

SUMMARY. U.S. government publications are valuable to collections supporting research on ethnic studies, but are underrepresented in collection building literature. Federal documents are no longer as difficult to identify and acquire as in the past and should be sought out for ethnic collections. This article describes relevant publications available from federal agencies, major federal and selected commer-

Linda Bowles-Adarkwa is Monographs Cataloger and Subject Specialist for Black Studies and Women Studies, and LaVonne Jacobsen is Government Publications Specialist and former Acting-Head of Acquisitions at J. Paul Leonard Library, San Francisco State University, 1630 Holloway Avenue, San Francisco, CA 94132.

[Haworth co-indexing entry note]: "U.S. Government Publications in Ethnic Studies: An Often Overlooked Source," Bowles-Adarkwa, Linda and LaVonne Jacobsen. Co-published simultaneously in *The Acquisitions Librarian* (The Haworth Press, Inc.) No. 9/10, 1993, pp. 183-219; and: *Multicultural Acquisitions* (ed: Karen Parrish and Bill Katz) The Haworth Press, Inc., 1993, pp. 183-219. Multiple copies of this article/chapter may be purchased from The Haworth Document Delivery Center. Call 1-800-3-HAWORTH (1-800-342-9678) between 9:00 - 5:00 (EST) and ask for DOCUMENT DELIVERY CENTER.

183

cial sources for identifying and acquiring publications and using depository libraries as resources. Appendix A profiles key agencies and Appendix B is a bibliography of "tantalizing" examples.

INTRODUCTION

Scope

In our experience at San Francisco State University, U.S. government publications are highly valued and routinely used by the students and faculty in the School of Ethnic Studies. That may also be true in many other libraries, but documents remain nearly invisible in the reviewing and indexing resources for ethnic studies and, in many cases, for librarianship. Coupled with the prevailing assumptions that documents are difficult to acquire, U.S. documents of interest to ethnic studies are surely underrepresented in non-depository libraries. We hope to persuade selection and acquisitions personnel who seldom work with U.S. government publications that documents are valuable resources for ethnic studies and less troublesome and mysterious than is often thought.

Although this paper has an academic emphasis, the observations and examples also should be of interest to public libraries. In our library, ethnic studies researchers using government publications are usually concerned with the same issues of concern to the surrounding community—for example, access to health care, retention of students, economic development, or affordable housing. The discussion and resource examples in this paper will be limited in scope to four major American ethnic groups: African Americans, Asian Americans, Latino/Hispanic Americans, and Native Americans. We will discuss ethnic studies as an academic discipline and the types of information available from federal agencies in relationship to ethnic studies, list major sources for selecting appropriate documents, and review basic acquisitions information. Some agencies and documents are cited within the text, but there are two appendices with more examples of specific agencies and documents to illustrate the range of materials and topics covered by federal publishing.

We have excluded legislative and legal sources, with the exception of a Native American treaty source and Congressional publications containing topical research. The legislative process and resources are extremely important to the study of ethnic groups in America but too extensive to include here. We have also excluded consumer and health materials for the layman which are not directed at a specific ethnic group. Such publications may be an important part of the library's collection and service to a multicultural community but are already profiled in the literature.

ETHNIC STUDIES AS A FIELD OF STUDY

Despite the fact that the population of the United States is represented by more than a hundred different ethnic groups (19, p.vi), it wasn't until the 1960's that ethnic studies emerged as an academic discipline. Prior to that time, much of the research on the traditionally identified American minority groups–Indians and Blacks–centered on the anthropological and sociological aspects of these groups' experience as interpreted against the larger Euro-American culture. According to one writer, "Minorities were believed to have little to contribute to human knowledge and the idea that they might have some history or culture worth knowing was regarded as the greatest insanity . . . No one ever believed that racial minorities might have their own point of view" (5, p. 1). During the decades that preceded the 1960's, however, a few trailblazing scholars, from various ethnic backgrounds and disciplines, were researching and documenting the contributions of Blacks, Indians, and Latinos, and providing new perspectives on these cultures. Black scholars, such as W.E.B. DuBois, Carter G. Woodson, and E. Franklin Frazier, and Mexican Americans, such as historian Carlos E. Castaneda and educational sociologist George I. Sanchez, stand out as pioneers in combatting the cultural bias in American scholarship.

It took the Civil Rights Movement of the 1960's, however, to bring to the wider attention of the American nation the presence and contributions of Blacks and other minorities. On college campuses, minority students demanded the inclusion of courses which were relevant to their experiences. Hastily, many colleges offered broad survey courses which failed to incorporate the unique perspectives of the groups studied. "In general the first courses should be described as 'cameo' appearances. They were traditional articulations of manifest destiny sporadically punctuated by polite bows to Blacks, Chicanos, and Indians" (5, p. 1).

Although the hasty introduction of ethnic studies programs into the curriculum during the 1960's and 1970's was accomplished without much forethought to the development of ethnic studies as an academic discipline, today it can be said that ethnic studies has evolved into a legitimate and important field of study. There are more than seven hundred programs and departments in ethnic studies in the U.S. offering various degrees or concentrations in American Indian Studies, Asian American Studies, Black Studies, and Latino Studies. In addition, there are five learned societies concerned with the scholarship of ethnicity: American Indian Studies Association, Asian American Studies Association, Chicano Studies Association, the National Council for Black Studies, and the National Association for Ethnic Studies.

Ethnic studies as a mature academic discipline is defined as an "interdisciplinary, comparative study of the cultures of U.S. people of color as they interact with each other and with the larger American culture" (2, p. 26). In addition to studying aspects of a group's culture or history, ethnic studies employs some of the methodologies of the humanities and social sciences to develop theoretical and historical frameworks for the experience of a group in relationship to other groups and societies. Ethnic studies research also expresses a global and international dimension and an emphasis not only on race, but also on gender and class.

As an academic program, ethnic studies has a strong community base and is directed not only towards theoretical research, but also emphasizes applied studies which have direct relevance to minority communities. Ethnic studies faculty often foster close ties to minority neighborhoods and may be involved in outreach efforts such as student recruitment and retention. Typically they also are concerned with the development of social policies which impact these communities and may serve as resource persons in community development projects.

U.S. GOVERNMENT PUBLICATIONS IN ETHNIC STUDIES RESEARCH

A literature search in *Library Literature* and *ERIC* for the years of 1975 to 1992 indicated that not many publications have been written on the relevance of U.S. government publications to ethnic studies and very few in recent years. Ford's chapter on "United States Government Publications as Sources for Ethnic Materials" (7, pp.46-62) discusses the types of government publications issued by various federal agencies, giving examples of important and interesting titles. References and bibliographies relating to U.S. documents and minorities appeared in Robinson's *Subject Guide to U.S. Government Reference Sources*[15] and Bailey's *Guide to Popular U.S. Government Publications*.[1] Articles and bibliographies concerning government documents and specific ethnic groups include: Tate's "Studying the American Indian Through Government Documents and the National Archives"[18] and Walshak's "Afro-Americans: a Bibliography of U.S. Government Documents Indexed in the Monthly Catalog of U.S. Government Publications, January 1970 through July 1982."[24] *Afro-American History: Sources for Research* edited by Clarke contains the papers from the National Archives Conference on Federal Archives as Sources for Research on Afro-Americans.[3]

Primary Sources

Government publications are an essential part of researching topics on ethnic studies research for the same reasons that they are important to other fields of scholarly study—currency, uniqueness, breadth of scope, and the availability of primary sources. As advanced researchers know, primary materials are indispensable to original research. Much of the process of uncovering and interpreting events from the ethnic studies scholar's perspective is based upon examining primary documents such as original treaties, manuscripts, letters, congressional testimonies, debates and proceedings. Despite the fact that such records preserve an "official" view, they are still necessary and important records. For example, for American Indian Studies, Tate reminds us that, "researchers will still find the National Archives to be the most substantial holding of sources on federal Indian relations for the past 200 years of American history" (18, p. 29). In approaching the records of the Bureau of Refugees, Freedmen, and Abandoned Lands, another writer points out that, "The skillful historian can, however, use the observations of whites to reveal much about black behavior which observers themselves did not understand, but nevertheless reported" (4, p. 75).

Within the U.S. government, the supreme source of primary materials, of course, is the National Archives. Fortunately, a scholar does not have to travel to the National Archives in Washington, D.C. to view every relevant record available. The National Archives microfilm publication Program, in operation since 1940, offers groups of Federal records that have a "high research value" according to the catalog. Efforts have been made to microfilm groups of related records by subject or geographic areas for the convenience of researchers. These microfilmed records are not available on depository and must be purchased.

The *National Archives Microfilm Resources for Research: a Comprehensive Catalog* (1990, $5.00) identifies these sales items and is arranged by agency with record group notations. Subject catalogs of National Archives microfilm publications are $2.00 each and include the following six catalogs which may be of interest to ethnic studies researchers: *American Indians* (1984), *Black Studies* (1984), *Diplomatic Records* (1986), *Genealogical and Biographical Research* (1983), *Immigrant and Passenger Arrivals* (1991), and *Military Service Records* (1985).[23]

Commercial vendors also offer U.S. archival government publications for sale; sometimes as the only source and sometimes as an alternative. Two important commercial examples are: *Papers of the U.S. Commission on Wartime Relocation and Internment of Citizens* (University Publications of America) and *Papers of the Society of American Indians, 1906-1946* (Scholarly Resources Inc.). Microform collections offered by commercial publishers, the National Archives, and the Library of Congress are frequently reviewed in sources such as *Microform Review* and *Choice*. Dodson's *Microform Research Collections: a Guide*[6] and Niles's *An Index to Microform Collections*[13] provide guidance to major sets of microforms.

From the acquisitions librarian's perspective microform purchases are usually expensive and must be acquired carefully. Also, added costs of microform reader/printers must be considered and additional considerations such as quality of reproduction and detailed accompanying guides to the microform set must be weighed.

Good primary sources are not just from the National Archives:

> I heard my husband call, and I suddenly realized that it was not an ordinary day. My heart pounded, my entire body suddenly felt weak with fright. The horror of the day dawned, and I quickly arose. My throat was dry, and my body was sore. I had cried for months, but not until I heard my own husband, a very strong and dependable person, weep under the blanket did I realize how helpless we were and how hopeless it was. . . The Tsukamotos were number 22076. Ojii san, (grandpa) Al's father, had come from Japan in 1892 to Florin and had been farming for more than 50 years. We found grandpa, now 75 years old, staring at the trees and vines that he had planted . . . We just couldn't believe that all of this was really happening to us in America. This shocking development must surely be only a bad dream. (20, p. 720)

The memories of Mary Tsukamoto, 71, evacuee, shared in 1986 with the members of a Congressional Committee, are part of a reservoir of oral history readily available in current Congressional publications. First person accounts by ordinary citizens may not predominate in Congressional publications, but even the testimony of experts has an immediacy that engages and informs the researcher whether school child, neighbor, or scholar. The Chair of our American Indian Studies program, Dr. Elizabeth Parent, makes a practice of bringing her new students to Government Publications in order to nurture exactly that sense of engagement and interest in research–to demonstrate the ties between the "real world" and the academic world. Personal connections are made when a student reads the testimony of a tribal leader or the original words of a treaty signed by his or her ancestors. Congressional documents also are vital for public policy research, of course.

Public Policy Studies

Many U.S. government publications are vital to research on current policy issues which affect minorities. Government agencies initiate policy studies of social problems in order to provide policy-makers with recommendations for solutions. Many contemporary social problems such as racial discrimination in employment, education and housing, inadequate health and mental care of recent immigrants, and underrepresentation in the business and political arena, are of special concern to minority communities. According to Wong, "There is an important reason why minority Americans have been concerned with policy research. The barriers experienced by minority groups in socioeconomic advancement, political participation, and the exercise of civil rights in general, are fundamentally institutional in nature. There is thus, a constant need to monitor and identify those institutional practices which limit opportunities or undermine the quality of life of minority Americans" (25, p. 3).

The ethnic studies researcher engaged in practical and socially active research in the community finds government documents to be particularly vital; for example, Congressional hearings on re-vitalizing the inner city, data collected on the issues facing minority students, health studies on the diseases affecting minorities such as diabetes and recently AIDS, and scores of other issues.

It must be pointed out, however, that the majority of such policy documents are concerned with Indians, Blacks, and Hispanic populations. For Asian Americans, governmental studies are scarcer. In searching the *Monthly Catalog* for the years 1976 to the present, most documents on Asian Americans were published in the late 1970's to mid-1980's and were almost exclusively concerned with Southeast Asian immigrants, the Japanese American wartime relocation experience, and studies on the educational and economic status of Asian Americans. Also, as Wong observed, Asian groups tend to be lumped together, rather than studied separately (25, p. 4).

New and Unique Information

Government agencies are often the first to publish information about current topics. Prime examples are the AIDS crisis information first disseminated by the Centers for Disease Control and the otherwise unpublished observations of experts testifying to Congressional committees. In particular, the most up-to-date statistics on AIDS by ethnic group are found in government documents from the CDC.

Many times government publications may provide unique, difficult to find, or otherwise extremely expensive information. The major statistical surveys are examples of data collection that only the government has the resources to do or which would be expensive, proprietary marketing data available only to a select few. For ethnic studies research, the decennial Census of Population and Housing Subject Reports, the surveys of minority business enterprises every five years, and the employment and earnings data from the Department of Labor are important baseline sources on ethnic groups. The value of unique government sources only emphasizes the importance of providing access to documents in libraries serving ethnic communities; particularly sources which encourage citizen participation. For example, the nature of data collected and the manner in which it is published can be affected by citizen input. The decennial census has been the target of citizen and local government activity regarding the quality of the minority count. Furthermore, plans to cut out valuable distinctions among population subgroups in the Census were also forestalled by lobbying.

Variety of Topics

Since the activities of the agencies of the federal government are far-ranging and cover many aspects of life, agency publications represent subjects of interest to a variety of users. Materials of interest to a general audience include citizenship manuals for new immigrants, ethnic cookbooks, cultural event calendars, and a variety of "how-to" literature. Historical biographies of famous minority people, or minorities in fields like science or the military, will appeal to educators in the elementary and secondary schools as might some of the posters and videos. Although U.S. government publications will not be published on every single topic of interest, or may not be available at exactly the level desired, there is a wealth of possibilities.

FACTORS LIMITING THE ACQUISITION OF U.S. GOVERNMENT PUBLICATIONS

As noted above, U.S. government publications are underrepresented in collection building literature in general and in the literature on multicultural collections. Furthermore, in spite of a stepped up marketing program by the Government Printing Office and increased efforts to publicize the depository library program, it seems that documents continue to be narrowly perceived in terms of subject coverage and continue to have a reputation for being hard to acquire. It is also possible that the prominent national policy battles over the scope, quantity, and format of federal publishing may lead librarians to assume that little of general interest is still published. Although challenges and limitations remain, the situation is more positive than its reputation and the materials published merit more attention by selectors for ethnic studies.

In the last several years, U.S. documents have become less troublesome to search and acquire although some special treatment is still necessary. As recently as 1989, Magrill characterized government publications as offering "special problems" such as being rarely available through commercial channels and as being especially difficult to search without offering encouragement about improvements in U.S. document acquisitions (12, p. 151-157). Robinson also emphasized bibliographic and other barriers to documents use in 1988 (16, p. 151-155). Certainly agencies and titles vanish, appear, or change suddenly (as do many other serials); some are out of print as soon as they leave the printing plant; and others never appear in widely available access sources. However, large numbers of U.S. documents are available without the need for extraordinary sleuthing, many mainsteam titles remain in print, and others can be acquired as out-of-print items.

The most significant improvement over the past is that a large percentage of U.S. government publications are now in national bibliographic databases such as OCLC and RLIN. The Government Printing Office and large research libraries contribute AACR2 cataloging for all publications distributed by the GPO and many others as well. With the availability of machine-readable records, libraries large and small have been integrating documents records into their online catalogs. Thus, the old difficulties with bibliographic searching and invisible, mysterious separate collections are fading away.

The difficulties in buying and borrowing U.S. documents have also been somewhat alleviated. Online documents records improve the chances of borrowing a document cost-effectively using routine automated systems. Coupled with the fact that federal documents are copyright-free, copying has become a more viable acquisitions alternative. Many commercial vendors are willing to handle U.S. documents according to our Acquisitions staff and some vendors specialize in documents acquisition (for example, Bernan Associates and Congressional Information Service). However, in spite of improved efforts by federal agencies to do sales marketing, there is still no centralized federal source for the purchase of U.S. government publications.

Federal documents have been controversial in the last several years because of several access issues, e.g., mandatory reductions in publishing, excessive security concerns, privatization, microforms publishing, and electronic formats. For readers who want to follow these issues, there have been numerous excellent articles in *Documents to the People* (GODORT), *Government Information Quarterly,* and *Government Publications Review* (for example, sources 9, 11). It is not practical to review the public policy debates related to these issues but the format issues can be briefly summarized.

One of the most visible results of attempts to limit the costs of federal publishing has been the relative explosion of microform and machine-readable publishing by agencies. U.S. documents have always been published in the same bewildering array of formats available commercially (plus ephemeral formats such as leaflets). At present, about 60% of GPO is in microfiche format; the majority of these being available in that format only. In addition to the lack of choice, until recently the GPO was having severe problems with microform contractor performance. There was an enormous publishing backlog which is nearing resolution; they hope to finish processing and distributing the backlog in 1993. [7]

The conversion to magnetic tape, floppy disks, and CD-ROM products has been a difficult transition for depository libraries. However, non-depository libraries which can acquire electronic formats may find federal sources easy to acquire and more affordable than private products (several agencies price their products to recover production costs but not research and development). Typically, the user interface software will be fairly simple and additional commercial software may be desirable.

IDENTIFYING AND ORDERING
U.S. GOVERNMENT PUBLICATIONS

Long-standing limitations on regular reviewing sources remain barriers to access. A thorough survey of reviewing sources is outside the scope of this paper, but a brief check of *Library Literature* and of major ethnic studies reviewing sources for the 1990's revealed few routine columns or review categories highlighting government publications. Specialized journals for online databases, microforms, documents, and maps are exceptions to the norm. *Library Journal, Booklist,* and *Collection Building* feature annual or occasional columns on government publications; in the last few years, none have focused on minority issues. *Choice,* and others, have had occasional bibliographic essays on topics such as civil rights documents or historical collections on microform which are quite useful.

In general, the selection sources for U.S. government publications will be the same sources used for bibliographic searching because of the few U.S. documents reviewed in mainstream sources. Those unfamiliar with U.S. documents may find O'Hara's book, *Informing the Nation: a Handbook of Government Information for Librarians*[14] or Schwartz's *Easy Access to Information in United States Government Documents*[17] helpful in addition to other sources cited above. Key federal sources and selected commercial sources are described below and out-of-print options noted where appropriate.

Although there is no single central distribution center among federal agencies, there are just a few major alternatives for non-depository libraries to consider: GPO, NTIS, NAVC, agency direct, and borrowing from depository collections. The Government Printing Office (GPO), the National Technical Information Service (NTIS) and the National Audiovisual Center (NAVC) sell publications produced by a wide variety of agencies; the differences will be outlined below. Agencies which are likely to produce interesting ethnic studies materials and which distribute many of their own publications are profiled in Appendix A. Depository libraries, those which automatically receive some or all materials distributed by the GPO, are important to other libraries as sources of acquisitions advice as well as sources of hard-to-find documents. The depository system also is outlined in more detail below.

Indexes and Catalogs

Major resources for identifying federal documents are listed below for the convenience of those not familiar with federal publishing. The emphasis is on sources provided by federal agencies rather than commercial resources although some of those are also mentioned. Most federal publications found in library collections were distributed by the GPO and therefore have classification numbers provided by the Superintendent of Documents–known as the "SuDoc" or "SD" number. The classification system is agency based; C numbers, for example, represent agencies within the Department of Commerce, Y4 numbers represent Congressional groups. Many libraries use the "SuDoc" system as a filing and access system. GPO publications for sale have a stock number (S/N) that is necessary when ordering. Many individual government agencies also publish sales catalogs or bibliographies; they can be identified in some of the sources listed below and in the depository library resources listed later.

Monthly Catalog

The *Monthly Catalog* database belongs in a category by itself because of its broad scope; it is a complete catalog of GPO sales and depository publications, but it is not a complete catalog of all publications from federal agencies.

> *Monthly Catalog of U.S. Government Publications.* Monthly with cumulative indexes. GP3.8: (year/no.); S/N 721-022-00000-5 (paper), $199/year; S/N 721-023-00000-1 (microfiche), $32/year. Available commercially on CD-ROM and online through services such as DIALOG, BRS, and CARL. Since July 1976, the *Monthly Catalog* has been produced as a machine-readable database with indexing by Library of Congress subject headings, title keywords, title, personal and corporate author, series/report numbers, contract numbers (for technical reports),

and GPO sales stock number. Entries have been cataloged according to AACR2 and include information such as OCLC number, Dewey and LC classification numbers, Superintendent of Document number, prices for GPO sales publications, depository selection item number, and format availability as part of the bibliographic description. The comprehensiveness of coverage for specific agencies varies with each agency's cooperation with the Government Printing Office.

The *Monthly Catalog* is easy to search when a comprehensive selection tool is needed because of its title keyword and LCSH indexes; as an online data base it is even more convenient. Each monthly issue is lengthy and arranged by agency, thus it is not convenient to use as a current awareness or browsing source. GPO sales catalogs (see below) and catalogs from specific agencies are handier for locating readily available and popular U.S. government publications.

GPO Sales Publications

The Government Printing Office (GPO) sales program constitutes the most easily acquired category of U.S. government publications. Up-to-date acquisitions information for GPO sales (including telephone numbers and addresses) is available in current issues of the *Monthly Catalog*. Currently, about 14,000 titles are being sold by the Government Printing Office. Publications can be ordered by mail, telephone, fax, teletype, or online through DIALOG/DIAL-ORDER. There are also 24 federal bookstores in larger cities throughout the United States which carry the most popular titles and will order those not in stock. The bookstores are listed in the front of individual issues of the *Monthly Catalog*.

How likely is it that documents of interest to ethnic studies are GPO sales items? With the exception of 2 NTIS documents and the non-book materials, the bibliography of sample relevant documents in Appendix B was compiled from the GPO database without regard for sales status. Of the nearly 100 titles, 45% are (or were) GPO sales publications, including titles available through the GPO Congressional Sales Office. Another 9% of those titles are available from ERIC. Several other titles are available from agencies such as the Census Bureau which have readily accessible sales programs as well.

While acquisitions of federal documents has become less troublesome in other ways, payment options remain somewhat limited. All GPO purchases must be prepaid; payments can be made by check, money order, credit card (MasterCard or VISA), or deposit account. Deposit accounts can be established with a $50 minimum and might be a good choice for libraries expecting to purchase federal documents regularly.

The following publications support the sales program; several are free on request and others are available at depository libraries. Send requests for free catalogs to the Superintendent of Documents, U.S. Government Printing Office, Washington, D.C. 20402 unless another address is given.

GPO Sales Publications Reference File (PRF). Bimonthly with monthly supplement, *GPO New Sales Publications,* and biweekly update of prices and status. Microfiche and magnetic tape only. Available by subscription and online through DIALOG; distributed to depository libraries and federal bookstores. GP3.22/3:(no/yr). Functions as "books in print" for GPO sales publications, including serials. Out of stock titles are transferred annually to an *Out-of-Print GPO Sales Publications File (OPRF)* and cumulated every six years.

Government Periodicals and Subscriptions Services (Price List 36). Quarterly; single issue free. GP3.9:36. Alphabetical by serial title with agency index; introductory pages include information on ordering, quantity discounts, claiming, and cancellation. Some publications available in microfiche and/or magnetic tape.

New Books: Publications for Sale by the Government Printing Office. Bimonthly; subscription free. GP3.17/6:(vol/no). Lists new sales titles by broad subject categories such as education, health, science, etc.; no annotations.

Subject Bibliography Index. Updated irregularly. Free. GP3. 22/2:599. Lists about 230 Subject Bibliographies available from the GPO and includes form for requesting free copies. These bibliographies list current sales publications on different topics, for example: *Africa* (SB-284); *Asia and Oceania* (SB-288); *Civil Rights and Equal Opportunity* (SB-207); *Immigration, Naturalization, and Citizenship* (SB-69); *Minorities* (SB-6). Format-specific bibliographies include *Posters, Charts, Picture Sets, and Decals* (SB-57) and *Motion Pictures, Films and Audiovisual Information* (SB-73).

U.S. Government Books: Publications for Sale by the Government Printing Office. Quarterly; single issue free. GP3.17/5: (vol/no). Annotated and illustrated catalog of approximately 1,000 best-selling and new publications.

Commercial Indexes and Reviewing Sources

Commercial indexes and bibliographies may also include U.S. government publications, but few do so with any degree of intensity. The Ethnic Studies indexes available in the San Francisco State University Library rarely include U.S. documents, i.e., the *Chicano Index* (which covers books as well as periodicals), the *Index to Black Periodicals,* and the *Hispanic American Periodicals Index (HAPI).* The primary non-documents index which does include major U.S. documents is *PAIS International in Print* (formerly *Public Affairs Information Service Bulletin*). It includes citations to federal publications on a wide variety of public policy issues of interest to ethnic communities such as immigration and equal access to health care. It is well-known for including significant statistical sources, as well. Subject headings are different from the Library of Congress ("Blacks" instead of "Afro-Americans," for example) but good cross-references are provided. Citations to documents include Superintendent of Documents numbers, ISBN numbers, GPO stock numbers, and prices when known. In libraries which already subscribe to it, *PAIS* might be a cost-effective way to select a small number of public policy documents related to ethnic groups.

Among the few commercial indexes to current federal documents, the products of the Congressional Information Service are probably best known; for example, the *American Statistics Index* and the *CIS/Index to Publications of the U.S. Congress*. They merit attention for subject selection because of the in-depth indexing which provides citations to portions of documents. In *CIS*, for example, it is possible to identify a Congressional hearing which included testimony by a local community leader. The publisher provides GPO sales information for each citation and also provides a CIS Documents on Demand sales service for current and historical titles. These sources would be important to use for special projects when a comprehensive search is needed.

Non-GPO Acquisitions and Out-of-Print Options

Lack of a centralized distribution agency remains a troublesome aspect of acquiring U.S. government publications. Regional offices of federal agencies publish numerous titles which never reach the GPO indexing and distribution system and many titles in the *Monthly Catalog* are not sold by the GPO. Larger vendors will attempt to supply federal documents, particularly those in the national bibliographic databases. In many cases, however, the only alternative is to contact the agency directly; some will send one copy at no charge but others will charge. Many agencies publish sales catalogs or bibliographies of publications which include non-depository, non-GPO titles. As an example, the Smithsonian Institution Press books are not distributed as documents but the catalog is a depository item (Sup.Doc. No. SI1.16/4).

In Appendix A, some of the federal agencies most likely to have interesting publications are profiled; many others were not included for space reasons. Less well-known agencies were located by simply browsing the indexes in the *United States Government Manual*. [21] Realistically, most libraries haven't the time to pursue more elusive government publications one by one, but don't overlook the possibility of making special arrangements to receive all publications from a local office. Local National Park Service offices, for example, may have historical pamphlets of interest to a particular ethnic community. The two agencies profiled below differ from the ones profiled in the appendix in that they sell publications from many agencies on a broad range of subjects. Like the GPO sales publications, their publications are more readily available and more likely to stay in print for awhile.

The National Technical Information Service is a self-supporting agency which is a clearinghouse for federally produced or sponsored information covering science, business, management, foreign and domestic trade, current technologies, health, social sciences (especially military history), environment, energy, and many other specialties. NTIS distributes GPO publications in addition to those of other federal agencies and of foreign sources. NTIS does not collect all publications but it adds about 70,000 titles each year to its collection and is committed to making them permanently available. Thus, NTIS is an important source to use when seeking out-of-print documents.

The agency publishes numerous catalogs and bibliographies by topic areas, but the principal access source is the *Government Reports Announcements & Index (GRAI)* in paper and *NTIS* bibliographic database online through several vendors. The *NTIS/GRAI* database provides ordering information and abstracts for each citation. Some ERIC documents are included although NTIS does not sell them. The clearinghouse offers publications in paper, microform, or machine-readable formats. As with the GPO, orders can be made by telephone, mail, fax, or online. Unlike the GPO, NTIS will accept purchase orders for an additional fee; state and local governments and state universities can get "immediate credit" and use purchase orders without the additional fee. Academic libraries qualify for a discount. Deposit accounts are also available. For further information, call for the *NTIS Catalog of Products and Services* [PR-827], (703) 487-4650.

The National Audiovisual Center is a little-known agency in the National Archives and Records Administration which markets audiovisual materials created by federal agencies; particularly VHS videotapes and audio-cassettes. NAVC sells or rents materials and makes referrals to free loan sources. Orders are accepted by telephone, fax, or mail and purchase orders are accepted in addition to payment by check, money order, or credit card. Their main catalog is the *Media Resource Catalog* supplemented by their *Quarterly Update*. They also have topical catalogs such as *Media for Black Studies*. Call 1-800-NAVC to be placed on the mailing list. For ethnic studies, the NAVC holdings are strongest in Black Studies and foreign language courses; sample titles are included in Appendix B, the bibliography.

With the exception of GPO, NTIS and NAVC sales titles, government publications often go out of print quickly. Significant historical and ethnographic documents are available from out-of-print dealers or reprint publishers; in fact, reprint publishers have been quite active in making more ethnic studies materials available. Out-of-print Congressional publications can be purchased individually through the CIS Documents on Demand Service. Lesser known government titles may be available from NTIS and will be available through the depository library system. Regional depository libraries are expected to lend from their comprehensive collections and selective depositories will do so as well. As noted previously, because federal publications are copyright free, permission is not needed to copy the entire publication. Some depository libraries may be able to supply microfiche copies of their microfiche holdings. The source of last resort for U.S. government publications (in any format) is the National Archives and Records Administration. The collection is said to number over 2.4 million items, some of which extend back to 1789. As permanent "record copies," materials are not loaned but reproductions can be ordered.

Depository Libraries and Satellite Locations

The depository library network is designed to provide public access to federal publications but it has also been envisioned as a community of librarians available as resources to surrounding non-depository libraries and librarians. More than 1400 depository libraries have been designated by Congressional representatives over the years; there will be at least two in most Congressional districts. There are 53 "regional" depository libraries which acquire nearly all GPO distributed publications. Most states have at least one regional which may provide advanced reference assistance and may be a source of out-of-print items through interlibrary loan and duplication services. The regionals are listed in each issue of the *Monthly Catalog*.

Interested readers are urged to follow up this brief survey by contacting the nearest depository collection. The Superintendent of Documents guidelines to depository libraries encourage community outreach and networking to reach the greatest number of users; depository librarians should welcome inquiries from other libraries. Local Congressional offices can provide information on which nearby libraries are depositories and should be able to provide a copy of the *Directory of U.S. Government Depository Libraries* from the Joint Committee on Printing (Y 4.P93/1-10:yr). A descriptive directory has been published by the Government Documents Roundtable of ALA and CIS.[10]

In addition to encouraging outreach and the lending of documents, probably the least known aspect of the depository program is the provision for satellite locations for depository publications. Non-depository libraries may enter into agreements with depository libraries to receive U.S. government publications on a regular basis through a program called "Selective Housing of Documents." This type of arrangement is useful and appropriate when specific categories of documents can be readily identified and forwarded to a library where they might be more widely available. Depository guidelines require a written agreement in which the receiving Library agrees to follow depository regulations regarding record-keeping and access; the lending Library agrees to assist in selecting new materials on an on-going basis.

The libraries entering into such an agreement need not be related administratively (e.g., in the same public or University system), but may simply be neighboring libraries with complementary collection needs. The advantages to the receiving library are obvious; however, this arrangement requires that all materials received be made available to the general public without charge. The advantages to the lending library may be less apparent. The lender gains space (possibly) and community good will; more importantly, the lender is supporting public access and community outreach goals of the depository system.

Libraries participating in such a program would want access to a few key titles from the Superintendent of Documents which guide depository libraries:

> *Administrative Notes* (Superintendent of Documents). GP3. 16/3-2:vol/no. Depository only. Biweekly newsletter to depository librarians.

Federal Depository Library Manual (1988) and *Instructions to Depository Libraries* (1992). GP3.29:D44/992. Guidelines and regulations for depository collections.

GPO Depository Union List of Item Selections. Depository only, microfiche. GP3.32/2:(year). Arranged by item selection numbers (from list below) and indicates which libraries select each item.

List of Classes of United States Government Publications Available for Selection by Depository Libraries. GP3.24:year/no. Quarterly, subscription or depository. Lists individual series or categories of publications for each agency available for depository selection; provides Item Selection Number.

This type of agreement is most easily administered when the materials to be forwarded fall into concrete categories such as posters, maps, or all materials in a certain item selection number. Federal guidelines do not require or recommend such limitations, however. The following are some examples from the *List of Classes:*

Bibliographies and Lists of Publications. National Archives & Records Service. AE1.110:(Cutter); Item # 0569-C-03.

Federal Textbooks on Citizenship. Immigration and Naturalization Service. Study guides for citizenship examinations. J21.9: (Cutter); Item # 0724.

Handbook of North American Indians. Smithsonian Institution. 9 of 20 volumes published to date (for list, see bibliography). SI1.20/2:(vol); Item # 0909-D-01.

Minority Business Today. Commerce Department. Bimonthly, microfiche only. C1.79:(yr/no); Item # 0126-C-03.

APPENDIX A: PROFILES OF SELECTED AGENCIES

The agencies selected for brief profiling emerged from subject-oriented literature searches and from browsing the two major directories of federal agencies published by the government: the *United States Government Manual* and the *Congressional Directory.* While this list includes some major agencies which may be of interest to most libraries, this list is not exhaustive. Again, each library may have some unique needs served by topics or agencies which have not been highlighted here.

Administration for Native Americans, Office of Human Development Services, Department of Health and Human Services.
  Represents the concerns of American Indians, Alaskan Natives, Native Hawaiians, and Native American Pacific Islanders in HHS policy development; focus issues include social and economic development, self-sufficiency, and self-determination. Provides technical assistance, administers grant programs and keeps constituent groups informed of HHS services and benefits. Typical publication: *Federal Funding Sources for American Indian Tribes,* HE23.5002:F96. Phone: (202)245-7776.
American Folklife Center, Library of Congress.
  Supports, preserves, and presents American folklife by maintaining collections, doing scholarly research, and presenting performances, exhibitions, workshops, etc. Collections include major holdings in music, oral traditions, and photographs. Covers all American ethnic groups; for examples of publications, see the bibliography. Phone: (202)707-6590.
Bureau of the Census. Department of Commerce.
  Publishes hundreds of documents each year, all distributed through the GPO or their own sales program. Major series which include race and ethnicity data are listed in the bibliography: decennial censuses, economic censuses and current population reports. Relevant material ranges from historical population data to projections for the 21st century and from city block statistics to international demographic data. Becoming an electronic publisher on a large scale; current data is available online in DIALOG files, on magnetic tape, floppies and CD-ROM, and through electronic bulletin boards. Community data is critical foundation for service provider studies, planning, etc. New Census Information Center pilot program developed to serve "special populations" works with five lead organizations: National

Urban League, National Council of LaRaza, Southwest Voter Research Institute, IndianNet Information Center, and Asian Pacific Data Consortium. Call (301)763-1384 for CIC information. The Census Bureau publishes a semiannual catalog updated by *Monthly Product Announcements. Census and You* is a useful newsletter available for $12/year. The scale of this agency is too large to do justice to in a profile; call for catalogs and further information: (301)-763-4100.

Bureau of Indian Affairs, Department of the Interior.
Established in 1824 under the War Department, transferred to Interior in 1849. As modified by laws in this century, BIA acts as trustee for lands and monies and works with Native Americans to develop educational opportunities, obtain social services, manage human and natural resources, and provide training opportunities. Publications vary from policy documents to health education pamphlets and may also include tourist information. Phone: (202)208-7315.

Commission on Civil Rights.
Collects and analyses discrimination and equal opportunity information, makes recommendations to the President and Congress, but has no enforcement authority. Serves as a national clearinghouse for civil rights information. Publications are frequently substantial reports on the status of discrimination in an industry or service sector. Phone: (202)376-8312.

Congressional Publications.
Several committees and subcommittees of Congress produce documents of considerable value for ethnic studies; representative examples appear in the bibliography. Hearings and Committee Prints generally represent the research and opinions of experts and citizens, not federal policy. Documents and Reports represent Congressional viewpoints and may be used differently by researchers. Current publications are sold by the GPO, for more information, call the Congressional Sales Office (202) 512-3030.

Educational Resources Information Center (ERIC), Office of Educational Research and Improvement, Department of Education.
Well-known network of clearinghouses for educational research; publishes indexes in paper and online and distributes reproduc-

tions of most titles in the system. Virtually all federal publications of substance on education and ethnic groups will be part of this system and also in the GPO database. Although GPO sells some education titles, more are available from ERIC. For more information, call ACCESS ERIC, (800)USE-ERIC.

Equal Employment Opportunity Commission.
Legacy of the Civil Rights Act of 1964. Monitors and investigates compliance with anti-discrimination laws by private employers and federal agencies. Provides educational and technical assistance to small and midsize employers and unions; surveys employers on racial, ethnic, and gender characteristics of employees. Publications directly reflect agency mission and include valuable data on employment status of minorities and on patterns of discrimination. Phone; (202)663-4900.

Indian Health Service, Public Health Service, Department of Health and Human Services.
Provides comprehensive health services delivery system for American Indians and Alaska Natives. Assists with health planning, health management training, and human resource development. Publications provide analytical data on Indian health status and health promotion materials. Phone: (301)443-1397.

Minority Business Development Agency, Department of Commerce.
Develops and coordinates a national program to encourage minority business enterprises. Provides technical assistance, promotes and assists similar efforts in other federal agencies, and coordinates opportunities in the private sector. Maintains an information clearinghouse on minority business. Phone: (202) 377-1936.

National Archives and Records Administration, General Services Administration.
Maintains and provides access to historically valuable records of the U.S. government dating from the Revolutionary War era to the recent past. Since the 1940's, has made many important records available for purchase on microfilm. Publishes several catalogs, some of which deal with Black, Indian, and immigrant history. Maintains 12 Regional Archives which have collections of primarily regional or local interest plus major microfilm sets

from the National Archives. These regional centers also publish guides to their local collections. Responsible for the National Audiovisual Center which sells or rents motion pictures, film-strips, slide sets, and video and audio tapes from many agencies. For further information on the services of the National Archives, phone: (202)501-5400.

Smithsonian Institution.

Created in 1846 in accordance with the wishes of James Smith-son, who gave his entire estate to the United States in order to further learning and research. The Institution is comprised of several museums, libraries, research institutes, and offices, some of which relate directly to ethnic studies. For instance, the Ana-costia Museum not only houses objects of interest to African American culture and life, it also conducts research in Black history, minority and ethnic studies. The Office of Folklife Pro-grams conducts research and gives presentations on American folklife traditions. It also prepares for publication materials amassed during previous Festivals of American Folklife. The Smithsonian has a non-government auxiliary, the Smithsonian Institution Press, which publishes major resources not included in government publications databases but available through com-mercial channels. For further information on the Smithsonian's activities, phone: (202)357-1300.

APPENDIX B: SELECTIVE BIBLIOGRAPHY

The entries in this bibliography were chosen as representative examples of U.S. government publications issued in the last fifteen years. This list is intended to be a set of examples which will inspire further exploration according to each library's unique and varied need. It is not a core collection, an in-print list, or otherwise com-prehensive.

Titles were selected from the *Monthly Catalog* database unless otherwise noted; there is a separate category at the end for examples of non-book materials. Citations include the Superintendent of Doc-uments classification number when available; sales order numbers and prices are given for items known to be in print in spring 1992.

GENERAL

Bigotry and Violence on American College Campuses By Lallie P. Dawson. Commission on Civil Rights. 1990. CR1.2:B48.

Enterprise Zones: Hearings, June 25 and July 11, 1991. Subcommittee on Select Revenue Measures, Committee on Ways and Means, House. 102nd Congress, 1st Session. 1992. Y4.W36: 102-52. Recent document on enterprise zones as solution to inner city problems; several titles on this issue going back to early 1980's.

Ethnic Folklife Dissertations from the United States and Canada, 1960-1980: a Selected, Annotated Bibliography. By Catherine Hiebert Kerst. American Folklife Center, Library of Congress. 1986.LC39.9:12. Lists multi-disciplinary selection of Ph.D dissertations on indigenous and immigrant ethnic folklife in the U.S. and Canada and includes information on obtaining copies.

Folklife Annual. American Folklife Center, Library of Congress. Annual since 1985. LC39. 14:(year) S/N 030-000-00230-0.

Health Status and Needs of Minorities in the 1990's: Hearing, June 8, 1990. Subcommittee on Health and the Environment, Committee on Energy and Commerce, House. 101st Congress, 2d Session. 1990. Y4.En2/3:101-185.

Higher Education Opportunities for Minorities and Women: Annotated Selections. Department of Education. Annual since 1982. ED1.42:(year) through 1985/86; later issues from ERIC. Listing of scholarship opportunities.

Housing Discrimination Study: Incidence and Severity of Unfavorable Treatment. Prepared by John Yinger. Housing and Urban Development. 1991. HH1.2:D63/18.

An Immigrant Nation: United Sates Regulation of Immigration, 1798-1991. Immigration and Naturalization Service. 1991. J21.1: Im6/14.

Job Patterns of Minorities and Women in Private Industry. Equal Employment Opportunities Commission. Y3.Eq2:12-7/989. Irregular, title varies.

Minority Student Issues: Racial/Ethnic Data collected by the National Center for Education Statistics Since 1969. By MacKnight Black. Department of Education. 1989. ED1.302:M66/2 and ERIC Doc #305416. Data covers such issues as student preparation, access and choice, transitions, persistence, school/instructional climate; elementary through post-secondary.

1980 Census of Population and Housing. Volume 2: Subject Reports. Bureau of the Census. C3.223/10:80-2-*(volume/section)* 30 reports were planned but not all were prepared; unlike earlier decennial censuses, none have been published on Black Americans or Hispanic Americans. Citations for Asian Americans and Native Americans are included in those selections below. The 1990 Census plans include comparable subject reports; printed reports will begin to be issued in 1993.

1987 Economic Censuses. Survey of Minority-Owned Business Enterprises. Bureau of the Census. 1991. Key parts: *Asian Americans, American Indians, and Other Minorities.* 1991. C3.258:87-3. GPO sales, O.P.

Black Americans. 1990. C3.258:87-1. S/N 003-024-06935-1; $4.75.

Hispanic Americans. 1991. C3.258:87-2. GPO sales, O.P.

Report on the Glass Ceiling Initiative. Department of Labor. 1991. L1.2:G46. *GPO* database; sold by NTIS; # PB92-120567/GAR; $17.00. Report acknowledging the "glass ceiling" barrier to management positions for minorities and women. Timing note: in Jan. 1992 *Monthly Catalog* and Apr. 1992 *GRAI.*

Report on Minorities in Higher Education: Hearing, September 13, 1988. Committee on Education and Labor, House. 100th Congress, 2d Session. 1988. Y4.Ed8/1:100-92.

Sourcing Program: to Identify Outstanding Women and Ethnic Minorities in Research and Research Management. Lawrence Livermore National Laboratory. 1991. NTIS; #DE92000097/GAR $19.00.

We, the Americans. Bureau of the Census. 1984. C3.2:Am3/6. O.P. Brief summary of the 1980 Census data including race; other pamphlets in the series include:

Nosotos=We [the Mexican Americans, the Puerto Ricans, the Cubans, and the Hispanics from other countries in the Caribbean, Central and South America, and from Spain]. 1985. C3.2:W37/5; O.P.

We, the Asian and Pacific Islander Americans 1988. C3.2:Am3/8; S/N 003-024-06869-9, $1.25.

We, the Black Americans. 1986. C3.2:Am3/6/no.3; S/N 003-024-05693-0, $1.25.

We the First Americans, 1989. C3.2:Am3/9; S/N 003-024-06902-4, $1.75.

Similar pamphlets are anticipated from the 1990 Census.

AFRICAN AMERICANS

Afro-American Life, History and Culture. United States Information Agency. 1985. IA1.27:Af8.

America's Black Air Pioneers, 1900-1939. By R.J. Jakeman. Air Command and Staff College, United States Air Force. 1988. Example of elusive publication, not in GPO or NTIS database; identified in a bibliography, found in OCLC [#20961081]; could be borrowed or photocopied.

America's Black Population, 1970 to 1982: a Statistical View. Bureau of the Census. 1983. C3.268:83-1. S/N 033-024-05624-1, $3.50.

Black Americans in Congress, 1870-1989. Office for the Bicentennial and Office of the Historian, House. 101st Congress, 2nd Session. 1990. Y1.1/7:101-117. S/N 052-071-00892-6. Bibliographic essay; arranged alphabetically by Congressional representative and includes photographs and bibliographic citations.

Black Americans in Defense of Our Nation. Department of Defense. 1991. D1.2:B56/991; S/N 008-000-00585-1, $17.00. Covers Colonial times through the Persian Gulf War; includes list of Medal of Honor winners and the role of Afro-American women.

Black News Digest: News from the U.S. Department of Labor, Office of Information and Public Affairs. Department of Labor. Weekly since early 1970's. L1.20/6:(date). Most libraries keep current year or five years only.

Black Population of the United States, March 1990 and 1989, Current Population Reports, Series P-20. Bureau of the Census. 1991. C3.186/P-20:no.448. Recurrent survey (has been annual) of standard characteristics: age, sex, education, income, earnings, marital status. This edition not based on 1990 Census.

Blacks in Science and Related Disciplines. Science and Technology Division, Library of Congress. 1989. LC33. 10:89-9.

Climbing Jacob's Ladder: the Rise of Black Churches in Eastern American Cities, 1740-1877. Smithsonian Institution. 1987. SI1.2:C61/740-877.

The Economic Status of African-Americans: Hearing, May 24, 1990. Subcommittee on Investment, Jobs, and Prices. Joint Economic Committee. 101st Congress, 2d Session. 1991. Y4.Ec7: St2/11.

The Economic Status of Black Women: an Exploratory Investigation. Commission on Civil Rights. 1990. CR1.2:B56/3.

Generations Past: a Selected List of Sources for Afro-American Genealogical Research. Library of Congress. 1988. LC1.12/2: Af8/4. GPO sales, O.P.

Recording of Slave Narratives and Related Material in the Archive of Folk Song: Reference Tapes. Library of Congress. 1981. LC1.12/2:Sli.

Selected Documents Pertaining to Black Workers Among the Records of the Department of Labor and its Component Bureaus, 1902-1969. By Debra L. Newman. National Archives and Records Service. 1977. (reprinted 1985). GS4.7:40.

Slavery in the Courtroom: an Annotated Bibliography of American Cases. Library of Congress. 1985. LC1.12/2:Sli/2; S/N 030-000-00163-0; $12.00. Lists materials from the Law Library and from the general collections, special collections and rare books collections of the Library of Congress.

Status of the Black Elderly in the United States. Report by the National Caucus and Center on Black Aged, Inc. Select Committee on Aging, House. 100th Congress, 1st Session, 1987. Y4.Ag4/2:E112/42.

The Traditionally Black Institutions of Higher Education, 1860 to 1982. Department of Education. 1985. ED1.310/2:262741. Available from ERIC.

ASIAN AMERICANS

Anti-Asian Violence: Oversight Hearing, November 10, 1987. Subcommittee on Civil and Constitutional Rights, Committee on the Judiciary, House. 100th Congress, 1st Session. 1989. Y4.J89/1: 100/116.

Asian and Pacific Islander Population in the United States, 1980. Volume 2: Subject Reports, 1980 Census of Population and Housing. 2 volumes. Bureau of the Census. 1988. C3.223/10: 80-2-1E/Sec.1-2. GPO sales, O.P.

Attainment Status of Asian Americans in Higher Education. Department of Education. 1988. ED1.310/2:297635. Available from ERIC.

Civil Rights Issues of Asian and Pacific Americans: Myths and Realities. Commission on Civil Rights. 1980. CR1.2:As4/3.

The Economic Status of Americans of Asian Descent: an Exploratory Investigation. Commission on Civil Rights. 1988. CR1.10:95.

Exceptional Asian Children and Youth. Office of Educational Research and Improvement, Department of Education. 1986. ED1.310/2:276178.

Japanese American Evacuation Redress: Hearing, July 27, 1983. Subcommittee on Administrative Practice and Procedure of the Committee on the Judiciary, Senate. 98th Congress, 1st Session. 1984.Y4.J89/2:S.hrg. 98-485.

Mental Health Issues: Indochinese Refugees: an Annotated Bibliography. Department of Health and Human Services. 1985. HE20.8113:In2.

A Mini-anthology of Korean American Literature: 7 Essays and 2 Poems on Korean Americans. Department of Health, Education, and Welfare. 1984. ED1.310/2:252098.

National Impact Project: National Pacific/Asian Resource Center on Aging. Administration on Aging, Department of Health and Human Services. 1986. HE23.3002:Im7.

Pacific Migration to the United States: Trends and Themes in Historical and Sociological Literature. Smithsonian Institution. 1977. SI1.40:2.

Personal Justice Denied: Report of the Commission on Wartime Relocation and Internment of Civilians. The Commission. 1982. Y3.W19/10:J98. Report on the forcible relocation on internment of Japanese American citizens and resident aliens during WWII; also includes Aleut citizens on the Pribilof Islands. Reprinted with new introduction by Rep. George Miller as Committee Print from the Committee on Interior and Insular Affairs, House. 102nd Congress, 2d Session. 1992. S/N 052-070-06800-1;

$14.00. Reprinted in support of the establishment of Manzanar Relocation Camp as a landmark.

Southeast Asian Mental Health: Treatment, Prevention, Services, Training, and Research. Office of Refugee Resettlement, National Institute of Mental Health, Department of Health and Human Services. 1985. HE20.8108:So8.

Success of Asian Americans: Fact or Fiction? Commission on Civil Rights. 1980. CR1.10:64.

HISPANIC AMERICANS

AIDS Knowledge and Attitudes of Hispanic Americans, United States: 1990: Provisional Data from the National Health Survey. By Ann E. Biddlecom and Ann M. Hardy. National Center for Health Statistics, Public Health Service. 1991. HE20.6209/3:207.

Chicano Students in Institutions of Higher Education: Access, Attrition, and Achievement. By Alfredo G.de los Santos Jr., Joaquin Montemayor, Enrique Solis. National Institute of Education. 1980. ED1.310/2:205360. Available from ERIC.

Diabetes Mellitus (NIDDM): an Unrelenting But Undeserving Threat to the Health of Hispanics. Report by the Select Committee on Aging, House. 102nd Congress, 2d Session. 1992. Y4Ag.4/2: D54/4.

Espanol! Hispanic Heritage Month Information Booklet: September 15-October 15, 1991. Bureau of Labor Statistics. 1991.

Hispanic Children and Their Families: a Key to Our Nation's Future: Hearing, September 25, 1989. Select Committee on Children, Youth, and Families, House. 101st Congress, 1st Session. 1989. Y4.C43/2:H62/2.

Hispanic Health Care: Today's Shame, Tomorrow's Crisis, Hearing, September 19, 1991. Select Committee on Aging and the Congressional Hispanic Caucus, House. 102nd Congress, 1st Session. 1992. Y4.Ag4/2:H62/4.

The Hispanic Population of the United States. Current Population Reports, Series P-20. Bureau of the Census. 1990. C3.186/14-2: 990. S/N 803-005-00048-6; $2.25. Recurrent survey (has been annual) of standard characteristics: age, sex, income, earnings, education, marital status.

Hispanics in America's Defense. Department of Defense. 1990. D1.2:H62/2/989. S/N 008-046-00133-2, $12.00. Includes Spanish exploration and conquest of North America (1492-1541), Hispanic participation in U.S. defense from the American Revolution through 1989, and Hispanic Medal of Honor winners.

Making Education Work for Mexican Americans: Promising Community Practices. ERIC Clearinghouse on Rural Education and Small Schools. 1990. ED1.310/2:319580. ERIC.

Noticias de Ia Semana: a News Summary for Hispanics from the U.S. Department of Labor, Office of Information and Public Affairs. Department of Labor. Weekly since early 1970's. Ll.20/6:(date).

Projections of the Hispanic Population: 1983 to 2080. Current Population Reports. Series P-25. no. 995. Bureau of the Census. 1986. C3.186:P-25/995; GPO sales, O.P.

The Spanish Black Legend: Origins of Anti-Hispanic Stereotypes. By Joseph P. Sanchez. Spanish Colonial Research Center, National Park Service. 1990. I29.2:Sp2. Not in GPO database; citation from scholarly essay on historical origins of anti-Hispanic attitudes. "Spanish Black" was coined in 1914 and refers to belief that Hispanics were inherently evil. Cataloged by research libraries into national bibliographic databases. Example of the need to work with local and regional offices of agencies.

Stress and Hispanic Mental Health: Relating Research to Service Delivery. National Institute of Mental Health. 1985. HE20.8 102:St8/2. GPO sales, O.P.

Temporary Safe Haven for Salvadorans: Hearing, June 18, 1987. Subcommittee on Immigration and Refugee Affairs, Committee on the Judiciary, Senate. 100th Congress, 1st Session. 1988. Y4.J89/2:S.hrg. 100-352.

NATIVE AMERICANS

AIDS is Also an Indian Problem. Native American AIDS Advisory Board, California Rural Indian Health Board. 1988. Prepared under contract to the U.S. Indian Health Service. HE20.9402: Ac7.

Ancient Indian Land Claims: Hearing, June 23, 1982. Select Committee on Indian Affairs, Senate. 97th Congress, 2d Session. 1983. Y4.In2/11:L22/5.

American Indian Civil Rights Handbook. 2d ed. Civil Rights Commission. 1980. CR1.10:35/2. Describes basic rights of Native Americans on and off reservations.

American Indians, Eskimos, and Aleuts on Identified Reservations and in Historical Areas of Oklahoma (Excluding Urbanized Areas), 1980 Census of Population, Volume 2. Subject Reports, Part 1D. Bureau of the Census. 1986. 3 volumes. C3.223/10:80-2-1D/pts. 1-2. GPO sales, O.P. Comparable report expected from the 1990 Census in 1993 or later.

American Indians Today: Answers to Your Questions. Bureau of Indian Affairs. 1991. I20.2:Am3/2/991.

Characteristics of American Indians by Tribes and Selected Areas: 1980. 1980 Census of Population. Volume 2, Subject Reports, Part 1C. Bureau of the Census. 1989. 2 volumes. C3.223/10:80-2-1C/sec.1-2. Distributed to depositories in 1992, not in GPO database. Comparable report will probably be published for the 1990 Census in 1993 or later.

Famous Indians: a Collection of Short Biographies. Bureau of Indian Affairs. 1975. I20.2:In2/26/974.

Federal Programs of Assistance to American Indians. Report by Richard S. Jones. Select Committee on Indian Affairs, Senate. 99th Congress, 1st Session, 1985. Y4.In2/11:S.prt.99-81.

Handbook of North American Indians. Smithsonian Institution. SI1.20/2:(vols). Planned as a twenty-volume set; nine volumes published and in print as of summer 1992:

> Vol. 4: History of Indian-White relations. 1989. S/N 047-000-00406-3, $47.00.
> Vol. 5: Arctic. 1985. S/N 047-000-00398-9, $29.00.
> Vol. 6: Subarctic. 1978. S/N 047-000-00374-1, $25.00.
> Vol. 7: Northwest Coast. 1990. S/N 047-000-00408-0, $38.00.
> Vol. 8: California. 1981. S/N 047-000-00347-4, $25.00.
> Vol. 9: Southwest [Pueblo Peoples]. 1979. S/N 047-000-00361-0, $23.00.
> Vol. 10: Southwest [non-Pueblo Peoples]. S/N 047-000-00390-3, $25.00.
> Vol. 11: Great Basin. 1986. S/N 047-000-00401-2, $27.00.
> Vol. 15: Northeast. 1978. S/N 047-000-00351-2, $27.00.

Indian Adolescent Mental Health. Office of Technology Assessment. 1990. Y3.T22/2:2In2/4. Ages 10 to 19. GPO sales, O.P.

Indian Affairs: Laws and Treaties. Edited by Charles J. Kappler. Department of the Interior. Il.107:(vol). 7 volumes published to date. Volumes 6 and 7 published as "Kappler's Indian Affairs, Laws and Treaties," and available through GPO; S/N 024-000-00813-4, $24.00. Earlier volumes available from reprint publishers.

Indian Nations at Risk: An Education Strategy for Action, Final Report. Indian Nations at Risk Task Force. Department of Education. 1991. ED1.2:N21/6. Recommends broad-based initiative to improve the quality of education for American natives; includes bibliography.

Indians in Agriculture: An Historical Sketch. By Henry W. Kipp. Task Force of the American Indian Agricultural Council, Bureau of Indian Affairs. 1988. I20.2:Ag8. Covers 1383 to 1987.

Keepers of the Treasures: Protecting Historic Properties and Cultural Traditions on Indian Lands. National Park Service. 1990. I29.2:T71/6. Report to Congress on funding needs concludes that Native Americans must have the opportunity to participate in the national historic preservation program on terms that respect their cultural values, traditions, and sovereignty.

Native American Libraries, Archives, and Information Services: Hearing. May 23, 1991. Select Committee on Indian Affairs, Senate. 102nd Congress, 1st Session. 1991. Y4.In2/11: S.hrg. 102-229. Examines current status and federal funding needs.

Native American Women: A Bibliography. Department of Education. 1981. ED1.17:N21.

Native American Children, Youth, and Families: Hearings: January 7, 9, and 10, 1986. Select Committee on Children, Youth, and Families, House. 99th Congress, 2d Session. 1986. Y4.C43/2:N2 1/pts. 1-3.

USDA Programs of Interest to American Indians. Department of Agriculture. 1983. A107.2:Am3.

NON-BOOK SAMPLES

For the most part, non-book materials are best selected from agency catalogs, although the GPO database includes some posters, maps, and electronic products. In addition to the National Audiovisual Center (NAVC) mentioned earlier, the Library of Congress and National Archives are especially useful for audio-visual materials.

Animal Tales Told in the Gullah Dialect by Albert H. Stoddard of Savannah, Georgia. 3 AUDIOCASSETTES. Edited by Duncan Emrich. Library of Congress. 1955. AFS L44-46, $8.95 each; pamphlet with program notes, texts, and glossary included with each cassette. LC Publications in Print, 1991.

Black Persons as a Percent of Total Population, 1990. MAP. Bureau of the Census. 1992. C3.62/2:B56. Graduations of color show data by counties in the U.S.; page-sized map.

Building a Nation of Neighbors: Fair Housing, 20 Years of Progress, 1968-1988. POSTER. Housing and Urban Development. 1987. HH1.98:H81/2.

Folk Art and Folklife: Missing Pieces, Georgia Folk Art, 1770-1976. POSTER. American Folklife Center and Georgia Council for the Arts and Humanities. 1978. LC1.13:F73Z/978.

Folk Music of Puerto Rico. LP PHONODISC. Edited by Richard A. Waterman. Library of Congress. 1974. AFS L18, $8.95. LC Publications in Print Catalog, 1991.

From Dreams to Reality–A Tribute to Minority Inventors. VIDEO and FILM. Patent and Trademark Office. 1986, color, 28 min. Golden Eagle Award, CINE, 1987. NAVC.

1990 Census of Population and Housing, Summary Tape File (STF) 1A on Compact Disc. Bureau of the Census. 1992. Each disc carries data on 1 to 7 states; $150.00 per disc. Data from short form (race, age, sex, marital status, etc.); state level down to the neighborhood level in census tracts or block groups. Software included provides menus for choosing data in standardized displays. Commercial spreadsheets or database managers needed to extract minority data only. Separate phone for ordering electronic formats: (301)763-4100.

PHOTOGRAPHS. The National Archives has extensive historical photograph collections from which duplicates may be made; catalogs published at irregular intervals.

Race Movies: The Popular Art of the 1920's. VIDEO. Anacostia

Museum, Smithsonian Institution. 1985. Color, 20 min, NAVC. VHS Video No. TCA16475, $45.00.

Records of the Bureau of Refugees, Freedmen, and Abandoned Lands (Record Group 105) MICROFILM. National Archives Trust Fund Board. 1984. Consists of several hundred rolls, including correspondence, personnel records, and a variety of standard reports concerning Bureau programs and conditions in the states. $23.00 per reel.

Slave Narratives: A Folk History of Slavery in the United States. MICROFILM. Library of Congress Photoduplication Service. 1971. 11 reels. $165.00.

REFERENCES

1. Bailey, William G. *Guide to Popular U.S. Government Publications.* 2d ed. Englewood, CO: Libraries Unlimited, Inc., 1990.

2. Butler, Johnnella. "Ethnic Studies: a Matrix Model for the Major," *Liberal Education,* 77(2): 26-32, March/April 1991.

3. Clarke, Robert L., ed. *Afro-American History: Sources for Research.* Washington, D.C.: Howard University Press, 1981.

4. Crouch, Barry A. "Freedmen's Bureau Records: Texas, a Case Study," in *Afro-American History: Sources for Research.* Edited by Robert L. Clarke. Washington, D.C.: Howard University Press, 1981.

5. Deloria, Vine, Jr. "Indian Studies–The Orphan of Academia," *Wicazo Sa* 2(2): 1-7, Fall 1986.

6. Dodson, Suzanne Cates, ed. *Microform Research Collections: a Guide.* 2nd ed. Westport, CT: Meckler, 1984.

7. "Federal Documents Update," *American Library Association Convention,* San Francisco, June 26, 1992. Sponsored by the Federal Documents Task Force, Government Documents Roundtable.

8. Ford, Barbara J. and Laurel Minott. "United Sates Government Publications as Sources for Ethnic Materials," in *Ethnic Collections in Libraries.* Edited by E.J. Josey and Marva L. DeLoach. New York: Neal-Schuman Publishers, Inc., 1983. p. 33

9. Hernon, Peter. "Government Publications and Publishing during the Reagan Years," *Government Information Quarterly,* 6(4): 395-410, 1989.

10. Horn, Judy, ed. *Directory of Government Collections and Librarians.* 6th ed. Bethesda, MD: CIS for Government Documents Roundtable, American Library Association, 1991.

11. "Interagency Conference on Public Access," *Government Information Quarterly,* 9(2): 187-198, 1992.

12. Magrill, Rose Mary and John Corbin. *Acquisitions Management and Collection Development in Libraries*. 2nd ed. Chicago: American Library Association, 1989.

13. Niles, Ann. *An Index to Microform Collections*. Westport, CT: Meckler. Volume 1, 1984; Volume 2, 1988.

14. O'Hara, Frederic J., ed. *Informing the Nation: a Handbook of Government Information for Librarians*. New York: Greenwood Press, 1990.

15. Robinson, Judith Schiek. *Subject Guide to U.S. Government Reference Sources*. Littleton, CO: Libraries Unlimited, 1985.

16. Robinson, Judith Schiek. *Tapping the Government Grapevine: the User-Friendly Guide to U.S. Government Information Sources*. Phoenix: Oryx Press, 1988.

17. Schwartz, Julia. *Easy Access to Information in United States Government Documents*. Chicago: American Library Association, 1986. p. 34

18. Tate, Michael L. "Studying the American Indian Through Government Documents and the National Archives," *Government Publications Review*, 5(3): 285-294, 1978.

19. Thernstrom, Stephan, ed. *Harvard Encyclopedia of American Ethnic Groups*. Cambridge, MA: Harvard University Press, 1980.

20. U.S. Congress. House. Committee on the Judiciary. *Civil Liberties Act of 1985 and the Aleutian and Pribilof Islands Restitution Act: Hearings before the Subcommittee on Administrative Law and Government Relations . . . on H.R. 442 and H.R. 2415 . . . April 28 and July 23. 1986; part 1*. 99th Congress, 2nd Session. Washington, D.C.: U.S.G.P.O., 1987.

21. U.S. General Services Administration. *United States Government Manual*. Washington, D.C.: U.S.G.P.O., annual.

22. U.S. National Archives and Records Administration. *Looking for an Out-of-Print U.S. Government Publication?* Washington, D.C.: NARA, 1990. AE1.113:28/990.

23. U.S. National Archives and Records Administration. *National Archives Publications. 1991*. Washington, D.C.: National Archives Trust Fund Board, 1991.

24. Walshak, Lynn G. *Afro-Americans: a Bibliography of U.S. Government Documents Indexed in the "Monthly Catalog of U.S. Government Publications."* January 1970 through July 1982. Springfield, VA: ERIC Document Reproduction Service, 1983. EDRS no. ED 229 328.

25. Wong, Paul. "Chinese Americans and Policy Research," *Chinese American Forum*, 7(1): 3-17, July 1991.

FOR OTHER CULTURES

Hispanic Collections
in the Public Library:
The Chicago Public Library Experience

Mary Ellen Quinn

SUMMARY. The growth of the Hispanic population in the United States presents a challenge to public libraries. There are a number of factors that complicate the acquisition of materials to meet the needs of this group, including language, characteristics of the Hispanic population, characteristics of the Spanish language book trade, lack of selection tools, and issues of access and availability. By adopting a variety of approaches that do not always conform to standard selection and acquisitions procedures, including profile-based standing orders, off-the-shelf buying, gift and exchange programs, and buy-

Mary Ellen Quinn is Director of Collection Development, The Chicago Public Library, Harold Washington Library Center, 400 S. State, Chicago, IL 60605.

[Haworth co-indexing entry note]: "Hispanic Collections in the Public Library: The Chicago Public Library Experience," Quinn, Mary Ellen. Co-published simultaneously in *The Acquisitions Librarian* (The Haworth Press, Inc.) No. 9/10, 1993, pp. 221-232; and: *Multicultural Acquisitions* (ed: Karen Parrish and Bill Katz) The Haworth Press, Inc., 1993, pp. 221-232. Multiple copies of this article/chapter may be purchased from The Haworth Document Delivery Center. Call 1-800-3-HAWORTH (1-800-342-9678) between 9:00 - 5:00 (EST) and ask for DOCUMENT DELIVERY CENTER.

221

ing at book fairs, The Chicago Public Library has been able to overcome some of the obstacles.

INTRODUCTION

The Hispanic population is one of the fastest growing demographic groups in the United States and presents a special challenge to public libraries. In some cases, response to this challenge has been made on a well coordinated, statewide level. California, for example, has taken a leadership role in developing model programs, such as the project "Developing Library Collections for California's Emerging Majority." This project, funded by the California State Library through the Library Services and Construction Act, and sponsored by The Bay Area Library and Information System, produced two tools to help librarians improve service to multicultural populations. One was a conference held in San Francisco in 1990. The second tool was a manual, *Developing Library Collections for California's Emerging Majority, a Manual of Resources for Ethnic Collection Development.*[1] In Illinois, the effort to develop effective library service for multicultural populations has been centered in Chicago. The Chicago Public Library (CPL) has a long history and tradition of service to its ethnic communities. The Hispanic community, because of its rate of growth and the urgent needs created by low income and low literacy levels of the more recent arrivals, has been a particular focus for the Library in recent years. CPL has learned that meeting the needs of this community requires flexibility and a variety of often nontraditional approaches.

THE CHICAGO PUBLIC LIBRARY
AND THE HISPANIC COMMUNITY

According to 1990 census figures, the Hispanic population in Chicago is about 545,000, a 29% rise since 1980. Of the 80 branches in The Chicago Public Library system, 11 have been identified as Hispanic branches (with 50% or more Hispanics in their area of service), and an additional 14 branches have been identified as Hispanic influence branches (20-50% Hispanic). CPL provides service at a variety of levels to this group. The Foreign Language Information Center of the Literature and Language Department, located in the Harold Washington Library Center, includes a sizeable Spanish language collection, as well as a Language Laboratory providing materials for the study of English as a Second Language. Spanish Information Services, located in the Foreign Language Information Center, serves primarily as a telephone-based reference center with materials in Spanish and English and a bilingual staff. The Hispanic Services Committee, an outgrowth of various Spanish language selection advisory committees, was formally organized in 1986. This committee includes staff from Foreign Language and from various administrative and support units, but its impetus came from concerned branch librarians who felt that the growing Hispanic population was being underserved. One of the first actions of the Committee was to recommend the reinstatement of the position of Hispanic Services Coordinator, a position which had been eliminated several years before. Together with the Hispanic Services Office, the Committee continues to take a strong advocacy role. Committee members have been particularly active in writing grants to bridge gaps in the traditional models of library service. Among some of the projects funded by the Illinois State Library through the Library Services and Construction Act are: "En sus Marcos. . .Listos . . . Fuera: Preparación de Lectura Para Niños," to set up Young Child Centers in branch libraries, housing books, educational realia, and parenting information; "Libro Means Book," to introduce bilingual children to the library through story hours and intensive school visiting; and "Salud–to Your Good Health," to provide materials and programs in Spanish on health-related issues. An LSCA Title I grant also provided funding for a Hispanic Services manual, written by the Hispanic Services Committee and published in 1990.[2] Finally, the construction of the Rudy Lozano Branch Library, which was dedicated in 1989, helped provide a new focus for the Library's efforts to serve the Hispanic community. This 18,000 square foot facility, located in Pilsen, a community that is 89% Hispanic of primarily Mexican origin, replaced a tiny storefront branch. Approximately 40% of the collection is in Spanish. In addition, Lozano is home to the Hispanic Heritage Collection, some 1,200 items in English dealing with the history and culture of Hispanics in the United States and Latin America, with emphasis on Mexicans and Mexican Americans.

Although the Library has been acquiring foreign language material for years, only recently has it begun to codify its commitment, in various documents and policies, to providing multicultural collections. These documents include its Mission Statement, and its Materials Selection Policy, revised in 1989. As described in the Hispanic Services manual, "The Chicago Public Library Materials Selection Policy serves as an example of a selection policy which encourages multi-ethnic collections."[3] The policy states, for example, that collections must reflect a community's ethnic and economic diversity, and that materials are collected in any language which meets community needs. In 1990, each branch library wrote a collection development plan that outlined priorities in terms of communities served. However, while it is important to have mission statements, policies, and plans that support multicultural service, the actual task of acquiring material and developing collections for the Hispanic community can be complicated, time consuming, and frustrating. There exist a number of barriers that make this task a more complex one than building standard library collections.

BARRIERS TO ACQUISITIONS

1. Language. Language barriers can impede not only the selection, acquisitions, and cataloging processes, but also the effective use of materials by public service staff.

2. Characteristics of the Hispanic population. It is easy to lose sight of the diverse nature of the Hispanic population. Although they share a common language and culture, there are important differences between the various nationalities–Mexican, Puerto Rican, Cuban, South and Central American–and these differences need to be considered when the library buys materials. At the very least, the library needs to make an effort to acquire books published in Latin America, rather than in Spain. Other differences are societal rather than national. Length of time the Hispanic population has been in the U. S., economic status, fluency in English, reading level in Spanish, and which languages the children read are some of the variables that the library needs to take into account when it decides

what services and materials to provide. Some patrons read only English, while others may be illiterate even in Spanish. Further complicating the library's efforts is the fact that some Hispanics, especially more recent arrivals, are unfamiliar with the concept of the public library. "Latin American libraries do not have the community orientation that libraries in the U.S. have developed. Historically they have been available mainly to an intellectual elite for research and educational purposes."[4]

3. Characteristics of the book trade. Librarians who have learned to expect certain standards and practices from the American book publishing industry find that their expectations must be different when they venture into the Spanish language publishing world. Bindings and paper quality are often inferior. Titles are printed in small runs and tend to go out of print quickly. Attempting to deal directly with publishers in Spain and Latin America is complicated by currency exchange rates, customs, and billing practices. For these reasons, many acquisitions librarians prefer to work with distributors who are based in the U.S., such as Bilingual and Lectorum in New York, and HBD in Tucson. Acquiring English language materials of interest to the Hispanic community can also be difficult, as these materials are often available only from small presses.

4. Lack of selection tools. Because of a lack of selection tools, such as regular, current review source, librarians are often not aware of what Spanish language materials are available. *Booklist* and *School Library Journal* periodically provide lists of Spanish language titles, but librarians who use these lists as selection tools cannot be sure that the books are still available for purchase when an order is placed. *Libros en venta,* the Spanish-language equivalent to *Books in Print,* is out of date before it is published, because of the short print runs. Bibliographies, such as Fabio Represto's *Spanish Language Books for Public Libraries*[5] and Isabel Schon's *Basic Collection of Children's Books in Spanish*[6] are excellent works, but cannot be used as sources for current information. Often, the catalogs issued by U.S.-based distributors of Spanish language books are a library's most current and useful selection tools. These catalogs, however, reflect only a limited range of Spanish language publishing.

5. Access vs. availability. Ideally, a permanent collection of titles

in Spanish requires the same catalog access that is given to English language collections. However, Spanish language materials, like other materials published outside the U.S., almost always require original cataloging. Such items are unlikely to have catalog access in OCLC, and almost certainly will not have been cataloged by the Library of Congress. ISBNs are in general use, but Spanish and Latin American publishers are not consistent in the use of the terms "edition" and "printing," so that extra time is required to determine whether a title is unique. Materials that are delayed in cataloging are not available to patrons. Some libraries have chosen to overcome this problem by putting their foreign language books in uncataloged, browsing collections. However, this approach limits access to the collection by patrons and staff.

THE COLLECTION DEVELOPMENT PLAN: SOME FACTORS TO CONSIDER

As noted by Eugene Estrada, "The information and recreation needs of the Hispanic patron are basically no different from those of any other kind of patron. Information about jobs, resources for schoolwork, a means of self-improvement, cultural enlightenment, all these traditional areas of library concern apply to Hispanics as well."[7] But because of the impediments listed above, the idea of doing real collection development for the Hispanic community sometimes seems Quixotic. The acquisition of materials in Spanish can be so frustrating that there is a tendency for libraries to take whatever they can get for their Spanish language collections. However, a library can make strides by writing a realistic collection development plan to help focus and guide the acquisitions process. The Chicago Public Library's Hispanic Services manual provides general guidelines on what to buy for the Hispanic community. These guidelines describe how different subject areas should be developed at both a basic and expanded level, and also consider various types of materials: bilingual and literacy materials, magazines, fotonovelas, and non-print. Bilingual materials are scarce, most are published in the United States, and most are for children. Literacy materials are often only available from community organizations teaching Spanish literacy. There is a wide variety of Spanish language periodicals, many available from U.S. distributors, and these can be an effective way to supplement a small book collection and ensure a steady flow of current information into the library. Yolanda Cuesta writes that the popularity of magazines and newspapers is "overwhelming": "All Hispanic groups demonstrate a high demand for material that keeps them informed of what's happening in their homeland."[8] Fotonovelas, or "photo novels," are the most widely read format in Latin America, and need to be considered for the public library collection, even though they don't fit traditional standards for selection. Non-book material, such as recorded music and videos, are also popular.

For children, the library needs to consider how fluent they are in English, how many children are in bilingual classrooms, how many children who speak Spanish are actually able to read it, and at what age children from Spanish-speaking homes begin to read English. Many of the Hispanic oriented branches in Chicago concentrate on buying board books, picture books, and other books for the young child for their Spanish children's collections, finding that, once the children have learned to read English, Spanish is no longer stressed in the schools. On the other hand, some neighborhoods are ports of entry, where older children who do not read English are continuously moving into the community. Other kinds of materials that should be considered for the children's collection are book cassette kits, puzzles, toys, and games. Several CPL branches have family learning centers that provide a variety of children's print and non-print material along with books for adults on parenting, to stimulate the development of pre-reading and reading skills and give parents the opportunity to learn with and teach their children.

When writing a plan for the Hispanic collection, it is important to remember that English language as well as Spanish language materials will be included. Linda Chavez makes a distinction between Spanish language collections, serving those whose first language is Spanish, and Chicano collections, predominantly in English, geared toward individuals of Mexican descent. As she notes, "A library serving a Mexicano/Chicano community needs to have both collections to adequately serve these patrons."[9]

ACQUISITIONS STRATEGIES

Once the library has a collection development plan in place, it needs to adopt a variety of acquisitions strategies to help meet collection development goals. While the acquisitions process–identification of vendors, placement of orders, receipt of materials–is centralized at CPL, the selection process is not. Selection specialists do the work of identifying titles and checking availability, but the actual decision of whether or not to buy an item rests with the public service librarians. This approach enables librarians to tailor collections to their communities, but also makes the ordering process cumbersome and slow. Over the years, it has become apparent that CPL's careful, individual, title-by-title approach has not worked well in the area of foreign language acquisitions. Among the alternative strategies used by CPL for the acquisition of Spanish language material are: profiles, direct off-the-shelf purchases, gifts and exchanges, and buying at book fairs. These strategies are designed, for the most part, to circumvent regular selection and acquisitions procedures.

1. Profiles. CPL has developed a plan to implement a profile-based approach to acquisition of newly published Spanish language material. Librarians who have chosen to participate have written profiles that outline priorities for both their adult and children's collections, and also have committed a portion of their budgets to the plan. Based on the needs described in the individual profiles, CPL has devised a system profile, parts of which will be assigned to three or four vendors with whom the Library has worked closely in the past, and who have had experience dealing with library profiles. On a standing or blanket order basis, new material will be sent to the Library once a month, and members of the Hispanic Services Committee will be responsible for assigning the books to participating branches. Staff have written a computer program that will keep track of assignments and funds. The computer program will also allow the Library to follow each title on this way through Acquisitions, Cataloging, and Processing, helping to identify where materials are delayed. It is anticipated that the steady flow of materials will help alleviate some of the logjams that occur at the cataloging and processing stages, as well as ensuring that new materials are always available to patrons. As noted by Robert B. Downs and

Norman B. Brown, "blanket orders may be the most satisfactory and effective plan to cover the current publishing production."[10] CPL already has standing order arrangements for the receipt of some kinds of Spanish language material, such as fotonovelas.

2. Off-the-shelf purchases. Chicago is fortunate to have several Spanish language bookstores with whom the Library has developed fruitful working relations. Though these bookstores are too small to supply all needed materials, librarians have taken advantage of their proximity to acquire replacements, items not available from the larger vendors, and any materials needed in a hurry. For a small library, or a library where there is a single budget for Spanish language material instead of multiple branch budgets, off-the-shelf buying can be one of the most effective means of acquisitions. It has worked well with other languages, such as Polish and Ukrainian, for which only one or two CPL branches have a need. CPL used off-the-shelf buying as a way to help create the opening day collection for Lozano Branch. In that case, there was not enough material available locally, so staff were sent to buy from the warehouse of a Spanish-language distributor in New York.

3. Gifts and exchanges. The Mexican government provides books to its consulates to be distributed to libraries. Between 1985-1986, approximately 5,000 books were given in custody to CPL for a period of 99 years, an arrangement called a "comodato." The books are housed at the Lozano branch, which has attracted other donations as well, including books from the Mexican Ambassador to the U.S., the Mexican Minister of Education, and the Mexican Solidarity Program, a literacy group. Other branches have also benefitted from the interest created by the new Lozano Branch. For example, the Mexican Consulate has acquired bilingual dictionaries for Clarence Darrow Branch, which is located at the Cook County Department of Correction and serves an inmate population that is increasingly Hispanic. CPL's Hispanic Services Coordinator has been instrumental in facilitating these donations, and also in setting up an exchange program between The Chicago Public Library and the National Library of Mexico, or UNAM. According to the terms of this agreement, CPL will provide UNAM with bibliographic records of foreign publications of Mexican interest, and, if possible, copies of the publications themselves; and UNAM will annually

deliver to Lozano Branch copies of titles which they have published and believe will be of interest to CPL. These types of agreements are fostered by events that bring together librarians from the U.S. and Mexico to discuss their mutual concerns, such as the Trans-border Library Forum co-sponsored by the Asociación Sonorense de Bibliotecarios, the Arizona State Library Association, the U.S.-Mexico Libraries Subcommittee of the International Relations Committee of the American Library Association, Asociación Mexicana de Bibliotecarios, and el Colegio Nacional de Bibliotecarios.

4. Book fairs. Book fairs are another way that CPL acquires Spanish language materials. For the past several years, there has been a small book fair in Chicago, organized by a local Spanish language bookseller. Librarians who attend the fair have the opportunity to examine and select materials available from a number of local dealers, and one dealer is authorized to act as CPL's purchasing agent. On a much larger scale is the book fair held each year in Guadalajara. The Guadalajara International Book Fair, or Feria Internacional del Libro (FIL), was organized in 1986 by the University of Guadalajara to promote the Latin American publishing industry. Guadalajara was chosen because of its proximity to the United States. In 1991, nearly 1,000 publishing imprints were represented, from 33 countries, including Mexico, Argentina, Brazil, Chile, Colombia, Venezuela, and Spain. Prior to the opening of Lozano Branch, CPL made arrangements with two U.S. distributors, one based in Chicago, and one in the Southwest, to acquire books at FIL based on profiles that outlined the branch's collection development needs. Since then, CPL has tried to send staff to FIL every year, to learn about Latin American publishing, make contact with publishers and distributors, and see what Spanish language materials are available. Besides the exhibits, another important component of FIL are the many events that provide opportunities for cooperation and cultural exchange. In 1991, there were several meetings especially for librarians, some co-sponsored by the Mexican Association of Librarians and ALA. Also in 1991, the first Latin American Book Industry Fair (SILAR), whose motto is "Por la Integración Editorial Latinoamerica" (For the Integration of the Latin American Publishing Industry), was held in conjunction with FIL. As noted in a *Publisher's Weekly* report on Fil '91, the organizers of SILAR

hope to create a kind of common market for Latin American publishing.[11] Partly because of FIL, Latin American publishers are
becoming more aware of the American market, and have begun to
change their business practices to facilitate doing business with
libraries and others in the U.S.

OTHER DEVELOPMENTS

There have been other recent developments that can only benefit
libraries and their Hispanic patrons. In 1990, Fondo de Cultura
Economica, the largest and oldest publishing house in Latin America, opened its first U.S. office in San Diego, in order to improve
availability of Spanish language books. Subsidized by the Mexican
government, Fondo de Cultura Economica has built a list of 4,000
titles, including works by Spanish and Latin American authors, and
translations of U.S. and European works focusing on Latin American interests.[12] A number of U.S. publishers are now publishing
Spanish translations of their books. Facts on File offers several
Spanish language titles, and McGraw-Hill has an entire catalog of
Spanish language books on business and health-related subjects.
For children, Children's Press, Raintree Steck-Vaughn, and Watts
have published nonfiction in Spanish; while Dutton, Farrar Strauss
Giroux, Putnam Grosset, and Viking have published picture books,
board books, and fiction. While acquiring Spanish language books
from U.S. publishers is no substitute for acquiring books published
in Spain and Latin America, U.S. publishers should be encouraged
to continue this trend.

CONCLUSION

Like other public libraries, CPL has found that the task of making
its collections relevant to the Hispanic population is not an easy
one. There is no single, foolproof formula for success. However,
knowing the needs and interests of the Hispanic community, working closely with vendors, being willing to explore creative, often
untraditional ways to overcome obstacles, and having a strong com-

mitment on the part of both administration and public service staff, can help the public library to meet the challenge offered by an increasingly important segment of U.S. society.

REFERENCES

1. Katharine T.A. Scarborough, ed. *Developing Collections for California's Emerging Majority, a Manual of Resources for Ethnic Collection Development.* Berkeley: Bay Area Library and Information System, 1990.

2. Hispanic Services Committee, The Chicago Public Library. *Hispanic Services Manual: A Practical Manual for the Public Librarian.* Chicago, 1990.

3. Ibid., p.1.

4. Ingrid Betancourt. "Libraries: Que Pasa?" *The U*N*A*B*A*S*H*E*D Librarian* no. 58, p.10.

5. Fabio Represto, ed. *Spanish Language Books for Public Libraries.* Chicago: ALA, 1986.

6. Isabel Schon. *Basic Collection of Children's books in Spanish.* Metuchen, N.J.: Scarecrow Press, 1986.

7. Eugene Estrada. "Changing Latino Demographics and American Libraries." In *Latino Librarianship: A Handbook for Professionals.* Jefferson, N.C.: McFarland & Company, Inc., 1990.

8. Yolanda Cuesta. "From Survival to Sophistication: Hispanic Needs = Library Needs." *Library Journal* (May 15, 1990): 26-28.

9. Linda Chavez. "Collection Development for the Spanish-Speaking." In *Latino Librarianship: A Handbook for Professionals.* Jefferson, N.C.: McFarland & Company, Inc., 1990.

10. Robert B. Downs and Norman B. Brown. "The Significance of Foreign Materials for U.S. Collections: Problems of Acquisitions." In *Acquisition of Foreign Materials for U.S. Libraries.* Metuchen, N.J.: Scarecrow Press, 1982.

11. Herbert R. Lottman. "Guadalajara: New Focus in Latin America." *Publisher's Weekly* (January 13, 1992): 32-34.

12. Lisa See. "Mexican House Plans to Publish Spanish Titles for U.S. Market." *Publisher's Weekly* (February 24, 1992), p.10.

U.S./Mexican Borderlands Acquisition: Defining and Pursuing the Materials

Theresa Salazar
Maria Segura Hoopes

SUMMARY. Collecting materials from and about the U.S. Mexican Borderland presents special challenges: (1) Defining the area and its literature in historical and contemporary terms. (2) Identifying publishers and sources. (3) Developing a policy to acquire the materials thus categorized. (4) Continually assessing to look for gaps or to formulate changes in orientation. This article describes how the University of Arizona recently approached the question anew and what considerations ruled this approach. Its objective is to help other would-be collectors of borderlands materials, or, in a general sense, collectors of any hard-to-define materials.

THE BORDER: A WORKING DEFINITION

The "borderlands" region of the United States and Mexico extends nearly 2000 miles across the U.S. states of Texas, New Mexi-

Theresa Salazar is Special Collections Librarian at The University of Arizona Library, Tucson, AZ 85721, and Maria Segura Hoopes is Reference Librarian also at The University of Arizona Library, Tucson, AZ 85721.

[Haworth co-indexing entry note]: "U.S./Mexican Borderlands Acquisition: Defining and Pursuing the Materials," Salazar, Theresa and Maria Segura Hoopes. Co-published simultaneously in *The Acquisitions Librarian* (The Haworth Press, Inc.) No. 9/10, 1993, pp. 233-246 and: *Multicultural Acquisitions* (ed: Karen Parrish and Bill Katz) The Haworth Press, Inc., 1993, pp. 233-246. Multiple copies of this article/chapter may be purchased from The Haworth Document Delivery Center. Call 1-800-3-HAWORTH (1-800-342-9678) between 9:00 - 5:00 (EST) and ask for DOCUMENT DELIVERY CENTER.

233

co, Arizona, and California and the Mexican states of Nuevo Leon, Coahuila, Tamaulipas, Chihuahua, Sonora, and Baja California Norte. Uneasiness, turbulence and often violence have characterized much of the history of this region, although the "borderlands" and the two countries abutting each other are also socially, culturally, politically, and economically intertwined. "The continuous stream of people and information that flows across the border has, over the years, exerted a strong influence on the cultures of both countries, while close trade relations, commercial and financial interests, and the demand for labor have bound the nations together economically."[1] As the U.S./Mexican relationship shifts, the borderlands region reacts to the issues and problems facing each country. This international zone has been identified as a world unto itself. The boundary line has not separated the people on either side. Rather, "Demographically, economically, linguistically and culturally the U.S. border area is functionally an extension of Mexico, and in a similar fashion, the Mexican border zone is an extension of economic, social, and cultural influences from the United States."[2] Thus a unique border culture has developed, made up of Native Americans, Mexicans and Chicanos, and more mainstream American populations (e.g., Western European). It is along the 2000 mile stretch of land that many pressing issues have arisen: economic development and exploitation; free trade; environmental concerns; women's, Native American, and minority rights; health and education; and drug trafficking to name but a few. Documentation of the history of and the contemporary life along the border has taken many forms.

HISTORICAL AND CONTEMPORARY PERSPECTIVES

European documentation of what is now the U.S. Mexico border region began in the sixteenth century as early explorers and missionaries were required to send back reports. Because of the church and state bureaucracies of the Spanish colonial empire, a written record of the landscape and people exists, thanks to the work of many chroniclers, such as Father Junípero Serra and Alvar Núñez Cabeza de Vaca. In addition to the ethnographic and geographic information found in these narratives, there exist thousands of administrative documents including judicial records, inspection records, military papers, and civil documents, such as petitions, wills, and materials relating to slave trade. Not the least in importance among these papers are land titles and mining registers. Ecclesiastical documents, such as baptismal records, tithe records, and Inquisition proceedings provide demographic, economic and social information in addition to church history.[3] These archival records are held in various libraries and repositories, among them many in the Southwest. The Spanish, and later the Mexican bureaucracy continued to produce records concerning the Southwest until the U.S. annexation of Mexico's territory in 1848.

"The high-spirited and jaunty voice of nationalism in early nineteenth century America split into different registers when the westward-pushing frontier collided with Mexico."[4] Both racism and "manifest destiny" presented different faces of what became the literature of the border.[5] Chroniclers of westward migration included explorers such as Zebulon Pike, John J. Audubon and Francis Parkman. Victory over Mexico produced the patriotic dime novels, full of nationalism and stories of Anglo military might.[6] A complex vision of the area that was to become the borderlands developed. Myth evolved around the romance of the Spanish grandees thought to have populated early California. Much early Anglo writing about the West was the writing of the area now called the Border. Mary Austin collected material from the natives and Cincinnatus Hiner Miller took the first name of his hero, the Mexican bandit Joaquin Murrieta.[7] The recognizable border literature of fiction, history, description and travel is often a mixture of fact and hyperbole, but economists, sociologists, political scientists, linguists and natural scientists, too, have written about the border, whether or not they define their geographical area using that term. Materials by or about Mexican Americans, regional indigenous peoples of both sides, Mexico-U.S. trade, migrant farm workers, quirky changes in boundary rivers and southwest deserts, are, per se, border literature. Students of religion and folklore, too, focus on this area, along with criminologists and ecologists. At present, there is a conscious readiness to define these materials as border-related. Collecting border literature has become a mission of numerous regional libraries. How does one go about this?

SOURCES

Publishers of materials concerning the borderlands are multitudinous. On both sides of the border universities, specialized research institutions, state and federal governments, business enterprises, the media (e.g., newspapers, magazines), trade and small press publishers, and special interest groups (Native Americans, Chicanos, religious groups) all produce literature and information on the border. Many outstanding bibliographies and reference tools exist to help librarians identify what is available. For the names of some of these institutes and publications, consult the annotated bibliography at the end of this article.

ACQUISITION OF CURRENT IMPRINTS

Like many libraries across the country, we at the University of Arizona have availed ourselves of the expertise of dealers who specialize in materials from Mexico. Because materials from Mexico are relatively inexpensive compared to material from other parts of the world, more can be collected for less. While at one time the challenge was getting anything on Mexico out of Mexico without going to Mexico, now many dealers have well-established and effective business operations.

What we perhaps have done differently in approaching collection development is to design a detailed collection policy for the area intended to cover not only its rich history but also to document the everchanging circumstances occurring along the border. In addition, our library has decided to concentrate on collecting comprehensively materials from and about the states of Arizona, New Mexico, southern California, Sonora, Chihuahua, and California Baja Norte, collecting only major university and trade publications from the other borderlands regions.

Both the United States and Mexico are made up of populations reflecting rich cultural diversity. In our area, Tohono O'Odham, Tarahumara, Apache and Yaqui Indians represent but a few of the Native American groups present in the borderlands region. While anthropological and sociological studies of Native American groups provide one kind of information, tribal newspapers and publications can provide an insider's point of view on many of the issues facing these groups.

Various provincial cultures have developed from state to state, in many ways tied to the economic development of the area. Mining towns, ranches, and burgeoning bordertowns are all related to the minerals, resources and manpower available along the border. A whole range of materials document these activities throughout the border states, ranging from annual reports, promotional brochures, to newsletters.

And the Mexican and Mexican-American experiences are very different realities needing documentation, via academic studies, creative writing, art and other such materials.

Of special concern to us is the area of Arid Lands Studies, as water use and conservation and ecology are crucial to the preservation and development of this fragile environment. Scientific reports, conference proceedings and dissertations all enrich the mainstream publications available for research in this field.

Timely issues like drug trafficking and human rights abuses which involve immigration policy and enactment of that policy by the border patrol are particularly of interest as we at the University establish more links to Mexican academic institutions. Along with the federal government, special interest groups such as the American Friends Service Committee monitor and report the situation along the border. By keeping apprised of timely events, we hope to gather documentation of the many events occurring along this ever-changing region.

Our intent in detailing our areas of concern for dealers is to allow for acquiring not only major trade and university publications, but also other more elusive publications being produced by less obvious publishers.

One problem area we have identified and have yet to solve is how to deal with periodicals. Often they contain the most current information on the topic and are the first place for new issues to receive voice. Periodicals are not only numerous, but erratic in their production. We have subscriptions to the more stable periodicals as well as samples of many of the wide range of publications produced in this area. We are currently discussing how to handle these materials, which are often timely but, because of that, transitory in nature.

ACQUISITION OF RETROSPECTIVE AND SPECIALIZED MATERIALS

At the University of Arizona the Southwestern Collection including holdings on Borderlands subjects is the major component of Special Collections. This Collection reflects a conscious effort on our part to collect a wide range of materials from our geographic region as well as materials from formerly underrepresented groups.

Besides the major monographs and periodicals published in the U.S. on the Southwest and most major monographs related to Sonora, Chihuahua and Baja California Norte, Special Collections contains rich retrospective holdings, including early printed books and manuscripts from all historical periods relating to these states. Collecting rare and unique materials involves identifying gaps in holdings as well as keeping abreast of what is available through purchase or gifts. We have compared our holdings against bibliographies like *Borderline*. In addition, we peruse dealers' catalogs specializing in Southwestern Americana and are continually adding to our holdings. With the help of the Friends of The University of Arizona Library, we were able to purchase Gaspar Pérez de Villagrá *Historia de la Nueva Mexico,* published in 1610.

While we do not actively purchase manuscript collections, we do try to identify material of potential interest to researchers and to cultivate relationships which will lead to gifts. One outstanding manuscript we were able to purchase this year is Lt. Frank West's journal, 1884-1885, which provides a unique opportunity to follow the course of the U.S. Army's campaign against the Apache Indians, including the Chiricahua Campaign against Geronimo.

Moreover, we have changed the scope of what we collect. Our older manuscript holdings reflect Spanish colonial and Anglo expansionism and settlement. Some of our more recent acquisitions reflect alternative points of view, documenting minority concerns and dissenting opinions. Included in the Manuscript Collection are the defense lawyers' transcripts and notes on the Sanctuary Movement Trials which document the illegal immigration of Central

Americans into the U.S. and the broad ecumenical support the immigrants received. The collection also includes the papers of the Alianza Hispano Americana, a fraternal organization concerned with helping Mexican workers in the U.S.

In addition, Field Historians, working for the Library have gathered copies of archival materials (photocopies and microforms), mostly from the state of Sonora. The Director of the Southwest Folklore Center, another component of the Library, has actively acquired "artifactual" materials, such as holy cards, commemorations of the Day of the Dead, etc. Also included in his archive are recordings of local musicians and singers, documenting the rich and vital musical scene along the border. Ideally, this type of field work is the best way to identify and gather ephemeral material about the U.S. border states and all types of material about Mexico and provides rich, original research materials for scholars.

Currently the Library is less able to support this kind of field work. Thus much of the other unusual materials we want to obtain are provided by local dealers in Arizona and New Mexico, who know of our interests. We try to collect materials that are not only mainstream publishing ventures, actively pursuing ephemeral materials of all sorts: posters, promotional programs, locally produced literature, including children's literature, commercial publications (e.g., railroad time schedules), unpublished reports from government offices, conferences, etc. Often reflected within ephemeral publications are timely topics of interest to researchers: popular culture, language retention, minority literature, and environmental concerns, to name but a few.

Special Collections also has strong photographic holdings, and we continue to collect documentary photographs of this region, again depending on local dealers specializing in our area of interest. We inform them of our areas of concentration and of what areas we want to develop. We collect both vintage photographs as well as recent images in documenting the southwestern U.S. borderlands. It has, however, been more difficult for us to find current photographic materials related to Mexico.

The University of Arizona made the decision to commit its resources for borderlands materials to the northwestern states of Mexico and the southwestern states of the U.S. While major trade and university publications are acquired to document all areas of the borderlands, our unique and extensive holdings on the Southwestern borderlands reflect a retrospective richness in the collection and a continuing commitment to building on that strength.

REFERENCES

1. Barbara G. Valk et al. *Borderline: A Bibliography of the United States–Mexico Borderlands* (Los Angeles: UCLA Latin American Center: Riverside: University of California Consortium on Mexico and the U.S., 1988), preface.

2. Oscar J. Martinez, *Troublesome Border* (Tucson: The University of Arizona Press, 1988), 145.

3. Thomas C. Barnes, Thomas H. Naylor, Charles W. Polzer, *Northern New Spain: A Research Guide* (Tucson: University of Arizona Press, 1981), 1-17.

4. Cecil Robinson, *With the Ears of Strangers: The Mexican in American Literature* (Tucson: The University of Arizona Press, 1963), 24.

5. Ibid., 24.

6. Ibid., 1-26.

7. Marcienne Rocard, *The Children of the Sun: Mexican Americans in the Literature of the United States,* translated by Edward G. Brown, Jr. (Tucson: The University of Arizona Press, 1989), 5.

THE BORDER/LA FRONTERA
AN ANNOTATED BIBLIOGRAPHY OF SOURCES

BORDERLANDS PERIODICALS

The Borderlands Journal. 1977- . Brownsville, TX: South Texas Institute of Latin and Mexican American Research, Texas Southmost College.
General coverage journal. Semi-annual. Indexed in HAPI.[1]

El Correo Fronterizo. 1984- . Tijuana, Baja California Norte: Colegio de Ia Frontera Norte.
Spanish language. Newsletter. Bi-monthly. No index.

---

1. For full name of index, consult the section dedicated to periodical indexes, below.

International Guide to Research on Mexico/Guia Internacional de Investigaciones Sobre Mexico. 1986- . La Jolla, CA:UCSD Center for Mexican Studies and Tijuana, BC: El Colegio de la Frontera Norte.
Annual guide to Borderlands-related research in various publications. Index at end allows subject approach.

Journal of Borderlands Studies. 1986- . Las Cruces, NM: Dept. of Economics. New Mexico State University.
Quarterly journal.

Maquiladora. 197- . Mexico, DF: American Chamber of Commerce of Mexico.
Trade publication. Published every two months.

Twin Plant News. 1985- . El Paso, TX: Nibbe, Hernandez and Associates.
Monthly trade magazine.

PERIODICALS FROM U.S. BORDER STATES

Arizona Review. 1952- . Tucson: University of Arizona College of Business and Public Administration. Division of Economic and Business Research.
Indexed in PAIS.

Arizona and the West. 1959- . Continues under new title: *Journal of the Southwest* after 1986.
Indexed by AZ INDEX; HIS.ABSTR.; AMERICA HISTORY AND LIFE; AHCI; CHIC. PER. IND.

California History/California Historical Society Quarterly. 1922- . San Francisco: California Historical Society.
Indexed by HIS. ABSTR.; AMERICA HISTORY AND LIFE; AHCI; CHIC. PER. IND.

Journal of the Southwest. 1959- . (Formerly *Arizona and the West*). Tucson: The University of Arizona.
Indexed by AZ INDEX; HIS. ABSTR.; AMERICA HISTORY AND LIFE; AHCI; CHIC. PER. IND.

Journal of the West: An Illustrated Quarterly of History and Culture. 1962- . Manhattan, KS: Journal of the West, Inc. 1962- . Indexed by HIS. ABSTR.; HUM. IND.; AMERICA HISTORY AND LIFE; AHCI; CHIC. PER. IND.

New Mexico Historical Review. 1926- . Albuquerque: University of New Mexico. Indexed by HIS. ABSTR.; AHCI; AMERICA HISTORY AND LIFE; CHIC. PER. IND.

New Mexico Magazine. 1923- . Santa Fe: Economic Development and Tourism Department. Indexed by ACCESS; CHIC. PER. IND.

Pacific Historical Review. 1932- . Berkeley, CA: University of California Press. Journals Division. Indexed by HIS. ABSTR.; HUM. IND.; AHCI; CHIC. PER. IND.

El Palacio: Magazine of the Museum of New Mexico. 1913- . Santa Fe: Museum of New Mexico. Indexed by HIS. ABSTR.; CHIC. PER. IND.

Social Science Quarterly. 1920- . (Formerly *Southwestern Social Science Quarterly*). Austin: University of Texas Press. Indexed by HIS. ABSTR; SSCI; SOC. SCI. INDEX.

Southwestern Historical Quarterly. 1897- . Austin: Texas Historical Association. Indexed by HIS. ABSTR.; SSCI; AHCI; CHIC. PER. IND.

Texas Historian. 1941- . Austin: Texas Historical Association. Indexed by HIS. ABSTR.

INDEXES TO PERIODICALS

America: History and Life. 1964- . Santa Barbara, CA: ABC-CLIO. Covers books, journals and dissertations pertaining to American History.

Arizona Index: A Subject Index to Periodical Articles about the State, compiled by Donald M. Powell and Virginia E. Rice. Boston: G.K. Hall, 1978.
This index covers numerous Arizona publications and covers periodicals from a time early in the century.

Arts and Humanities Citation Index (AHCI). 1978- . Philadelphia: Institute for Scientific Information.
Similar in organization to the *Social Science Citation Index* (see below) this source covers the journal literature in the arts and humanities, including art, architecture, classics, drama, film, folklore, history, linguistics, literature, music, philosophy, and religion. The citation approach allows one to search the literature for authors who have written in the past and are currently being cited.

Business Periodicals Index. 1958- . New York: H.W. Wilson. Covers accounting, banking, labor, business, management, economics and advertising. Suggested subject headings: *Mexico–boundaries; Mexico–industries*.

Chicano Periodical Index: A Cumulative Index to Selected Chicano Periodicals. . . (CHIC. PER. IND). 1981- . Berkeley: Chicano Studies Library Publication Unit.
Its volumes index Mexican American periodical literature. Spans a time period from 1967 to date.

Handbook of Latin American Studies. 1936- . Austin: University of Texas Press.
Annual coverage since 1935. Volumes alternate: one year Social Sciences, the next, Humanities. Traditional source for books and periodicals on Latin America. More appropriately called a bibliography, it is included here because it has a subject index.

HAPI. Hispanic American Periodicals Index. 1975- . Los Angeles: UCLA Latin American Center Publications. University of California.
Covers 350 journals in the fields of social sciences and humanities. Indexes by subject and author.

Historical Abstracts (HIS. ABSTR.) 1955- . Santa Barbara: ABC-
  CLIO.
Two parts *Twentieth Century* (1914 to present) and *Modern History*
(1450-1914). Sample subject heading: Mexico (Chihuahua).

Humanities Index (HUM. IND.) 1974/75- . New York: H.W. Wilson.
Covers over 250 English language publications in archaeology,
history, folklore, philosophy, religion, literature and the arts. Preceded by the *Social Sciences and Humanities Index* and, before that,
by the *International Index*.

Public Affairs Information Service. Bulletin. (PAIS) 1915- . New
  York: Public Affairs Information Service.
Provides access to books, pamphlets, periodical articles and government publications on economic and social conditions, public
administration and international relations from throughout the
world.

Readers' Guide to Periodical Literature. 1915- . New York: H.W.
  Wilson.
Familiar standby indexes periodicals of general interest by subject
or author. Dates back to 1900.

Social Sciences Citation Index (SSCI) 1979- . Philadelphia: Institute
  for Scientific Information.
This complex indexing set allows a number of approaches to an
enormous amount of information from social science-related journals. For subject access, consult the volume labelled *Permuterm
Subject Index*. This will give an author name; look up the author
name in the *Source Index* for a citation to the article. First-time
users should consider consulting a librarian for best results. This set
retrospectively has indexed materials back to 1952.

Social Sciences Index (SOC. SCI. IND.) 1974-1975- . New York:
  H.W. Wilson.
Indexes more than 250 English-language periodicals in the social
sciences including, economics, law, sociology, psychology, political
science and anthropology. Preceded by the *Social Sciences and
Humanities Index* and, before that, by the *International Index*.

Sociological Abstracts. 1952- . La Jolla, CA: Sociological Abstracts.
Indexes journal literature in sociology as well as proceedings and other materials. Suggested headings: *Borders, Immigration, Mexican Americans.*

BIBLIOGRAPHIES AND REFERENCE GUIDES

Borderlands Sourcebook: A Guide to the Literature on Northern Mexico and the American Southwest edited by Elwyn B. Stoddard, Richard L. Nostrand, and Jonathan P. West. Norman: University of Oklahoma Press, 1983.

Cumberland, Charles C. "The United States-Mexican Border: A Selective Guide to the Literature of the Region," in *Supplement to Rural Sociology* 25 (June 1960), pp. 1-211.

Demografia de la Frontera Norte de Mexico. Mexico: Consejo Nacional de Poblacion, 1988.

Sklair, Leslie. *Maquiladoras: Annotated Bibliography and Research Guide to Mexico's In-Bond Industry. 1980-1988.* La Jolla, CA: Center for U.S.-Mexican Studies, University of California, San Diego, 1988.

Statistical Abstract of the United States-Mexico Borderlands, ed. by Peter L. Reich. Los Angeles: UCLA Latin American Center, 1984.

Valk, Barbara G. et al. *Borderline: A Bibliography of the United States-Mexico Borderlands.* Los Angeles: UCLA Latin American Center; Riverside: University of California Consortium on Mexico and the U.S., 1988.

SERIAL PUBLICATIONS

Border Issues and Public Policy. 1982- . Irregular Series. El Paso, TX: Center for Inter-American and Border Studies, The University of Texas at El Paso.

Border Perspectives. 1983- . Irregular Series. Center for Inter-American and Border Studies, The University of Texas at El Paso.

Border-State University Consortium for Latin America. *Occasional Papers.* 1970- . San Diego: Institute of Public and Urban Affairs Press, San Diego State University.

Borderlands Research Monograph Series. 1985- . Las Cruces: Joint Border Research Institute, New Mexico State University.

Estudios Fronterizos Mexico-Estados Unidos. 1982- . Irregular. Tijuana, BC: CEFNOMEX.

Noroeste de Mexico. 1976- . Irregular Series. Hermosillo, Sonora: Centro Regional del Noroeste. Instituto Nacional de Antropologia e Historia.

Developing the Library Collection for Native American Studies

Donna E. Norton
Saundra E. Norton

SUMMARY. The article examines the development of the adult and children's library collection for Native American studies. The discussion of Native American studies includes a review of the types of literature that should be in the library acquisitions, a list of criteria for evaluating Native American literature, a discussion of examples of literature that meet the criteria, and a review of issues that concern the development of the collection. The library collection discussed meets the needs of students, scholars doing research in Native American studies, and general readers who are interested in the subject.

INTRODUCTION

When developing the Native American collection, librarians must meet the basic requirements for students, scholars, and general readers who are interested in the study of Native American people,

---

Dr. Donna Norton is Professor of Children's Literature in the Department of Curriculum and Instruction, Texas A&M University, College Station, TX 77843. Saundra E. Norton is Research Associate and Lecturer in the Department of English, Texas A&M University, College Station, TX 77843.

[Haworth co-indexing entry note]: "Developing the Library Collection for Native American Studies," Norton, Donna E. and Saundra E. Norton. Co-published simultaneously in *The Acquisitions Librarian* (The Haworth Press, Inc.) No. 9/10, 1993, pp. 247-266; and: *Multicultural Acquisitions* (ed: Karen Parrish and Bill Katz) The Haworth Press, Inc., 1993, pp. 247-266. Multiple copies of this article/chapter may be purchased from The Haworth Document Delivery Center. Call 1-800-3-HAWORTH (1-800-342-9678) between 9:00 - 5:00 (EST) and ask for DOCUMENT DELIVERY CENTER.

247

their culture, and their literature. They must also, however, be equally concerned with the quality and authenticity of the literature and the references. A special sensitivity is required as librarians approach the selection of materials, the categorizing of the materials, and the possible issues related to those selections. A case in point is Forrest Carter's *The Education of Little Tree*.[1] When the book was reissued it received the 1991 American Booksellers Association's ABBY award, given to the book that booksellers most enjoyed hand-selling that year. At this point it was advertised as a sensitive, evocative autobiographical account of a Cherokee boyhood in the 1930s and was on the *New York Times* best-seller list for nonfiction. After revelations about the author's background, the book was moved from nonfiction to fiction on the same best-seller list of the *New York Times*. The book has carefully developed characterization, historical settings, and believable conflict, but it is not an autobiography of a Cherokee boy. Instead, it is historical fiction. These distinctions are important for librarians and for the scholars and students who are studying Native American literature.

The focus of this article is the development of a Native American collection that provides guidelines and sources for students, scholars doing research in Native American studies, and general readers who are interested in the subject. The article is written from the point of view of the authors who conduct research in multicultural literature, teach university courses in children's and young adult literature that emphasize multicultural literature, direct graduate studies in research about multicultural literature, and conduct in-service for librarians and teachers who are adding multicultural materials to the curriculum. Throughout this article, we will emphasize some of the materials that have been the most helpful to us when we are in these various roles.

TYPES OF LIBRARY ACQUISITIONS

The Native American collection requires journal and research volumes that encourage scholarly research and provide background information. Without these sources, scholars and students may not understand the complex nature of the Native American culture and the literature. In addition, they may not be able to identify, analyze, and authenticate the Native American values, beliefs, history, and culture developed within the literature. Sources such as *Guide to Research on North American Indians*[2] by Arlene Hirschfelder, Mary Gloyne Byler, and Michael Dorris are excellent. This text published by the American Library Association provides annotated references to 1,100 books, articles, government documents, and other written materials. The text covers Indian tribes from across North America and is divided into areas of study such as history and historical sources; economic and social aspects; and religion, arts, and literature. Guides such as this identify many of the books and journals that focus on Native American studies. Journals provide both historical and contemporary materials for Native American studies. Journals such as *Ethnohistory, American Indian Culture Research Journal,* and *Journal of American Folklore* are particularly beneficial for conducting research and developing understanding.

Books on literary criticism are important to all readers of Native American literature. For example Susan Scarberry-Garcia's *Landmarks of Healing: Study of House Made of Dawn*[3] analyzes the significance of stories and rituals in the text and discusses how Momaday blends oral tradition and fiction within his award-winning book. Likewise, Julian Rice's *Black Elk's Story: Distinguishing Its Lakota Purpose*[4] analyzes this popular biography and presents the belief that Neihardt's translations are influenced by his own Christian beliefs. *Narrative Chance: Postmodern Discourse on Native American Indian Literatures,*[5] edited by Gerald Vizenor, presents a collection of essays on works written by Native American authors.

Any worthwhile collection must have sources of children's, young adult, and adult literature that includes examples under each genre. A thorough understanding of the literature and the culture requires collections of folklore that emphasize the traditional beliefs and values of the people and that allow readers to identify the types of stories that dominate the literature and to analyze the characteristics of the folklore. This folklore collection must include sources from numerous Native American tribal areas across North America. There are many examples of folklore collected from the Great Plains, the Southwest, the Pacific Northwest, and the Eskimo regions of North America. Within each of these areas there are numerous collections of folklore from specific tribes such as the Blackfoot, the Cherokee, and the Inuite. Readers and researchers need sufficient examples to read, compare, and draw conclusions about the literature and the people.

The collection also needs sources such as historical documentation, biography, and autobiography that present a view of the earlier period in Native American history and the interactions of the people with the European culture. Adult sources such as Hana Samek's *The Blackfoot Confederacy, 1880-1920*,[6] Robert Utley's *The Indian Frontier of the American West, 1846-1890*[7] and juvenile sources such as Brent Ashabranner's *Morning Star, Black Sun: The Northern Cheyenne Indians and America's Energy Crisis*[8] and Albert Marrin's *War Clouds in the West: Indians & Cavalrymen, 1860-1890*[9] provide valuable background information for both researchers and readers. Readers need to authenticate autobiographies and biographies by comparing the information with other sources of historical nonfiction.

The collection should include examples of historical fiction so that readers can evaluate the literature according to authenticity of settings, conflicts, characterizations, themes, language, and traditional beliefs and values. They should be able to compare the conflicts and settings in historical fiction with the nonfictional autobiographies, biographies, and historical information written about the same time period. For example, before authenticating Scott O'Dell's historical fiction, *Sing Down the Moon*,[10] readers need to understand the government policy that forced the Navahos to leave Canyon de Chelly in 1864 and be relocated in Fort Sumner.

The collection also needs sources of contemporary fiction, biography, and poetry. Through the contemporary literature, readers analyze for recurrent themes across literature and search for threads that may be found in the literature as the authors build upon their own cultural experiences or try to write stories that reflect another culture. Readers discover contemporary values, beliefs, and problems as the literature reflects the culture of the people. By including both adult and juvenile literature, readers can compare the themes, conflicts, and characters in books such as N. Scott Momaday's Pulitzer Prize winning text *House Made of Dawn*[11] and juvenile texts such as Jamake Highwater's *Legend Days,*[12] *The Ceremony of Innocence,*[13] and *I Wear the Morning Star.*[14]

It is also beneficial if the collection includes numerous writings by Native American authors. For example, the children's and young adult literature collection should include examples of the works of Native American authors such as Byrd Baylor, Nanabah Chee Dodge, Jamake Highwater, Virginia Driving Hawk Sneve, Paula Spencer, and White Deer of Autumn. There are also writers who are not Native American, but who write about Native American experiences. Authors such as Brent Ashabranner, Jean Craighead George, Paul Goble, Jan Hudson, Scott O'Dell, and Joyce Rockwood write historical fiction and nonfiction and retell Native American folklore. Readers and scholars benefit from comparing the writings of the two groups. Without including the writings of these last authors, certain genres of literature would be almost deplete of titles. For example, most of the historical fiction about Native American experiences written for children and adolescents is not written by Native American authors.

CRITERIA FOR EVALUATING NATIVE AMERICAN LITERATURE

Two types of criteria should be considered when evaluating the Native American literature for library acquisition: the generic criteria that may be used with any Native American literature and the criteria that applies to specific genre within the literature.

The following generic criteria is useful when evaluating Native American literature (Norton, 1992):[15]

1. Are the Native American characters portrayed as individuals with their own thoughts, emotions, and philosophies? The characters should not conform to stereotypes or be dehumanized.
2. Do the Native American characters belong to a specific tribe, or are they grouped together under one category referred to as Indian?
3. Does the author recognize the diversity of Native American cultures? Are the customs and ceremonies authentic for the Indian tribes?

4. Is the Native American culture respected, or is it presented as inferior to the white culture? Does the author believe the culture is worthy of preservation or that it should be abandoned? Must the Indian fit into an image acceptable to white characters in the story?
5. Is offensive and degrading vocabulary used to describe the characters, their actions, their customs, or their lifestyles?
6. Are the illustrations realistic and authentic, or do they reinforce stereotypes or devalue the culture?
7. If the story has a contemporary setting, does the author accurately describe the life and situation of the Native American in today's world?

In addition to generic criteria, there are also specific criteria for each genre. For example, folklore must reflect the oral tradition of the Native American people and the specific tribes from which the stories are told. Sources such as John Bierhorst's *The Red Swan: Myths and Tales of the American Indians*[16] and *The Mythology of North America*[17] provide information about tribal areas and characteristics of folklore. For example, *The Red Swan: Myths and Tales of the American Indians* identifies the following four categories found in Native American mythology: (1) myths that emphasize "setting the world in order," in which the world is created out of or fashioned from the chaos of nature; (2) myths that emphasize "family drama" by centering on various conflicts and affinities rising out of the kinship unit; (3) myths that emphasize "fair and foul," such as the trickster cycle tales in which the hero progresses from a character of utter worthlessness to one that displays a gradual understanding of social virtue; and (4) myths that emphasize "crossing the threshold" by depicting the passage from unconsciousness to consciousness, the ordeal of puberty, the passage into and out of death, and the transition from nature to culture. Bierhorst identifies examples of stories that represent these various categories of myths. Examples that reflect the categories are also found in single stories and anthologies that include tales passed down in tribes across the North American continent. The folklore collection should include examples that reflect these types of Native American folklore.

When choosing historical fiction about Native American people, the settings must be authentic in every respect and encourage readers to understand time and place. If the setting is the antagonist, as in Farley Mowat's *Lost in the Barrens,*[18] the author must describe the setting so that readers understand the harsh reality of nature. If changes in setting, such as found in Scott O'Dell's *Sing Down the Moon,*[19] are important to the story, the author must describe these settings in detail so that readers can compare the peaceful Canyon de Chelly with the harsh windswept reality of Fort Sumner. The conflicts must also be authentic for the time period. The conflicts should reflect the times and the attitudes of the people. The author needs to develop characters whose actions, beliefs, and values are true to the time period without depending on stereotypes. Themes should respect the Native American culture, values, and beliefs. The authors' language should be authentic for the time period. If possible, the language and style of writing should develop the mood and the image of Native American life during that time period.

Evaluation criteria for biographies is especially important when choosing Native American literature for the library. The biographies should be based on research and reflect the real situations of the biographical character. For example, librarians should consider the following questions if the biography is about an historical character who lived during the time of the early interactions with the European soldiers, settlers, and missionaries. Does the biography present a true picture of the conflicts over land as exemplified by the displacement of people or the impoverishment of the people? Does the biography reflect truthful conflicts resulting from the intrusion of conflicting beliefs, values, customs, and religion? Does the biography present a truthful description of how the biographical character may have responded to the interaction with this alien culture? Norton[20] compared autobiographies and biographies written for adults with those written for children and found that biographies written for children and adolescents frequently ignored conflicts caused by cultural confrontation, especially differences in values and beliefs. The inference in many of these biographies written for younger audiences is that the Native American biographical characters experienced few conflicts due to cultural clashes. Both scholars and general readers need opportunities to read and analyze various accounts of historical personages.

Contemporary works, whether prose or poetry, need to reflect the settings, life styles, conflicts, and themes that are important for contemporary Native American people. Contemporary prose and poetry frequently includes many of the same values and beliefs as found in the earlier folklore. Conflicts in the stories may develop when the people are forced to ignore their traditional ways of life. The themes in these stories and poems suggest that traditional values such as close harmony with nature are still respected in contemporary life. The poems in *Songs From This Earth On Turtle's Back: Contemporary American Indian Poetry*,[21] edited by Joseph Bruchac, are especially meaningful for analysis. In addition, the tribal association of each poet is identified.

Nonfiction informational books about Native Americans need to be accurate through both text and illustrations. As in other nonfictional books, the facts should be accurate, stereotypes should be eliminated, illustrations should clarify the text, and the style should stimulate interest. This next section identifies some of the books that meet these guidelines.

EXAMPLES OF LITERATURE
THAT MEET THE CRITERIA

To meet the criteria cited above for folklore, the collection requires both anthologies of literature and single volume texts. A major requirement for researchers and scholars is that the folklore be identified according to tribal affiliations and to sources for the translations or transcriptions. Anthologies written for adults such as *American Indian Mythology*,[22] collected by Alice Marriott and Carol K. Rachlin are especially beneficial because they are divided into categories for the tales (for example, "The World Beyond Ours," "The World Around Us," "The World We Live In Now," and "The World We Go To") and each tale is identified according to tribal affiliation. Numerous folklore anthologies reflect the collection of tales from one tribal group. For example, sources such as Frank Hamilton Cushing's *Zuni Folk Tales*,[23] Roger Welsch's *Omaha Tribal Myths and Trickster Tales*,[24] Edwin S. Hall's *The Eskimo Storyteller: Folktales From Noatak, Alaska*,[25] and James Mooney's *Myths of the Cherokee and Sacred Formulas of the Cherokees*[26] provide both information about the particular tribal folklore and numerous tales that exemplify Bierhorst's categories of Native American folklore. Anthologies of children's literature are also essential for the collection. Virginia Hamilton's *In the Beginning: Creation Stories from Around the World*[27] includes several myths from various identified Native American tribes. Jean Monroe and Ray Williamson's *They Dance in the Sky: Native American Star Myths*[28] includes myths on the particular subject collected from various tribal areas. There are also children's literature collections of tales gathered from one area such as tales from the Northwest coasts of United States and Canada. Christie Harris's *The Trouble With Adventurers*[29] and *Mouse Woman and the Vanished Princesses*[30] emphasize how heroes venture onto the unpredictable sea and overcome perils associated with the ocean wilderness.

Highly illustrated single editions of folklore are also necessary for the collection. Many of these tales are categorized as children's or young adult literature. For example, John Bierhorst's *The Ring in the Prairie: A Shawnee Legend*[31] includes elements that exemplify several of the categories identified by Bierhorst including fair and foul tricksters, crossing thresholds, and family drama. Paula Underwood Spencer's *Who Speaks for Wolf*[32] is a "Native American Learning Story" that develops the importance of living in harmony with nature by chronicling the experiences of the Oneida as they move to a new location, only to discover that they have failed to consider the rights of the animals. Illustrated folklore from the Great Plains such as Olaf Baker's *Where the Buffalos Begin*[33] and Paul Goble's *Buffalo Woman*[34] develop the strong interactions between buffalo and the Great Plains Indians. Trickster tales from the various tribal groups are of special interest to many readers. For example, Paul Goble's *Iktomi and the Boulder: A Plains Indian Story*[35] and *Iktomi and the Berries*[36] develop the fair and foul side of Iktomi, a trickster character from the Great Plains Indians. The collection should include stories of trickster characters from throughout North America. Iktomi is the Sioux name for trickster. On the northwestern coast of the Pacific Ocean, the trickster is called Raven. Coyote, who may be a creator or a trickster, is a popular character in the plains.

Two award-winning books from the United States and two

award-winning books from Canada exemplify the characteristics of excellent historical fiction about Native Americans written for juvenile audiences. The Newbery Honor books by American authors, Scott O'Dell's *Sing Down the Moon*[37] and Elizabeth George Speare's *The Sign of the Beaver*[38] meet the criteria listed earlier. O'Dell's book focuses on the mid-1860s, when the U. S. Cavalry forced the Navaho to make the three-hundred-mile long walk from their productive home in Canyon de Chelly to the stark Fort Sumner. O'Dell realistically describes the setting, but also develops strong protagonists who are able to survive both spiritually and physically. Speare's book develops both the setting for the Maine wilderness of the 1700s and the values and survival skills of the Penobscot Indians. This book is especially strong because the themes of friendship, faith, moral obligation, working together, and love for the land are shown to be equally important for both the pioneer boy and his Indian friend. The Canadian Library Association Book of the Year, Jan Hudson's *Sweetgrass*[39] and Farley Mowat's *Lost on the Barrens*[40] are developed on strong historical content. Hudson focuses on a young Blackfoot girl's struggle for maturity as she faces a life-and-death battle during the 1837 smallpox epidemic. The values and beliefs of the people are carefully developed. Hudson's use of figurative language that closely relates to the Native American setting and protagonist is excellent. Mowat's story takes place in a remote arctic wilderness, hundreds of miles from the nearest town. The setting becomes an antagonist for a Woodland Cree and a white Canadian orphan when the two boys are separated from a Cree hunting expedition and must prepare for the rapidly approaching winter. The book portrays how the boys develop a close relationship and an understanding of each other.

Biographies and autobiographies are especially important for the Native American collection. The *Guide to Research on North American Indians*[41] includes an annotated bibliography of autobiographies and biographies about Native Americans. The text is divided according to tribal areas in North America. The books in this source are adult literature and provide sources for scholars doing comparative studies between adult and juvenile literature. Many of the juvenile sources are less candid than the adult sources and infer different consequences for the Native American characters who interacted with the European settlers. Several juvenile biographies are exceptions and provide historically accurate depictions of the time period and the characters. For example, Dorothy Morrison's *Chief Sarah: Sarah Winnemucca's Fight for Indian Rights*[42] is one of the strongest biographies as the author develops the numerous conflicts the biographical character faces as she tries to gain rights for her people and preserve their culture.

There are fewer contemporary realistic fiction novels and poetry selections written by or about Native Americans. In the adult collection there should be books by Native American authors such as N. Scott Momaday, Leslie Silko, Simon Ortiz, and James Welch. The children's and young adult collection will benefit from books such as White Deer of Autumn's *Ceremony–In the Circle of Life*.[43] This contemporary story is closely related to traditional values and beliefs. Works by Virginia Driving Hawk Sneve frequently develop understandings about the past to help their characters respect their heritage. In *High Elk's Treasure*,[44] Sneve uses flashbacks to 1876, when the Sioux were taken to the reservation following the defeat of General Custer at the Battle of the Little Big Horn. Symbolism, traditional values, tribal customs, and conflict with contemporary society are all found in Jamake Highwater's Ghost Horse Cycle that includes *Legend Days*,[45] *The Ceremony of Innocence*,[46] and *I Wear the Morning Star*.[47] Most of these books develop the conflict that Native American characters face as they try to adjust to a world that no longer allows them to live in their traditional ways. The themes in contemporary poetry vary depending on the age level of the audience. Poems such as Jamake Highwater's *Moonsong Lullaby*[48] present the beauty of and the love for nature and tradition felt by the Native American people. Likewise, Virginia Driving Hawk Sneve's collection *Dancing Teepees: Poems of American Indian Youth*[49] emphasizes a belief in many of the traditional values. The poetic texts written by Byrd Baylor reveal both contemporary and traditional life styles and values. Baylor's *The Desert Is Theirs*[50] communicates the Papago Indians' closeness to nature. In *When Clay Sings*,[51] Baylor ponders the secrets of prehistoric people as seen through their drawings on pottery. Contemporary poetry written for adult audiences frequently develops themes related to inner conflicts as the poets try to retain their Native American values. Poetry collections such as *Songs From This Earth On Turtle's Back: Contemporary American Indian Poetry*[52] allow readers and researchers to understand these contemporary conflicts. For example, poems by Maurice Kenny (Mohawk) develop the poet's strong love for nature. Poems by Simon Ortiz (Acoma) explore contemporary conflicts with society.

There are numerous nonfictional texts that meet the criteria for accuracy. Many of the children's and young adult sources emphasize contributions of Native Americans, their history, and their struggles for survival against overwhelming odds when Europeans began claiming the continent. Marcia Sewall's *People of the Breaking Day*[53] focuses on the Wampanoag nation of Southeastern Massachusetts before the English settlers arrive. Some of these texts are enriched by photographs and paintings taken from an earlier time. For example, Russell Freedman's *Buffalo Hunt*[54] is illustrated with reproductions of paintings by such artists as George Catlin and Karl Bodmer. The titled and dated illustrations add considerable interest to the text. Maps, early photographs, archive illustrations, and references provide additional information in Albert Marrin's *War Clouds in the West: Indians & Cavalrymen, 1860-1890.*[55] Books that trace the Native American people from earlier times to contemporary life are especially beneficial. Brent Ashabranner's *Morning Star, Black Sun: The Northern Cheyenne Indians and America's Energy Crisis*[56] traces the Northern Cheyenne from their early migrations into Montana to their recent conflicts with power and mining companies. Ashabranner characterizes the Northern Cheyenne as people who have strong values, such as respect for the land and animals, regard for bravery and wisdom, and reverence for religious principles. Contemporary life is the focus of both Ashabranner's *To Live in Two Worlds: American Indian Youth Today*[57] and Arlene Hirschfelder's *Happily May I Walk: American Indians and Alaska Natives Today.*[58] These books are beneficial for the collection because they include interviews with young people living on both reservations and in urban environments and discussions about contemporary topics such as tribal governments, education, and economic life.

Numerous additional Native American sources for children and young adults are found in Donna Norton's *Through the Eyes of a*

Child: An Introduction to Children's Literature[59] and in Anna Lee Stensland's *Literature by and About the American Indian.*[60]

ISSUES OF CONCERN
WHEN DEVELOPING THE COLLECTION

Many multicultural books go out of print faster than other books. This is of considerable concern to the acquisitions librarian. In a study of the books that went out of print between editions of *Through the Eyes of a Child: An Introduction to Children's Literature,* Norton[61] found that an average of 7 percent of the books went out of print between editions. When analyzed according to genre and type, however, the range was between 0 percent and 30 percent. The highest 30 percent of the literature was classified as multicultural. Of the multicultural books, 35 percent of the Native American books went out of print between editions.

In order to have a better understanding of the possible reasons for the high out of print phenomena, we need to review various influences on the writing, interpretation, and acceptance of Native American literature. These influences also emphasize many issues of concern when developing the Native American collection. A review of the scholarly journals in the past fifteen years reveals five major areas that influence Native American literature: (1) the identification, recognition, and nonacceptance of negative stereotypes found in literature from the past; (2) conflicts over sovereignty of the stories; (3) disputes over translations of poetry, folklore, and biography/autobiography; (4) disagreements over literal versus metaphorical interpretations; and (5) censorship issues.

Stereotypes are one of the greatest concerns when acquiring the Native American collection. Earlier books written for children and adolescents may cause particular problems. Researchers who analyze the books published prior to the mid-1970s are particularly critical of the stereotypes that are likely to be found in the books. For example, Byler[62] analyzed Native American books written for children and concluded:

> There are too many books featuring painted, whooping, befeathered Indians closing in on too many forts, maliciously

attacking "peaceful" settlers or simply leering menacingly from the background; too many books in which white benevolence is the only thing that saves the day for the incompetent childlike Indian; too many stories setting forth what is "best" for American Indians. (p. 28)

Herbst[63] analyzed the images of Native Americans in these earlier children's books and identified three common stereotypes that characterize Native Americans as (1) savage, depraved, and cruel; (2) noble, proud, silent, and close to nature; or (3) inferior, childlike, and helpless. Terms and comparisons suggesting negative and derogatory images often reinforce such stereotypes. A white family, for example, may be said to consist of a husband, a wife, and a child; members of Native American families, in contrast, may be called bucks, squaws, and papooses. White authors often dehumanized Native Americans by comparing them to animals. Even Native American language is often described as 'snarling,' 'grunting,' or 'yelping.' *The Matchlock Gun*,[64] by Walter Edmonds, compares the nameless Indians to trotting dogs, sniffing the scent of food. In this earlier literature, Native American characters may be depersonalized by not being given names, which implies that they are not individuals, or even full-fledged human beings.

Herbst also identifies three stereotypical ways in which the Native American culture has been portrayed in children's literature. First, the culture may be depicted as inferior to the white culture. In this case the author treats the abandonment of the Native American way of life as an improvement. Native American characters are often depicted making this gain by going to white schools or taking on the values of the white culture, leaving their culture and even their people behind. A common theme in such literature is that white people must be responsible for remaking Native Americans.

Second, the culture may be depicted as valueless, and thus not worthy of respect. The rich diversity of spiritual beliefs and ceremonies, moral values, artistic skills, and life-styles in Native American cultures may be ignored in favor of depicting violence as the chief Native American value. Authors may be ignorant of the fact that Native American peoples have many different cultures.

Third, the culture may be depicted as quaint or superficial, without depth or warmth. White characters in children's literature of the past commonly ridicule or scorn customs that have spiritual significance to Native Americans. They disparage sacred ceremonies, medicine men, ancient artifacts, and traditional legends as belonging to "heathen savages." Any of these three stereotypical portrayals is offensive. More current books, however, especially those written by Native American authors or other authorities on Native American culture, are usually sensitive to the heritage and individuality of the native peoples of North America.

Conflicts over sovereignty also cause issues related to writing, publishing, and reading Native American literature. One viewpoint states that Native American people should have total sovereignty over their traditions and their past. Advocates of this viewpoint maintain that Native American literature should be protected against the desecration committed by the imposition of alien cultures and American/European standards of literacy. Consequently, only Native Americans can translate their traditions or write about their history with an accurate perspective. The contrasting viewpoint encourages informed sensitivity among any writer who would write about the Native American traditions and history in a scholarly manner for the instruction and enlightenment of all audiences. The journals explore and debate such questions as: Should anyone but a member of that ethnic group write about the group? Who should be the audience for ethnic literature? Must members of an ethnic group be spokespersons for that group, or may they write about any subject?

Disputes over translations are closely related to issues of sovereignty and audience. Should the literature be changed so that it is more accessible to and understood by a broader audience? Or, should the literature retain its total context within the Native American culture. Changes in translation are frequently found in folklore, chants, poetry, and autobiography, especially the literature written for younger audiences. Advocates of changes in translations argue that the materials must be presented in such a way that they are understandable and accessible to audiences who are not Native American. In contrast, many Native American scholars argue that Native American literature should retain the total Indian context. Dorris[66] argues against diluting the literature so that it can be understood by a broader audience, but he maintains that scholars and readers need to develop an understanding of Native American literature by taking part in a study that progresses from an awareness of the language and philosophy of creation stories; proceeds through reading of myth cycles; continues to historical sagas; proceeds to reading riddles, songs, and religious chants; continues to treaties, diaries, and autobiographies; and concludes with modern authors from the culture. Norton[67] modifies Dorris' approach to identify appropriate Native American literature and a sequence of study that helps children and adolescents understand Native American culture and literature. To accomplish this type of study, the library collection must include these different types of literature.

A related area of concern focuses on the translations of early Native American autobiographies. In a study of these early autobiographies, Norton[68] found that if individuals wanted their life stories told, they usually had to rely on interpreters to translate language and editors to make these translations follow the prose style and the literary standards of the time period. In addition, editors often added information to put the narrative in a context for their audiences to understand. This tendency obscures the definition of autobiography and raises issues related to the authenticity of some of the texts.

Disputes over literal versus metaphorical interpretations influence the acceptance and interpretation of Native American literature. Critics argue over the interpretations of visions such as those described by Black Elk in the autobiography *Black Elk Speaks*[69] and by Plenty-Coups in *Plenty-Coups: Chief of the Crows*.[70] Plenty-Coups states that his strong belief in the literal interpretation of his medicine dreams controlled his actions throughout his life, and saved his people when other tribes were destroyed by the white man. How should these visions be interpreted in children's and adolescent literature?

Issues related to censorship may have the greatest impact on the publishing, acceptance, and reading of the literature for all multicultural groups. On one side, groups provide guidelines on what is, and what is not acceptable in ethnic literatures and argue for the inclusion of books that develop positive images and for the removal of certain books because of negative stereotypes or incorrect interpretations. In contrast, other groups may attack multicultural literature for different purposes. For example, some groups object to mythology, stories about cultures they consider to be pagan, supernatural literature, and books that include negative statements about the founding fathers of this nation. This final list of subjects that are considered objectionable by some groups shows that many of the materials in the Native American collection could be depleted if librarians are not sensitive to the cultural values and beliefs.

CONCLUSION

The Native American, or any multicultural literature, collection is extremely important for library acquisitions. A heightened sensitivity to the needs of all people has led to the realization that libraries should include literature by and about members of all cultural groups. Literature is appropriate for building respect across cultures, sharpening sensitivity toward the common features of all individuals, and improving the self-esteem of people who are members of racial and ethnic minority groups. These goals make the inclusion of Native American literature important for all readers.

REFERENCES

1. Carter, Forrest. *The Education of Little Tree*. New York: Delacorte, 1976, Albuquerque: University of New Mexico Press, 1986.

2. Hirschfelder, Arlene; Byler, Mary Gloyne; and Dorris, Michael. *Guide to Research on North American Indians*. Chicago: American Library Association, 1983.

3. Scarberry-Garcia, Susan. *Landmarks of Healing: Study of House Made of Dawn*. Albuquerque: University of New Mexico Press, 1990.

4. Rice, Julian. *Black Elk's Story: Distinguishing Its Lakota Purpose*. Albuquerque: University of New Mexico Press, 1991.

5. Vizenor, Gerald. *Narrative Chance: Postmodern Discourse on Native American Indian Literatures*. Albuquerque: University of New Mexico Press, 1989.

6. Samek, Hana. *The Blackfoot Confederacy, 1880-1920*. Albuquerque: University of New Mexico Press, 1987.

7. Utley, Robert. *The Indian Frontier of the American West, 1846-1990*. Albuquerque: University of New Mexico Press, 1984.

8. Ashabranner, Brent. *Morning Star, Black Sun: The Northern Cheyenne Indians and America's Energy Crisis.* New York: Dodd, Mead, 1982.

9. Marrin, Albert. *War Clouds in the West: Indians & Cavalrymen, 1860-1890.* New York: Athenaeum, 1984.

10. O'Dell, Scott. *Sing Down the Moon.* Boston: Houghton Mifflin, 1970.

11. Momaday, N. Scott. *House Made of Dawn.* Harper & Row, 1969.

12. Highwater, Jamake. *Legend Days.* New York: Harper & Row, 1984.

13. Highwater, Jamake. *The Ceremony of Innocence.* New York: Harper & Row, 1985.

14. Highwater, Jamake. *I Wear the Morning Star.* New York: Harper & Row, 1986.

15. Norton, Donna E. *The Effective Teaching of Language Arts,* 4th edition. Columbus: Merrill/Macmillan, 1992.

16. Bierhorst, John, editor. *The Red Swan: Myths and Tales of the American Indian.* New York: Farrar, Straus & Giroux, 1976.

17. Bierhorst, John. *The Mythology of North America.* New York: Morrow, 1985.

18. Mowat, Farley. *Lost in the Barrens.* Toronto: McClelland and Stewart, 1956, 1984.

19. O'Dell, Scott. *Sing Down the Moon.* Boston: Houghton Mifflin, 1970.

20. Norton, Donna E. "The Intrusion of an Alien Culture: The Impact and Reactions as Seen Through Biographies and Autobiographies of Native Americans." *Vitae Scholasticae.* 6 (Spring 1987): 59-75.

21. Bruchac, Joseph, editor. *Songs From This Earth on Turtle's Back: Contemporary American Indian Poetry.* New York: Greenfield Review Press, 1983.

22. Marriott, Alice and Rachlin, Carol K. *American Indian Mythology.* New York: New American Library, 1968.

23. Cushing, Frank Hamilton. *Zuni Folk Tales.* Tucson: The University of Arizona Press, 1901, 1986.

24. Welch, Roger. *Omaha Tribal Myths and Trickster Tales.* Chicago: Swallow, 1981.

25. Hall, Edwin S. *The Eskimo Storyteller: Folktales From Noatak, Alaska.* Knoxville: The University of Tennessee Press, 1975.

26. Mooney, James. *Myths of the Cherokee and Sacred Formulas of the Cherokees.* Nashville: Charles and Randy Elder-Booksellers, 1982.

27. Hamilton, Virginia. *In the Beginning: Creation Stories from Around the World.* Orlando: Harcourt Brace Jovanovich, 1988.

28. Monroe, Jean and Williamson, Ray. *They Dance in the Sky: Native American Star Myths.* Boston: Houghton Mifflin, 1987.

29. Harris, Christie. *The Trouble With Adventurers.* New York: Atheneum, 1982.

30. Harris, Christie. *Mouse Woman and the Vanished Princesses.* New York: Atheneum, 1976.

31. Bierhorst, John. *The Ring in the Prairie: A Shawnee Legend.* New York: Dial, 1970.

32. Spencer, Paula Underwood. *Who Speaks for Wolf.* Austin: Tribe of Two Press, 1983.

33. Baker, Olaf. *Where the Buffalos Begin.* New York: Warne, 1981.

34. Goble, Paul. *Buffalo Woman.* New York: Bradbury, 1984.

35. Goble, Paul. *Iktomi and the Boulder: A Plains Indian Story.* New York: Orchard, 1988.

36. Goble, Paul. *Iktomi and the Berries.* New York: Watts, 1989.

37. O'Dell, Scott, 1970.

38. Speare, Elizabeth George. *The Sign of the Beaver.* Boston: Houghton Mifflin, 1983.

39. Hudson, Jan. *Sweetgrass.* New York: Philomel, 1989.

40. Mowat, Farley, 1956.

41. Hirschfelder, Arlene; Byler, Mary Gloyne; and Dorris, Michael, 1983.

42. Morrison, Dorothy. *Chief Sarah: Sarah Winnemucca's Fight for Indian Rights.* New York: Atheneum, 1980.

43. White Deer of Autumn. *Ceremony–In the Circle of Life.* Milwaukee: Raintree, 1983.

44. Sneve, Virginia Driving Hawk. *High Elk's Treasure.* New York: Holiday, 1972.

45. Highwater, Jamake, 1984.

46. Highwater, Jamake, 1985.

47. Highwater, Jamake, 1986.

48. Highwater, Jamake. *Moonsong Lullaby.* New York: Lothrop, Lee & Shepard, 1981.

49. Sneve, Virginia Driving Hawk. *Dancing Teepees: Poems of American Indian Youth.* New York: Holiday, 1989.

50. Bayler, Byrd. *The Desert is Theirs.* New York: Scribner's, 1975.

51. Bayler, Byrd. *When Clay Sings.* New York: Scribner's, 1972.

52. Bruchac, Joseph, editor, 1983.

53. Sewall, Marcia. *People of the Breaking Day.* New York: Atheneum, 1990.

54. Freedman, Russell. *Buffalo Hunt.* New York: Holiday, 1988.

55. Marrin, Albert, 1984.

56. Ashabranner, Brent. *Morning Star, Black Sun: The Northern Cheyenne Indians and America's Energy Crisis.* New York: Dodd, Mead, 1982.

57. Ashabranner, Brent, 1984.

58. Hirschfelder, Arlene. *Happily May I Walk: American Indians and Alaska Natives Today.* New York: Scribner's, 1986.

59. Norton, Donna E. *Through the Eyes of a Child: An Introduction to Children's Literature*, 3rd edition. Columbus: Merrill/Macmillan, 1991.

60. Stensland, Anna Lee. *Literature by and About the American Indian.* Urbana Ill: National Council of Teachers of English, 1979.

61. Norton, Donna E. "The Rise and Fall of Ethic Literature." Paper presented at the National Council of Teachers of English, Phoenix, 1989.

62. Byler, Mary Gloyne. "American Indian Authors for Young Readers." In *Cultural Conformity in Books for Children,* edited by Donnarae MacCann and Gloria Woodard. Metuchen, NJ: Scarecrow, 1977.

63. Herbst, Laura. "That's One Good Indian: Unacceptable Images in Children's Novels." In *Cultural Conformity in Books for Children,* edited by Donnarae MacCann and Gloria Woodard. Metuchen, NJ: Scarecrow, 1977.

64. Edmunds, Walter. *The Matchlock Gun.* New York: Dodd Mead, 1941.

65. Herbst, Laura, 1977.

66. Dorris, Michael. "Native American Literature in an Ethnohistorical Context." *College English.* 41 (October 1979): 147-162.

67. Norton, Donna E. "Teaching Multicultural Literature in the Reading Curriculum." *The Reading Teacher.* 44 (1991).

68. Norton, Saundra E. "Fabricating Lives: Cultural Authenticity and the Autobiography." Paper presented at the International Society of Education Biographer's Conference, Chicago, Ill., April 1992.

69. Black Elk, as told through John G. Niehard. *Black Elk Speaks: Being the Life Story of a Holy Man of the Oglala Sioux.* Lincoln: University of Nebraska Press, 1961, 1932 edition, Morrow.

70. Plenty-Coups, edited by Frank B. Linderman. *Plenty-Coups: Chief of the Crows.* Lincoln: University of Nebraska Press, 1962.

71. Norton, Donna E., 1989.

Ethnic Diversity in a Northern Climate

Annette Salo

SUMMARY. Despite a budget cutback of 7% in 1991, the Saint Paul (Minnesota) Public Library continues to build a strong collection and service program to meet the needs of the city's growing ethnic population. According to 1990 census data, Saint Paul had a 612% increase in its Asian American population in the last decade. Library staff established a cooperative program with Lao Family Community of Minnesota (a mutual assistance organization) which introduced over 800 families to library services, provided bookmobile services to all public housing areas of the city, created a Launch a Young Reader Service for child care providers, established a Book Buddy Project, hired a bilingual Hmong Management Trainee, and received a three-year grant to increase the holdings of the world language collections.

INTRODUCTION

Saint Paul, Minnesota, has made national headlines in the past few years hosting the World Series, Super Bowl, Final Four, and Special Olympics. But, yet another dramatic event has occurred

Annette Salo is Area Librarian, Lexington Branch Library, Saint Paul Public Library, 1080 University Avenue, Saint Paul, MN 55104.

[Haworth co-indexing entry note]: "Ethnic Diversity in a Northern Climate," Salo, Annette. Co-published simultaneously in *The Acquisitions Librarian* (The Haworth Press, Inc.) No. 9/10, 1993, pp. 267-274; and: *Multicultural Acquisitions* (ed: Karen Parrish and Bill Katz) The Haworth Press, Inc., 1993, pp. 267-274. Multiple copies of this article/chapter may be purchased from The Haworth Document Delivery Center. Call 1-800-3-HAWORTH (1-800-342-9678) between 9:00 - 5:00 (EST) and ask for DOCUMENT DELIVERY CENTER.

which has not been reported in the national news. The descendants of the city's German, Irish, Italian and Scandinavian immigrants have been joined by a growing number of Southeast Asian immigrants. The 1990 Census shows 19,200 Asian and Pacific Islanders in the city–a 612% increase in the past decade.[1] With the help of mutual assistance organizations, immigrants from Vietnam, Cambodia and Laos have settled in the Minneapolis/Saint Paul area. The majority of these new immigrants, an estimated 16,000, are the Hmong who escaped political persecution in Laos by fleeing to refugee camps in Thailand after the end of the Vietnam War. Most Hmong in the United States settled in the Central Valley area of California to farm or came to Minnesota to live near 20 clan leaders who settled in this area.[2] The Twin City area houses the largest urban concentration of Hmong in the United States.[3] Saint Paul's Southeast Asian population makes up about 7.1% of the city and is about the same size as the city's African American population. The African American population increased 50% during the 1980's; the Hispanic population increased 45.9% during this period.[4] The city is currently experiencing an increase in Jewish immigrants from the nations of the former Soviet Union with more than 800 families settling here in 1991.[5] All of the immigrants and refugees have helped enrich the cultural diversity that is Saint Paul's legacy.

THE COLLECTION

Saint Paul has not been spared the budget reductions of the 1990's. The public library budget was cut 7% in 1992 and faces further cutbacks. Library Director, Gerald Steenberg, reports that the library's circulation increased 37% and requests for information increased 66.5% during the past decade.[6] Saint Paul is a medium-sized urban library system with a strong central library, ten branches, a kiosk library in a shopping mall, and a bookmobile. Selection of popular materials is managed centrally by a Collection Librarian; selection of subject materials and duplicate orders are initiated by Central Library Subject Specialists and Branch Librarians. Eighteen languages are collected for adult readers by the Social Science and Literature (SSL) Department at the Central Library. Eighteen languages are collected for adult readers by the Social

Science and Literature (SSL) Department at the Central Library. All world-language materials are ordered by SSL librarian Marilyn Rehnberg who then selects rotating collections to be sent to branch libraries as needed. Twelve languages are collected by Central's Youth Services Department and branches.

To update these collections, the Friends of the Saint Paul Public Library granted $30,000 for a three-year period. A world language committee was formed to share the responsibility for ordering. Collection Librarian, Cheryl Anderson, designed a questionnaire for community input towards the selection process. The questionnaire gathered information on the demographics of the community, projected immigration or expansion, educational and reading levels in English and native languages, and suggested sources for materials. Hmong, Vietnamese, Cambodian, Laotian, Hispanic and Russian community advisors, educators and immigrants participated in the survey. The World Language committee suggested renaming these library collections from foreign language to world language to reflect the many languages integral to the community. Circulation in the world languages was up 28% in 1991.[7]

Despite this extensive community input, building these collections has not been easy. City policies restrict the library from ordering materials directly from publishers outside of the United States or Canada. The library does not have staff fluent in all languages collected and has found it time-consuming and not always practical to rely on volunteers for assistance. Many titles available from distributors are geared to academic collections. Through 1991, the library has been ordering specific titles and is just beginning to use approval plans. For the small size of its collections and limited budget, approval plans appear to be more cost-effective.

Materials in Spanish are readily available; the Central Library and the Riverview Branch Library have popular fiction, photonovellas and magazines. Russian materials are a challenge. At the Highland Park Branch Library, recent Russian immigrants quickly utilize the English as a Second Language (ESL) collection and want to continue reading in their native language. It is difficult to find current popular Russian works from U. S. distributors to add to the old classics currently in the collection. Popular Vietnamese novels are regularly added to the collection and at the Lexington Branch

Library, periodicals in Vietnamese such as *Tien Phong* and English language editions of the *Bangkok Post, Trans-Pacific, Asian Business News, Asian Pages* and *Asian-American Press* provide international and local news for all the city's Southeast Asians.

Building the Hmong collection for the Lexington Branch Library has been a struggle. The Hmong culture did not have a formal, written language until the 1950's, making the number of published materials scarce. A Macalester (Saint Paul, Minnesota) professor, Dr. Charles Johnson, translated many Hmong folktales into ESL booklets and these form the basis of the collection. Pamphlets on public health, safety, legal aid and driver's education are included in the collection. English-language folk stories, cookbooks, needlework and art books, and more scholarly materials are housed in the "Hmong History and Culture" collection which is housed beneath a large "pa Ndau" needlework piece. Library users are immediately drawn to the collection.

The "Black History and Culture" collection and novels by African American authors have high circulation at Lexington. Popular African American magazines such as *Jet, Essence, Ebony, Black Enterprise,* along with local newspapers, add to the collection.

In addition to a commitment to provide special collections that reflect their neighborhoods, branch libraries provide tours and orientation sessions for ESL and literacy classes and youth groups. One example of this is the close cooperation between the Lexington Branch Library and the Lao Family Community of Minnesota. Since 1990, over eight hundred families have visited the branch, received library cards, and attended service talks focusing on sharing books with children. All of these services are part of the Quarterly Orientation Session for the Family English Literacy Program at Lexington.

BILINGUAL STAFF

In July 1991, the library hired Na Ly, a Hmong Management Trainee, to assist with translation and to help facilitate the use of the library among Hmong immigrants. Ly's salary is funded by the Southeast Asian Access Project, a federal grant from the Community Revitalization Program, which also funds trainees for the Public

Health Department and the Mayor's Complaint and Information Office. Ly has translated at child-care provider workshops, ESL classes, and storytimes and has spoken at the Hmong New Year Celebration, Southeast Asian Access Fair, and various youth, religious, women's and veteran's organizations. Ly staffs the bookmobile at stops with a large Hmong population.

LAUNCH A YOUNG READER

Saint Paul's Mayor, James Scheibel, is nationally recognized for implementing programs that affect the quality of life for children and families within the city. Child care has been a major initiative for Saint Paul. With this strong support, Youth Services Coordinator, Alice Neve, developed a pilot project for at-risk children served by the Lexington Branch Library. Launch a Young Reader (LYR) services began in September, 1990, introducing library services to children and providers in a child-care setting. Funded by a $55,000 grant from the Friends of the Saint Paul Public Library, Neve selected city planning districts with a prevalence of low-income and single-parent families. More than twenty child-care centers, pre-schools, and headstart programs care for 1200 children in the target area.[8] LYR Coordinator, Charlene McKenzie, created sixty story-time kits which circulated 604 times between September, 1990, and June, 1991.[9] Each kit contains at least two books, finger/body play ideas, poetry, flannelboard stories, and activity suggestions on a single theme. Everything needed to present a storytime such as *Count Me In, Silly Willies* or *Many Lands, Many Stories*, is provided in these kits. Workshops to introduce child-care providers to books, activities, and library resources are presented semiannually by LYR staff. Quarterly newsletters are mailed to all licensed family providers and child-care centers in the city. Child-care centers in the target area are invited to storytimes at Lexington. For those centers unable to come to the library, McKenzie and Storytime Specialist Peg Doheny make on-site visits. Of the 1,315 children attending storytimes in 1991, 48% were African American and 22% were Southeast Asian.[10] A $25,000 materials grant provided a fresh supply of positive, multicultural picture books, folk and fairy tales, easy nonfiction and children's music. To provide assistance to adult care-givers, a "Child Care Provider's Corner" houses preschool curriculum guides, activities for children, child-development resources, and materials on the business of day care. This focus on cultural diversity included the development of a slide show on multicultural books, multicultural booklist, LYR workshop for child-care providers, workshop for staff on multicultural children's materials, window displays and a special collection of juvenile multicultural titles at the Lexington branch.

BOOK BUDDIES

The Book Buddy Project was established in July, 1991, at the Central Library to promote reading and literacy among homeless children in Saint Paul. Volunteer Coordinator, Laura Samargia, and Alice Neve trained volunteers to read one-on-one or in small groups to children at a downtown family shelter. The Book Buddy Project was awarded a National Achievement Citation from the Public Library Association in 1992. The project has expanded to three family shelters. Books are collected for use at these sites. Book Buddy volunteers read to children at the shelters, and at the Lexington Branch Library.

BOOKMOBILE SERVICES

Saint Paul is one of the remaining cities to provide bookmobile services to senior high-rises, public housing communities, and areas of the city where physical and social barriers prevent easy access to a public library. In 1990, the Friends purchased a new mobile unit. More than 76% of public housing community residents are Southeast Asian.[11] At stops such as McDonough Homes, 97% of the households have incomes below poverty level.[12] Circulation at these stops is incredible. More than 150 children are waiting when the bookmobile arrives at McDonough. At the Martin Luther King Center, four day-care classes eagerly await the arrival of the bookmobile. User comments say it all: From a Hmong mother, "We have no books at home. The only books my children read are from the bookmobile"; and from a child who won a paperback in the Summer Reading Program, "I have never had a book of my own before."

STAFF TRAINING

Staff training, even during the time of cutbacks, is an important aspect of city services and library philosophy. The library had to eliminate a half-time training coordinator and shift some duties to the Staff Training and Development Committee. It designs at least two workshops for staff each year. A cultural diversity workshop focusing on Southeast Asian use of the library, and leadership training for library staff at all levels were the latest offerings. The City Training Department offers programs such as "Diversity Awareness Training" and the public schools offer a Hmong language class for service providers. A librarian serves on the Mayor's Work Group on Diversity, which promotes awareness of diversity and its value in the workplace.

CONCLUSION

Saint Paul Public Library's success with materials and services for its ethnic populations is a direct result of a caring and creative staff. With library hours cut to a one-shift schedule and 14 full time equivalent employees laid off in 1991, the library has not increased its materials budget. Strong Friends support, federal grants, and the use of volunteers for special projects supplements the reduced budget, allowing a dedicated staff to develop programs to meet the needs of its changing population.

REFERENCES

1. Saint Paul 1990 Census Report #1. City of Saint Paul. Department of Planning and Economic Development: p.5.

2. *Hmong Forum*. Haiv Hmoob Inc. P.O. Box 11314, Minneapolis, MN. volume 1. 1990: p.27

3. Blanton, Geoffrey, Lao Family Community in Minnesota. Civic Organization Partnership Proposal, 1992: p.2.

4. Saint Paul 1990 Census Report #1.: p.6-7.

5. Kunz, Virginia. *Saint Paul: The First 150 Years*. Saint Paul Foundation, Saint Paul, MN., 1991: p. 107.

6. Saint Paul Public Library Annual Report, 1990.

7. Saint Paul Public Library Annual Statistics, 1991.

8. Saint Paul Public Library. Launch A Young Reader Fact Sheet, 1990.

9. Stockdill, Stacey, Ph.D. EnSearch. Evaluation Report Regarding: Launch A Young Reader Pilot Project, September 1991: p.2.

10. Ibid., p.4.

11. Chase, Richard A., Ph.D. Amherst Wilder Foundation, Wilder Research Center, 1295 Bandana Blvd, Saint Paul, MN, 55108. Saint Paul PHA Family Survey, June 1990: p.2.

12. Ibid.

United States Women's History: A Bibliography

Jean Kemble

SUMMARY. This is a selective, partially annotated bibliography on the history of women in the United States. It was created to provide a list of the most significant books available on this subject.

INTRODUCTION

This selective bibliography is intended both for the general reader who wishes to learn about the history of women in the United States, and for acquisitions librarians in small college and large public libraries, who want to provide their users with a selection of the most significant books in this field. The bibliography is divided into major sections, reflecting both the periodization of women's history, as well as the major areas of contemporary research. A large number of the works included have been annotated, but many are only cited. Generally it is the more accessible works which have been reviewed.

Jean Kemble is a recent graduate of the MLS program at Suny Albany, in Albany, NY. She can be reached c/o F. Tripoli, P.O. Box 148, Gilbertville, MA 01031.

[Haworth co-indexing entry note]: "United States Women's History: A Bibliography," Kemble, Jean. Co-published simultaneously in *The Acquisitions Librarian* (The Haworth Press, Inc.) No. 9/10, 1993, pp. 275-308; and: *Multicultural Acquisitions* (ed: Karen Parrish and Bill Katz) The Haworth Press, Inc., 1993, pp. 275-308. Multiple copies of this article/chapter may be purchased from The Haworth Document Delivery Center. Call 1-800-3-HAWORTH (1-800-342-9678) between 9:00 - 5:00 (EST) and ask for DOCUMENT DELIVERY CENTER.

Until two decades ago, most historians were concerned almost exclusively with the public spheres of politics, the marketplace, and the military. Since women were not involved in determining the nation's political, economic, and military policy, they were virtually absent from these records of United States history. However, in the late 1960s, many feminists began demanding that women's experiences and contributions to American society receive the attention which they had long been denied. Initially the historians who responded to these demands did so either by researching the lives of famous women, or by tracing the history of the women's suffrage movement. It soon became apparent that these histories ignored the experiences of the vast majority of women who had spent their lives building a home, caring for their families, and contributing to the family's economic well-being through the barter and exchange of home-made goods, or wages earned in low-paying, low-status jobs.

As the 1970's progressed, an increasing number of women's historians began exploring the lives of these "ordinary" women. In particular they focused upon the continuity and change in women's roles responsibilities, both in their family and their community, women's status and identity, and women's relations with men and other women. These historians also began to explore how the dominant images and ideals of "women's place" altered over time, and how women responded to these images. Also, several historians began to explore the notion of a female culture that was different to that of men. During the 1970s, most research was centered upon the experiences of white women in the North East United States. Particularly important was the impact of industrialization upon these women's lives. In the mid-1980s, this bias was partially corrected by the publication of a number of works about both African-American women, and immigrant women from Ireland, Italy, and Eastern Europe. Today the amount of information that exists about women's lives is remarkable when one considers that women's history has been considered a major field of research for only two decades. However, there remains enormous potential for challenging research, making this one of the most vibrant areas of American history.

GENERAL WORKS

Banner, Lois W. *Women in Modern America: A Brief History.* New York: Harcourt, Brace, Jovanovich, 1974.

This work examines the history of women of all classes and races in the United States, from 1890 to the early 1970s. It illustrates clearly and effectively how industrialization, urbanization and commercialization have affected the lives of American women, and how they have responded to these social changes. Banner compares the realities of these women's lives with the images of women pervasive in the mass media, and considers the various types of discrimination that women have endured both in the work place and at home. She also examines the rise and fall of feminism. *Women in Modern America* is commendable for its excellent use of photographs and illustrations (almost every page has one or the other). It is very accessible, and contains a careful balance of historical facts and interpretation.

Cott, Nancy F. and Elizabeth H. Pleck. *A Heritage of Her Own: Toward a New Social History of American Women.* New York: A Touchstone Book, published by Simon and Schuster, 1979.

First published more than a decade ago, *A Heritage of Her Own* remains one of the best collections of articles on U.S. women's history. The contributors are pioneers in the field, and the vast majority of the articles included were followed by monographs. This collection covers many major areas, providing the reader with a brief examination of a wide variety of topics. Subjects include the experience of white women in the southern colonies, marital and sexual norms of slave women, women's lives during the Great Depression, feminism and the contemporary family, family and community networks among ethnic immigrants, and the "hidden" history of career women in the twentieth century. Although scholarly, these articles are quite accessible, and do not assume a familiarity with the field.

Evans, Sara M. *Born For Liberty: A History of Women in America.* New York: The Free Press, 1989.

Kerber, Linda X. and Jane deHart Matthews, eds. *Women in Ameri-*

ca: Refocusing the Past. New York: Oxford University Press, 1978.

Riley, Glenda. *Inventing the American Woman: A Perspective on Women's History.* Arlington Heights, Ill: Harlan Davidson Inc., 1987.

Riley states that *Inventing the American Woman,* is intended as a study of the work, socialization, roles, activities, and cultural values of American women. Throughout the work she compares the model that was to direct American women's behavior with women's reactions to this model, and "examines from a historical perspective the lives and activities of women who lived uneasily with the invented American woman." The work is divided chronologically in a manner consistent with the common periodization of women's history, and the author intersperses the narrative with an analysis of the changing interpretations of each era. Each chapter is followed by a fine bibliography.

Woloch, Nancy. *Women and the American Experience.* New York: Alfred A. Knopf, 1984.

NATIVE AMERICAN WOMEN

Albers, Patricia and Medicine, Beatrice. *The Hidden Half: Studies of Plains Indian Women.* Washington D.C.: University Press of America Inc., 1983.

The editors of this collection of research papers explain that their intention was to amass studies that review and critique past evaluations of the role and status of Plains Indian women, and to reassess their position in the light of recent empirical and theoretical developments in anthropology and women's studies. The studies vary in their accessibility–several do not presume a familiarity with the field, while others are too theoretical to be interesting to the more general reader. The papers cover a wide range of topics, including popular images of Plains Indian women, and their work, status and identity. Several Native American groups are included. All but two of the papers deal with women's lives in the pre-reservation period.

Niethammer, Carolyn. *Daughters of the Earth: The Lives and Legends of American Indian Women.* New York: Collier Books, 1977.

WOMEN IN THE COLONIES

Karlsen, Carol F. *The Devil in the Shape of a Woman: Witchcraft in Colonial New England.* New York: W.W. Norton & Company, 1987.

During the past decade or so a number of reputable works have appeared on the subject of witchcraft in the American colonies. Most of these have argued that economic instability, and bitter land and religious disputes, were responsible for the charges of witchcraft that were made against both men and women during this period. In *The Devil in the Shape of a Woman,* however, Carol F. Karlsen looks at the reason why the vast majority of the accused were women. Using demographic and economic data she illustrates that married, wealthy women were rarely prosecuted, while those who were moderately well-off or quite poor, both married and single, were far more vulnerable. A group that was particularly at risk were single women who stood to benefit from inheritance disputes, especially if it was believed that they ignored gender norms, or failed to adequately acknowledge the supremacy of God. In Puritan society hierarchy and order were sacred, and those who worked against either were considered evil. Since single women did not fulfill the expected female roles of mother and "helpmate" and dependent, they were a threat to stability. Somewhat academic, this work provides a fascinating look at the structure of colonial society, and its religious beliefs and gender roles. Her explanation of the behavior of those who claimed to be possessed by the accused is particularly noteworthy.

Spruill, Julia Cherry. *Women's Life and Work in the Southern Colonies.* New York: W. W. Norton, 1972.

Ulrich, Laurel Thatcher. *Good Wives: Image and Reality in the Lives of Women in Northern New England, 1650-1750.* New York: Alfred A. Knopf, 1982.

Skillfully organized and beautifully written, this scrupulously researched book describes the rich variety of roles assumed by ordinary women in colonial New England, and examines the expectations and behavioral codes associated with each. Two fascinating chapters speculate on the power and influence wielded by heroic frontier women and so-called "deputy husbands," women responsible for male duties. The author's interpretations are enriched by her familiarity with the secondary literature on American colonial life.[1]

THE REVOLUTION AND THE EARLY REPUBLIC

Akers, Charles W. *Abigail Adams: An American Woman.* Boston: Little, Brown and Company, 1980.

Chambers-Schiller, Lee Virginia. *Liberty, A Better Husband: Single Women in America, The Generations of 1780-1840.* New Haven: Yale University Press, 1984.

Cott, Nancy. *The Bonds of Womanhood: "Woman's Sphere" in New England, 1780-1835.* New Haven, Conn.: Yale University Press, 1977.

Jensen, Joan M. *Loosening the Bonds: Mid-Atlantic Farm Women, 1750-1850.* New Haven: Yale University Press, 1986.

Kerber, Linda. *Women of the Republic: Intellect and Ideology in Revolutionary America.* Chapel Hill: University of North Carolina Press, 1980.

Norton, Mary Beth. *Liberty's Daughters: The Revolutionary Experience of American Women, 1750-1800.* Boston: Little, Brown, 1980.

With the publication of *Liberty's Daughters,* Mary Beth Norton challenged two common theories of American women's history. First, the notion that the colonial era represented some kind of "golden age" for women, and second, the assumption that the

---

1. This review appeared in *Library Journal,* vol 107, March 1, 1982, p 550.

Revolutionary War exerted no influence upon the lives of American women. Opposing the first theory, Norton uses diaries and letters to illustrate both the sense of dissatisfaction many colonial women felt at the narrowness of their lives. She then argues that although women did contribute a great deal to the economic well-being of their family, their status was clearly inferior to that of men legally and politically. Examining the Revolutionary War, Norton argues that women's involvement in boycotts of British goods, was the first in a series of historic steps that increased their politicization, gender consciousness, and awareness of their ability to use economic power to effect social change. Their management of family farms while their husbands were away at war, fostered a great sense of their own ability, and awakened men's recognition of their wives' ability to act independently. Norton goes on to examine the impact of the new ideology of republican motherhood–that is, the importance of the mother's role in raising good citizens–upon women's status and identity.

Thatcher Ulrich, Laurel. *A Midwife's Tale: The Life of Martha Ballard Based On Her Diary, 1785-1812.* New York: Alfred A. Knopf, 1990.

In the beginning of this work, Laurel Thatcher Ulrich comments that other historians had previously looked at this diary, which was housed in the Maine State Archives, yet none had considered it particularly important, due to its "dailiness and repetitive nature." However, it is this dailiness that Ulrich considers to be its strength, since for this New England woman, "living was to be measured in doing. Nothing was trivial." The diary is doubly important when one considers how few records were left by women living at this time. Ulrich's painstaking research allows her to use the diary as a means of illuminating a wealth of information about life in a small community in Maine in the early years of the Republic. Some of the major themes include the medical practices of the era, the relationship between doctors and midwives, male and female roles and responsibilities, female rituals during marriage, pregnancy and childbirth, and women's relationships with their husbands, family, and community.

WOMEN IN THE ANTE-BELLUM SOUTH

Bleser, Carol, ed. *In Joy and Sorrow: Women, Family, and Marriage in the Victorian South, 1830-1900.* New York: Oxford University Press, 1991.

Fox-Genovese, Elizabeth. *Within the Plantation Household: Black and White Women of the Old South.* Chapel Hill: University of North Carolina Press, 1988.

Lebsock, Suzanne. *Free Women of Petersburg: Status and Culture in a Southern Town, 1784-1860.* New York: W.W. Norton, 1984.

In this work Suzanne Lebsock examines how and why the status of white and free black women changed, during the period 1784-1860. She also considers the extent to which these women had a distinct culture of their own, and how different their values and attitudes were from those of men. Using court deeds, letters, diaries, and journals she argues that many women did become more autonomous during this period through greater employment, lower rates of marriage, and greater ownership of property. However, women became less autonomous in the public sphere, both because men coopted women's causes, and the new women's organizations, such as temperance, became auxiliaries to male organizations. Examining female values, Lebsock illustrates that unlike men, women were guided by "personalism," that is personal relationships, in their moral choices and decisions about the division of property. Lebsock provides much new information about the lives of free black women in the South. The majority of these women worked as laundresses, domestics, or in the tobacco factories. The number of black women acquiring property during this time increased substantially. Approximately half of the free black households in Petersburg were headed by women, whereas this was true of only 15% of white women.

Jones, Jacqueline. *Labor of Love, Labor of Sorrow: Black Women, Work and the Family from Slavery to the Present.* New York: Basic Books, 1985. See under *AFRICAN-AMERICAN WOMEN.*

Scott, Anne Firor. *The Southern Lady: From Pedestal to Politics, 1830-1930.* Chicago: University of Chicago Press, 1970.

The author notes that this study emerged from her observation of a discrepancy between the image of Southern women's role and the reality of their participation in political reform movements. The fourfold purpose of the book is to: describe the culturally defined image of "the lady"; trace the effect this definition has had on women's behavior; describe the realities of women's lives which were at odds with this image; and describe and character-ize the struggle of women to free themselves from the confines of cultural expectation to find a way to self-determination. The book deals mainly with women from wealthy families, for to the slaves and to white working women the Southern notion of femi-ninity had no relevance.

White, Deborah. *Ar'n't I A Woman: Female Slaves in the Plantation South.* New York: W.W. Norton, 1985. See under *AFRICAN-AMERICAN WOMEN.*

"A WOMAN'S PLACE"

Chafe, William H. *The American Woman: Her Changing Social, Economic, and Political Roles, 1920-1970.* New York: Oxford University Press, 1972.

Cott, Nancy. *The Bonds of Womanhood: "Woman's Sphere" in New England, 1780-1835.* New Haven, Conn.: Yale University Press, 1977.

Filene, Peter. *Him/Her Self: Sex Roles in Modern America.* Balti-more: John Hopkins University Press, 1986.

Jensen, Joan M. *Loosening the Bonds: Mid-Atlantic Farm Women, 1750-1850.* New Haven: Yale University Press, 1986.

Lerner, Gerda. *The Majority Finds Its Past: Placing Women in History.* New York: Oxford University Press, 1979.

O'Brien, Sharon. *Willa Cather: The Emerging Voice.* New York: Fawcett Columbine, 1987.

This biography is significant for the light it sheds upon nine-teenth century definitions of femininity, female sexuality and identity, female friendship, the experiences of a woman entering a male dominated field, and the ways in which women dealt with society's expectations. O'Brien examines the way in which Cather's perception of her own femaleness alters from a complete rejection of Victorian notions of femininity during her adolescence, which is best illustrated by her posing as a man for several years, to a personal acceptance of her female identity and a rejection of stereotyped gender roles in her literature by 1913. O'Brien is the first biographer to state categorically that Cather was a lesbian, and to explore the implications of Cather's lesbianism for her personal and literary development. Examining Cather's development as an artist, O'Brien illustrates how difficult it was for Cather to find an authentic voice in a field that was dominated by men. It was not until meeting Sarah Orne Jewett, one of the most accomplished and respected local color writers of the late nineteenth century, that Cather recognized the existence of a female literary tradition from which she could benefit. This discovery enabled her to realize that her experiences as a child in Virginia and Nebraska, where she had witnessed worlds of female work, friendship, and storytelling offered her infinite material to explore through fiction. Drawing on this material Cather finally achieved a style of her own.

Osterud, Nancy Grey. *Bonds of Community: The Lives of Farm Women in Nineteenth Century New York.* Ithaca: Cornell University Press, 1991.

In *Bonds of Community,* Nancy Grey Osterud examines the meaning of gender in the lives of New York agricultural women, in the second half of the nineteenth century. Specifically she addresses how gender structured their interactions, their place in the farm family economy, and their participation in community organizations. Osterud states that the dominant paradigm of gender relations in nineteenth century women's history has been "separate spheres." She argues that unlike urban women whose position was increasingly defined by their difference to men, rural women were defined through their relations with men. Although women undoubtedly did create strong ties with other women, they also worked and socialized with their husbands and male kinsmen. This work is divided into four sections. First Osterud examines the structure of the rural community. Then she looks at women's lives, focusing in particular on courtship, marriage, childbearing, and widowhood. Discussing women's work, Osterud shows that where a gender based division of labor did exist, it was generally flexible, and varied within and between families. She argues that both female relations and their work culture was quite different from those of males. While men's relations with male kin were mediated by the transference of property, and their cooperative work with men was mediated by market models, women's kinship bonds depended on personal assistance, and cooperative work depended on ties forged through mutual assistance. Finally, looking at patterns of sociability, Osterud argues that both formal and informal events tended to counteract and overcome rather than extend and reinforce separation between women and men.

Smith-Rosenberg, Carroll. *Disorderly Conduct: Visions of Gender in Victorian America*. New York: Oxford University Press, 1985.

Welter, Barbara. *Dimity Convictions: The American Woman in the Nineteenth Century*. Athens: Ohio University Press, 1976.

The nine essays in this work provide a comprehensive overview of the role, identity, and status of middle-class white American women during the nineteenth century. Some of the subjects considered include: the cult of true womanhood, 1800-1860; medical views of American women, 1790-1865; the femininization of American religion, 1800-1860; and anti-intellectualism of American women; and the coming of age for American girls during this period.

WOMEN AND REFORM

Addams, Jane. *Twenty Years at Hull House*. New York: MacMillan, 1911.

Buhle, Mary Jo. *Women and American Socialism, 1870-1920*. Urbana: University of Illinois Press, 1981.

Epstein, Barbara. *The Politics of Domesticity: Women, Evangelism and Temperance in Nineteenth Century America.* Middletown, Conn.: Wesleyan University Press, 1981.

Foner, Philip S. *Women and the American Labor Movement From World War I to the Present.* New York: The Free Press, 1980.

Giddings, Paula. *When and Where I Enter: The Impact of Black Women on Race and Sex in America.* New York: William Morrow, 1984. See under *AFRICAN-AMERICAN WOMEN.*

Ginzberg, Lori D. *Women and the Work of Benevolence: Morality, Politics, and Class in the Nineteenth Century United States.* New Haven: Yale University Press, 1990.

In the introduction to this study of women's benevolence, Lori D. Ginzberg states that "to a degree astonishing to our pluralistic society and secular way of thinking about social change, middle and upper-middle class women of the ante-bellum era shared a language that described their benevolent work as Christian, their means as fundamentally moral and their mandate as uniquely female." A large number of middle and upper-middle class women had full time careers in benevolence during this period. Their societies were financially and culturally significant institutions in many large cities. Since their activities often involved government assistance, they necessarily became involved in petititioning and lobbying for new laws and appropriations. Ginzberg looks at the reasons behind female involvement in issues such as temperance, abolition, asylum building, and national relief organizations. She examines the ways in which this participation changed during the nineteenth century. She argues that until the 1850s, these women had been especially conscious of the "female" quality of their work. However, after this time the societies were increasingly aware of the need to stress the efficiency of their work, rather than its femininity if they were to maximize their potential. After the Civil War the ideology of female benevolence did persist, but the younger reformers emphasized the need for business skills and an unsentimental analysis of social ills.

Gordon, Linda. *Woman's Body, Woman's Right: A Social History of Birth Control in America.* New York: Grossman Press, 1976.

Hayden, Delores. *The Grand Domestic Revolution: A History of Feminist Designs for American Homes, Neighborhoods, and Cities.* Cambridge, Mass: MIT Press, 1981.

Hersh, Blanche G. *The Slavery of Sex: Feminist Abolitionists in Nineteenth Century America.* Urbana: University of Illinois Press, 1978

Smedley, Agnes. *Daughter of Earth.* New York: The Feminist Press, 1987.

Raised in the poverty stricken Missouri farmland in the 1890s, Marie Rogers, (who we can read as being Agnes Smedley herself), bears witness to deeply entrenched sexism and classism. She matures in a family fraught by domestic violence, and a community in which a basic level of education is rarely attained. In her late teens, Marie begins her life-long analysis of both the conditions in which working class women must live, and the inequalities within American society. At an early age Marie decides that "love expressed in sex enslaves and humiliates married women," and that this kind of love exacts too high a price to pay for economic protection. She is vehemently opposed to pregnancy, believing that children make the equality of the sexes an impossibility. As the work progresses, Marie struggles to live independently in all senses–economic, political, and emotional. After moving to New York City, her intellectual education coincides with World War I, and the growth of communist and socialist movements. Marie herself becomes involved in the socialist organization the International Workers of the World. This work is a powerful study of one woman attempting to come to terms with what it means to be working class and female in the United States, and the actions she takes to further the cause of human equality.

WOMEN AND WORK

Baxandall, Rosalyn, Linda Gordon, and Susan Reverby, eds. *America's Working Women: A Documentary History–1600 To The*

Present. New York: Vintage Books, A Division of Random House, 1976.

The editors' definition of work includes wage and slave labor, and unpaid household labor. They chose not to examine the work of professional women in this volume, since these women have always been a minority. Instead they decided to "focus on the majority, to correct a political distortion–the virtual exclusion from history of working class women." They "offer this book as a political act . . . to help restore a history to working class women because we believe they can reconstruct society." The materials used in this documentary history include union records, short stories, poems, songs, statistical studies, advertisements, letters, first person narratives, diaries, and social workers' reports. The work is divided into seven chronological periods with the majority of the study concentrating on the nineteenth and twentieth centuries. (Indeed the first half of U.S. history is covered in approximately a tenth of the total pages.) Each chronological period is prefaced by an introductory essay, three to four pages in length, which provides an overview of the era. Then each document is preceded by a couple of paragraphs which provide background information. The range of topics covered is impressive. Included are: an oral history of a slave woman, the rules and regulations governing the behavior of mills girls working for the Lowell Manufacturing Company, letters from black migrants to the North in the early twentieth century, an interview with a prostitute in the 1850s, letters to Margaret Sanger the advocate for birth control at the turn of this century, the diary of a woman welder during World War II, and testimony on the Equal Rights Amendment in 1970.

Benson, Susan Porter. *Counter Cultures: Saleswomen, Managers, and Customers in American Department Stores, 1890-1940*. Urbana: University of Illinois Press, 1986.

Davies, Margery W. *Woman's Place Is At The Typewriter: Office Work and Office Workers, 1870-1930*. Philadelphia: Temple University Press, 1982.

Groneman, Carol and Mary Beth Norton, eds. *To Toil The Livelong*

Day: America's Women at Work, 1780-1980. Ithaca: Cornell University Press, 1987.

Katzman, David. *Seven Days A Week: Women and Domestic Service in Industrializing America.* Urbana: University of Illinois Press, 1981.

Kessler-Harris, Alice. *Out To Work: A History of Wage-Earning Women in the United States.* Oxford: New York: Oxford University Press, 1982.

This scholarly work provides a critical analysis of women's participation in the American labor market from the colonial period to the present. Kessler-Harris explains how the nation's transition from an agricultural, barter economy to one based on industry and free market forces impacted women's work experience. As well as examining many different types of work, Kessler-Harris explores the work experiences of immigrant women, women's involvement in the labor movement, and the ways in which women have attempted to balance their responsibilities in the home and in the workplace. Throughout the work the author highlights employment discrimination against women, and the reasons why most women have consistently taken low-paying, low-status positions. She provides a comprehensive account of the actions that have been taken by women (for example membership in trade unions) and on their behalf (for example protective labor legislation) in order to improve their employment conditions and prospects.

Kessler-Harris, Alice. *Women Have Always Worked: A Historical Overview.* New York: McGraw-Hill, 1982.

Milkman, Ruth. *Gender at Work: The Dynamics of Job Segregation by Sex during World War II.* Urbana: University of Illinois Press, 1987.

Osterud, Nancy Grey. *Bonds of Community: The Lives of Farm Women in Nineteenth Century New York.* Ithaca: Cornell University Press, 1991. See under *A WOMAN'S PLACE*

Sachs, Carolyn E. *The Invisible Farmers: Women in Agricultural Production.* Totowa, NJ: Rowman & Allanheld, 1983.

Schwartz, Ruth Cowan. *More Work For Mother: The Ironies of Household Technology from the Open Hearth to the Microwave.* New York: Basic Books, 1983.

Strasser, Susan. *Never Done: A History of American Housework.* New York: Pantheon, 1982.

Weiner, Lynn Y. *From Working Girl to Working Mother: The Female Labor Force in the United States, 1820-1980.* Chapel Hill: University of North Carolina Press, 1985.

FEMINISM AND WOMEN'S RIGHTS

Buhle, Mary Jo and Paul Buhle, eds. *The Concise History of Woman Suffrage: Selections from the Classic Work of Stanton, Anthony, Gage, and Harper.* Urbana: University of Illinois Press, 1978.

DuBois, Ellen Carol. *Feminism and Suffrage: The Emergence of an Independent Women's Movement in America, 1848-1869.* Ithaca, NY: Cornell University Press, 1978.

DuBois states that her concern in this work is less with how women won the vote, than with how the issue of the vote generated a movement of increasing strength and vitality. In the antebellum era, the struggle for women's rights was only one aspect of reform politics. DuBois examines the slow growth of the movement, and illustrates how the abolitionist movement provided it with invaluable organizational resources, and opportunities for women to learn how to manage a large campaign. She then explores the reasons behind the split between these two groups in the post-bellum period, and looks at the relationship between the advocates of women's rights and both the political parties and working class women. This work provides a significant contribution to this field, however it should be pointed out that it does not adequately appreciate the importance of other organization's (such as temperance) upon the growth of the movement. Also there is a strong East coast bias, which results in too much emphasis on the role of leadership, and too little attention to the grass roots support.

Flexnor, Eleanor. *A Century of Struggle: The Woman's Rights Movement in the United States* 1959, rev. ed., Cambridge, MA: The Belknap Press, 1975.

This work was written by a woman outside of the academy, before the women's rights movements of the 1960s had influenced the work of social historians. Today it remains one of the most interesting and accessible accounts of the early women's rights movement. The author explains that the work was not intended to be "a history of American women, or a rounded sociological study of the changes that gradually took place in their status." For this reason she provides only a brief survey of their lives during the colonial and revolutionary periods, before the women's rights movement itself can be properly said to have begun. She then traces the movement from its beginnings in the mid-nineteenth century, to the enactment of the Nineteenth Amendment in 1920. As well as giving a well researched account of the movement itself, Flexnor also provides excellent portraits of the women responsible for the movement, their relations with each other, and their unwavering commitment to their cause.

Lerner, Gerda. *The Grimke Sisters from South Carolina: Pioneers for Woman's Rights and Abolition.* New York: Schocken, 1966.

IMMIGRANT WOMEN

Deutsch, Sara. *No Separate Refuge: Culture, Class, and Gender on the Anglo-Hispanic Frontier in the American Southwest, 1880-1940.* New York: Oxford University Press, 1987.

In the introduction to *No Separate Refuge,* Sara Deutsch states that as she conducted her research, she found that her basic hypothesis–that Hispanic women, being so oppressed in their villages would find the move North for wage labor to be a liberating experience–was being undermined. She then realized that due to the gap in historical work on Hispanic women, she had accepted conventional stereotypes about their lives, and that these stereotypes were far from accurate. Deutsch's detailed study of the traditional Hispanic community, shows that women had a great deal of autonomy, independence, and respect. Their status became far more tenuous when they had to work for wages, in the mining towns and sugar beet fields in Colorado. Here, not only did they make less money than their husbands, but they were also unable to perform their traditional functions–such as raising animals and tending a garden. As well as looking at these two distinct areas of the female Hispanic experience, Deutsch also examines the relationship between these women and the female Protestant missionaries that went out west at the end of the nineteenth century. Unlike previous historians, Deutsch illustrates that the Hispanic women did not accept wholesale the advice of the missionaries concerning childcare, and household responsibilities. Rather, they selected what they wanted from Anglo women, for example help with health care, and the education of their children. This work, although intended for an academic audience is quite accessible, and provides a fascinating portrayal of the experiences of an immigrant group that has often been ignored.

Diner, Hasia. *Erin's Daughters in America.* Baltimore: Johns Hopkins University Press, 1983.

In the first part of *Erin's Daughters,* Diner examines Irish society before the Great Famine of the 1840s and the mass migration to the United States. She pays particular attention to gender roles, and shows that although the society was patriarchal, women did exercise authority over domestic spending, child care, and the decision to migrate. Irish migration in the nineteenth century can be differentiated from that of other groups by the fact that more than half of all migrants were female, and many of these women were single. The main reasons for this were both the shortage of land in Ireland, and the vigorous recruiting of young women by American factories. If they chose not to work in factories or mills, single women invariably worked as domestics, work that provided them with a safe and healthy environment, and wages that allowed them to pay for the passage of other family members. Since marriage promised only economic hardship and constant motherhood, many of these women followed old world patterns of late marriage, or spinsterhood. Diner illustrates that Irish women were very active in the labor movement since it was culturally acceptable for women to be assertive in the market-place. She also examines the role of religion in these women's lives, and the support societies that they established to benefit the Irish community. This work is both comprehensive and highly readable.

Ewen, Elizabeth. *Immigrant Women in the Land of Dollars.* New York: Monthly Review Press, 1985.

In this work, Elizabeth Ewen examines the experiences of the Jewish and Italian women who settled in the Lower East Side at the turn of the century. Particularly central to the study are the ways in which migration affected women's roles and responsibilities both within their family and in the larger ethnic community, women's relationship with Americans (in particular social workers), and mother-daughter relations. Ewen also examines the ways in which young immigrant women attempted to balance their desire to maximize their opportunities for work and enter-tainment, while simultaneously fulfilling their more traditional duties. *Immigrant Women in the Land of Dollars* is both well-written and very accessible.

Maxine Schwartz Seller, ed. *Immigrant Women.* Philadelphia: Temple University Press, 1981.

This work provides a wide variety of materials about immigrant women who have settled in the United States, from all parts of the world, during the past one hundred and fifty years. The majority of documents included are first person accounts, or materi-als by relatives, sympathetic social workers, or researchers who had direct contact with the women themselves. Also included are excerpts from novels, short stories, and oral histories. The work is divided into eight sections including "Why They Came," "Work," "Family," and "Social Activists." There is an introduc-tory essay before each section, which provides an historical and scholarly context for the selections that follow. Brief head-notes precede each selection. The work illustrates women's par-ticipation in their own institutions, such as church societies and ethnic and cultural organizations, their struggles to adapt to life in a new society while maintaining as many old world customs as possible, their relations with their families and communities, and their experiences in the labor market and on the frontier.

Smith, Judith. *Family Connections.* Albany: State University of New York at Albany Press, 1985.

Judith Smith notes that in the process of migration, family ties directed immigrants from communities in Europe to particular cities and neighborhoods in the United States. In this work she examines the significance of family relations in the lives of Jewish and Italian families who migrated to Providence, Rhode Island at the turn of the century. She focuses in particular on the types of work taken by parents and children, the economic cooperation of the extended family's members, and parent-child relations and responsibilities. *Family Connections* provides a large amount of information about women's roles at home, as well as the economic contributions they made to the family through taking care of boarders, and taking in piece work. It also illustrates how daughters were able to take jobs in factories, since their mothers generally lived close by and were able to take care of the children. Also, their fluency in English and their familiarity with American culture enabled them to get jobs in offices and department stores. Like Ewen's work, *Immigrant Women in the Land of Dollars,* this work is both informative and accessible.

PIONEER WOMEN

Faragher, John Mack. *Women and Men on the Overland Trail.* New Haven: Yale University Press, 1979.

For this study, Faragher examined the personal narratives of almost two hundred men and women, as means of determining the impact of the move westward upon male and female roles, responsibilities, and status. Faragher argues that both on the trail and once settled out west, most wives worked an equal number of hours as their husbands. However, the former were not accorded equal status in any sphere–social, political, or economic. The women were excluded from the council meetings on the trail, and once settled out west their involvement in the public sphere was equally restricted. An analysis of men's journals shows that they evinced little regard for their wives work, since it was not related directly to the production of marketable goods. Faragher notes that the isolation felt by many women is illustrated by their frequent use of the word "I" in their letters, diaries, and journals. This is in marked contrast to the men's frequent use of the word "we." This study is quite accessible, and provides a vivid portrayal of life on the overland trail.

Hampsten, Elizabeth. *Read This Only To Yourself: The Private Writings of Midwestern Women, 1880-1910.* Bloomington: Indiana University Press, 1982.

Jeffrey, Julia F. *Pioneer Women: The Trans-Mississippi West, 1840-1880.* New York: Hill and Wang, 1979.

In this work Julia F. Jeffrey illustrates how the experiences of pioneer women were shaped by their cultural perspective. In particular she discusses the impact of the "cult of domesticity," and the dominant notion of women's role as guardians of moral and cultural values upon the roles, status, and identity of these women. Jeffrey admits that when she started research for the book, she had hoped to discover that pioneer women would have tried to "liberate themselves from stereotypes and behavior which I found constricting and sexist." However, it soon became apparent that although thousands of women did assume "male" responsibilities when necessary, the vast majority chose not to "disrupt cultural arrangements between the sexes and question sexual ideology." Instead they "found comfort and reinforcement in their own sphere," no matter how far short of its standards they may have fallen. Jeffrey is clearly left with a profound respect for the women that worked so hard to create some semblance of normalcy for their families in conditions that were often extremely difficult.

Kaufman, Polly Welts. *Women Teachers on the Frontier.* New Haven: Yale University Press, 1984.

Riley, Glenda. *The Female Frontier: A Comparative View Of Women And Men On The Prairie And The Plains.* Wichita: University of Kansas Press, 1988.

Glenda Riley was the first historian to illustrate a consistent "female frontier," that existed irrespective of time or place. She argues that the experiences and responsibilities of all women moving west, were shaped primarily by gender. In contrast, men's frontier experience was shaped by the geography and resources, by the presence of prairie, gold, or cattle. Even for those women who were not married, their experiences were limited to the opportunities available to them *as women.* Examining the diaries, letters, and daybooks of prairie and plains women, Riley illustrates that the female frontier had its own mode of operation, culture, and value system. She argues that although there were slight differences in how women's chores were accomplished according to region and era, the important point is that these chores were *always* women's work. Factors such as race, social class, and religion did not alter this fact. Clearly women's lives on the plains and prairies were far more alike than different.

Stratton, Joanna. *Pioneer Women: Voices From The Kansas Frontier.* New York: Simon and Schuster, 1981.

Pioneer Women is based upon the memoirs of approximately eight hundred Kansas pioneer women, which were gathered by Stratton's grandmother during the 1920s. The majority of these women were Protestant wives and mothers, whose lives revolved around the home, and who had a "firm dedication to the welfare of their families and to ultimately civilizing the frontier itself." The work provides an excellent portrayal of the everyday chores and responsibilities of these women, as well as a comprehensive account of the difficulties faced by them in times of drought, floods, fires, Indian raids, and grasshopper invasions. Stratton also evaluates the status of pioneer women in comparison to the women back East, and concludes that the former were on a more equal footing with men.

AFRICAN-AMERICAN WOMEN

Fox-Genovese, Elizabeth. *Within the Plantation Household: Black and White Women of the Old South.* Chapel Hill: University of North Carolina Press, 1988.

Giddings, Paula. *When and Where I Enter: The Impact of Race & Sex in America.* Toronto, New York: Bantom Books, 1984.

Giddings argues that until her book, black women were invariably token women in black texts, and token blacks in feminist ones. This treatment has been far from adequate since black women have a distinct history of their own that reflects their particular concerns, values, and contributions to American society. Giddings draws on the speeches, diaries, and letters of black women as well as periodical literature. She acknowledges that this may have biased the history somewhat, since these materials reflect the experiences of the literate, who were themselves a minority. The majority of this work is devoted to the post-Civil War period. Prominent in the text are black women's involvement in clubs and associations organized to improve the health, education and morality of their community; their involvement in the movements for female suffrage and later women's liberation, and their relationship with the white women who formed the majority of these movements. She illustrates their participation in the various periods of struggle for civil rights, and examines their attempts to adequately fulfill their role as wife and mother while working outside of the home in menial and low-paying jobs. Throughout the work Giddings examines the status and identity of black women both in their community and society at large, and looks at their attempts both to fit and to redefine society's image and understanding of what it means to be black and female.

Janiewski, Dolores. *Sisterhood Denied: Race, Gender, and Class in a New South Community.* Philadelphia: Temple University Press, 1985.

Jones, Jacqueline. *Labor of Love, Labor of Sorrow: Black Women, Work, and the Family from Slavery to the Present.* New York: Basic Books. 1985.

Jones argues that throughout the 1970s, there was a northeastern bias implicit in much of the scholarship of feminist historians, and an over-riding concern with the impact of industrialization upon women's lives. Since the vast majority of African-American women in the nineteenth century and early twentieth century were slaves and/or southern agricultural laborers, rather than industrial workers or middle class consumers, they were omitted from the historical landscape. Throughout her work Jones examines the myths and realities of African-American women's lives, the consequences of the double discrimination they have perpetually faced both as slaves and since the Civil War, the distinctive nature of both black and black women's culture, and the ways in which black women have constantly sought opportunities that would enable them to subjugate the demands being made by their employers to the requirements of their families, and the contributions they have made to their communities economically, politically and spiritually.

Lerner, Gerda. *Black Women in White America: A Documentary History.* New York: Vintage Books, 1973.

Moody, Anne. *Coming of Age in Mississippi.* New York: A Laurel Book, Bantom Dell Doubleday Publishing Inc. 1968.

This autobiography of a black woman growing up in Mississippi during the 1950s, powerfully illustrates what it means to have grown up in a segregated society, where the black community is constantly plagued by poverty and white violence in the form of harassment, arson, lynchings, police brutality, and hypocrisy. Anne Moody recognizes at an early age that something is not quite right in southern society. She spends much time and effort trying to uncover the secret behind white superiority, and the superiority that "yellow" African Americans feel over their darker neighbors. As she matures, her curiosity turns to anger at the injustice that is apparent everywhere. At college she joins the movement for civil rights that is evolving on campuses across the South. She is actively involved in student chapters of the NAACP, CORE, and SNCC, despite the threats that her family receive from her home town sheriff that she would be unable to return home if she continued to participate in the "Movement." This work is remarkable for its straightforward prose, and the insight it provides into the black community, the lives of black women, the grass roots of the civil rights movement, and race relations in the South at this critical moment in the nation's history.

Sterling, Dorothy. *We Are Your Sisters: Black Women in the Nineteenth Century.* New York: W.W. Norton & Co., 1984.

Walker, Margaret. *Jubilee.* Boston, Mass: Bantom Books, Houghton Mifflin Co, 1966.

This novel provides a refreshing alternative to the majority of novels set at the time of the Civil War. The novel's protagonist is Vyry, the daughter of a plantation owner and his favorite black mistress. The first third of the novel provides much insight into Southern society in the ante-bellum period, including everyday life on a plantation, the relations between the slaves and their masters and overseers, and gender relations in both the slave community and "The Big House." The second third is devoted to the impact of the Civil War on the plantation, and the experiences of Vyry's husband, a free black as he works for the northern war effort as a blacksmith in Tennessee. In the final part Vyry tries to establish a new life in Alabama for herself, her family and her second husband during Reconstruction. The obstacles to their progress are severe, not the least of them including poverty, and intimidation from the Ku Klux Klan. Yet Vyry herself never loses hope that some day her children will achieve an education, and will not suffer in the ways her generation were forced to.

White, Deborah. *Ar'n't I A Woman: Female Slaves and the Plantation South.* New York: W.W. Norton, 1985.

Until the publication of *Ar'n't I A Woman,* and Jacqueline Jones' *Labor of Love, Labor of Sorrow,* historians had defined the slave experience solely in terms of the lives of male slaves. White illustrates that the experience of female slaves was quite distinct from that of their male relatives. She examines the threefold responsibilities of these women: their work in the fields and in the "Big House"; the duties they carried out in their own family, cooking, cleaning, sewing, child care; and their roles within the slave community, healing and mid-wifery. She also looks at the relations between the slave women. Generally cooperation was very common, yet there were incidences of rivalry for men and positions, violence, and witchcraft. Finally White looks at slave women's experiences as wives and mothers, including marriage rituals, childbirth, the gender division of labor, divorce, and the frequent fears of being separated from a spouse. This work is extremely accessible.

THE TWENTIETH CENTURY

Anderson, Karen Tucker. *Wartime Women: Sex Roles, Family Relations, and the Status of Women During World War II.* Westport, CT: Greenwood Press, 1981.

Campbell, D'Ann. *Women at War With America: Private Lives in a Patriotic Era.* Cambridge, MA: Harvard University Press, 1984.

Hartman, Susan M. *American Women in the 1940s: The Homefront and Beyond.* Boston: Twayne Publishing, 1982.

May, Elaine Tyler. *Great Expectations: Marriage and Divorce in Post-Victorian America.* Chicago: University of Chicago Press, 1981.

In this scholarly work, Elaine Tyler May examines both the reasons for the enormous increase in the divorce rate during the late nineteenth and early twentieth centuries, and also how the reasons for divorce altered during this time. She argues that the reason given by most historians for the increase in the divorce rate–the rise of the women's rights movement–is too simplistic, and fails to adequately address the complex issue of changing gender roles, and the way in which social forces such as urbanization, and commercialization impacted the private sphere. May's sources include extensive complaint forms of over 750 divorce cases in Los Angeles and New Jersey, as well as numerous letters between the spouses and their friends, and statements of witnesses, doctors, and social workers. The work provides an interesting and persuasive account of this phenomena.

Scharf, Lois. *To Work and Wed: Female Employment, Feminism, and the Great Depression.* Westport, CT: Greenwood Press, 1980.

Ware, Susan. *American Women in the 1930s: Holding Their Own.* Boston: Twayne Publishing, 1982.

Westin, Jeanne. *Making Do: How Women Survived the Depression.* Chicago: Follett Publishing Co., 1976.

THE MODERN WOMEN'S RIGHTS MOVEMENT

Cott, Nancy. *The Grounding of Modern Feminism.* New Haven, Conn: Yale University Press, 1987.

In this scholarly work Cott challenges the notion that after the passage of the Nineteenth Amendment there was a rapid loss of interest in women's rights. She argues instead that this period was one of transition, during which time the major issues of modern feminists were first articulated. Some of the topics in this work include the formation and growth of the National Women's Party, and the nature of voluntarist politics during the 1920s, during which time women lobbied for health, safety, moral and welfare issues via women's clubs and associations. Cott examines the conflict between those arguing for the passage of an Equal Rights Amendment, and those who felt that this would erode critical protective legislation. She also examines the impact of birth control and smaller families, urbanization, and the growth of mass consumerism, upon the experiences of women. She illustrates that then as now one of the most important questions for women was how they were to combine the responsibilities at home and in the work place.

Evans, Sara. *Personal Politics: The Roots of Women's Liberation in the Civil Rights Movement and the New Left.* New York: Alfred A. Knopf, 1979.

Personal Politics provides an examination of the origins of the women's liberation movement of the late 1960s and early 1970s. As well as using traditional literary and archival sources of information, Evans also draws upon her interviews with dozens of women across the United States who had been involved in the civil rights movement, the New Left (student movement), and finally women's liberation. Looking at the civil rights movement, she examines the reasons behind white women's involvement, real and imagined differences in the roles and responsibilities of black and white women in organizations such as the Student Non-Violence Coordinating Committee, and the tensions that led to white students leaving these organizations. In the New Left, Evans argues that movement women experienced rampant sexism, most evident in the sexual division of labor, and the way in which women were invariably called upon to work in background organization and community projects, but were rarely involved in policy formulation and the writing of position papers. Their frustration at these arrangements combined with the confidence they had gained in years of organizing to persuade them that they had to create their own movement to address their own concerns, and to challenge the inequality they experienced as women both in society and in their personal lives.

Friedan, Betty. *The Feminine Mystique.*

This book, which was to become one of the classic texts of the modern women's movement, originated from responses to a questionnaire Friedan sent to her Smith College classmates in 1957, fifteen years after graduation. These responses confirmed to Friedan that she was not alone in experiencing a great difference between the reality of her own life, and the image to which women were supposed to be conforming–the image which she called "the feminine mystique." Everywhere women turned in postwar America they "heard voices of tradition and of Freudian sophistication informing them that they could desire no greater destiny than to glory in their own femininity." They were told that the truly feminine woman "does not want a career, higher education, political rights, and independence and opportunity that old fashioned feminists fought for." Yet Friedan discovered that the vast majority of her housewife classmates, as well as those women she later interviewed for the book, expressed dissatisfaction with their lives.

Friedan explores the roots of "the feminine mystique," and the reasons why it became so powerful in the 1940s-50s. Some of the areas she focuses on include: American society's need for security in the post-war period, the impact of the advertising industry, women's magazines and mass consumerism, the role of Freud and the functionalists, sex-directed education, "the sexual sell," and the rise and fall of feminism. The work ends with a plea that women start to reassert their sense of self and their individuality, and begin on the difficult path to the realization of their full potential.

Friedan, Betty. *It Changed My Life: Writings on the Women's Movement.* New York: W.W. Norton, 1985.

In the introduction to this work, Friedan writes that more than twenty years after the publication of *The Feminine Mystique,* women continue to tell her how it changed their lives. For Friedan, also, the publication of the book ensured that her life would inevitably be linked to the modern women's rights movement. *It Changed My Life* contains a wide variety of materials including excerpts from the letters that Friedan received after the publication of *The Feminist Mystique,* excerpts of feminist speeches she gave to gatherings throughout the late 1960s and early 1970s, articles written during this period about abortion, the Equal Rights Amendment, the Women's Strike for Equality in 1970, the creation of the National Women's Political Caucus, and Friedan's testimony against Nixon's appointment of Judge Carswell to the Supreme Court. In the section entitled the Betty Friedan Notebooks, 1971-73, Friedan reflects on marriage, the movement, and the nature of sexuality. The final section of the book contains essays about her meetings with Pope Paul, Simone de Beauvoir, and Indira Gandhi.

Morgan, Robin. ed. *Sisterhood Is Powerful: An Anthology of Writings from the Women's Liberation Movement.* New York: Random House, 1970.

Acknowledged as one of the most widely read books of the women's movement, this work contains essays, poems, and critical reviews covering all aspects of women's experiences. In the section entitled *The Oppressed Majority* topics include women in the professions, "the secretarial proletariat," women and welfare, and women and the Catholic Church. *The Invisible Woman* contains work on media images of women, birth control and female liberation, lesbianism and prostitution. *Changing Consciousness* includes essays on women in the black liberation movement, and Chicana women. There are also a significant number of women's liberation documents, including the National Organization of Women Bill of Rights, Principles of the New York Radical Women, and the Redstockings Manifesto.

SPECIAL TOPICS

Female Sexuality

Banner, Lois W. *American Beauty.* New York: Alfred A. Knopf, 1983.

In *American Beauty,* Lois Banner looks at what the fashion and beauty norms of any particular era reveal about American society's beliefs and expectations concerning the behavior, status, and identity of women. The sources used are extensive and include contemporary diaries, autobiographies, novels, fashion magazines, beauty and etiquette manuals, foreign travellers' accounts, and general periodical literature. The bulk of the work is concerned with the period 1800-1920, during which time the major institutions of American beauty culture were established. Some of the issues the author addresses include the origins of fashion ideas, and the ways in which these ideas permeate society in general, the constant battle between fashion and feminists, the role of the beauty contest, and the development of the modern fashion business. Although the vast majority of the work concerns the relationship between women and fashion, one chapter is devoted to the changing male fashions and standards of attractiveness, and illustrates what fascinations with beards, cigarette and cigar smoking, and sports, can tell us about the changing masculine ideal.

Barker-Benfield, G.J. *The Horrors of the Half Known Life: Male Attitudes Towards Women and Sexuality in Nineteenth Century America.* New York: Harper and Row, 1976.

D'Emilio, John and Freedman, Estelle B. *Intimate Matters: A History of Sexuality in America.* New York: Harper and Row, 1988.

Birth Control and Abortion

Gordon, Linda. *Woman's Body, Woman's Right: A Social History of Birth Control in America.* New York: Grossman, 1976.

Mohr, James C. *Abortion in America: The Origins and Evolution of National Policy, 1800-1900.* Oxford, New York: Oxford University Press, 1978.

This history of abortion in the United States, from 1800 to the present provides a balanced, chronological account of a highly controversial subject. Until 1800 "no jurisdiction in the United States had enacted any statutes on the subject of abortion" and in the absence of any statutes, abortion was governed by traditional British common law, which permitted abortion until quickening– or the first perception of fetal movement by the woman herself. During the nineteenth century a number of states began enacting abortion legislation. The author provides a cogent account of the role of the medical profession in the rapid increase in this legislation, stemming from their threefold desire to oust their competitors (non-qualified "quacks"), to establish professional standards and ethics, and to recapture their place among society's policy makers. Not only did the medical profession seek to eliminate the traditional quickening rules, and to revoke common law immunities for women seeking abortions, but they also enlisted the peripheral powers of the state to prevent the advertisement of abortion services that provided many women with their only source of information about abortion assistance. This work is reasonably accessible, and provides a fascinating look at the intersection between personal lives, public policy, and the political impact of wealthy interest groups.

REFERENCE BOOKS

Buhle, Mary Jo. *Women and the American Left: A Guide to the Sources.* Boston: G.K. Hall, 1983.

This annotated bibliography covers the period, 1871-1981. The 595 entries are concerned with the struggles of American women for the equality of the sexes, as well as their involvement in the labor movement. The materials are arranged within four major periods of the American Left: 1871-1900, 1901-1919, 1920-1964, and 1965-1981. Within each of these periods sources are grouped under specific headings: general works and histories, autobiographies and biographies, books and pamphlets that address the "Women Question," and periodicals with a socialist-feminist content, and works of fiction. The annotations provide a comprehensive account of the contents of each work. There is a combined subject, title, and author index.

Conway, Jill K. *The Female Experience in Eighteenth and Nineteenth Century America: A Guide to the History of American Women.* With the assistance of Linda Kealey and Janet E. Schulte. New York: Garland, 1982.

This work is arranged according to six broad subject sections: American culture and society 1750-1840; industrialization and women's work, 1810-1910; women's religious life, 1790-1860; women and politics, 1776-1930; and biology and domestic life, 1830-1900. Rather than simply listing her annotated citations, Conway has written many informative and interesting bibliographic essays in which she discusses the contributions of each work to the field. This work is accessible and useful for both academic historians and lay readers alike.

Harrison, Cynthia et al. *Women in American History: A Bibliography.* 2 vols. Santa Barbara, CA: ABC-Clio, 1979-85.

This work contains over 7,000 abstracts from about 600 serials and anthologies. The vast majority of entries were selected from *America: History and Life,* (1964-84). The majority of the material is arranged topically within chronological divisions, with a number of sections devoted to teaching and research, general works, and regional studies. The subject index is broad ranging and well organized. There is also an author index. Users of this work need to bear in mind that subjects covering more than two periods will appear in the "general works" section.

Kennedy, Susan Estabrook. *America's White Working Class Women: A Historical Bibliography.* New York: Garland. 1981.

This bibliography points users towards information concerning women in a wide variety of occupations. It is arranged chronologically, and is sub-divided into topics such as employment, community, and class. The citations are to papers, dissertations, books, articles and government documents. The well organized subject index should ensure that this work is fully utilized.

Krichmar, Albert. *The Women's Rights Movement in the United States, 1848-1970.* A Bibliography and Sourcebook. Metchuen. NJ: Scarecrow Press, 1972.

This work lists over 5,000 works covering the legal, political, economic, religious, educational, and professional status of women. The books, articles, and government documents are arranged by subject with author and subject indexes. One chapter describes over 400 manuscripts and has its own index. Especially noteworthy is the biography section, which contains citations on a number of women not included in *Notable American Women.*

Papachristou. Judith. *Bibliography in the History of Women in the Progressive Era.* Bronxville, NY: Sarah Lawrence College, 1985.

This bibliography cites nearly 650 secondary sources concerning women during 1890-1930. It is arranged into nine broad subjects areas including "Gender and the Family," "Feminism and Suffrage," and "Minority Women." The emphasis is on social, economic and political works, rather than works on art and literature. Most of the entries are books, articles, and chapters from books. Dissertations are not included. The citations are not annotated which is a drawback, although the subject index will undoubtedly help to improve access.

Sims, Janet L. *The Progress of Afro-American Women: A Selected Bibliography and Resource Guide.* Westport, CT: Greenwood Press, 1980.

This unannotated bibliography lists more than 4,000 titles concerning the position of black women within 34 subject areas including education, family life, science, and sex. It includes dissertations, books, and articles (many of these articles are taken from black journals or newspapers). This work is a much needed addition to the field of women's history, which until recently failed to pay adequate attention to minority women. It is not a definitive work, but provides an excellent starting point.

Watson, G. Llewellyn. *Feminism and Women's Issues: An Annotated Bibliography and Research Guide.* New York: Garland, 1990.

This two volume 2,000 page bibliography is divided into broad subject areas, all of which have many sub-headings. Examples of the subjects included are "Women and Education," "Women and Health," and "Sexism." Many works are cross referenced. There is no author or title index, which could be problematic.

Acquisition of Feminist Books in Community College and Public Libraries: A Discussion and a Study

Laura Pattison

Laura Pattison

SUMMARY. It is important for libraries to take account of the influence of feminism, in order to fully serve their communities of users. This article discusses library acquisition of feminist books and reports on a study undertaken to examine the extent to which feminist materials have been purchased and made available to library users. The specific purpose of the study was measurement of acquisitions of non-fiction books listed in core bibliographies of feminist books, by nine public and community college libraries.

INTRODUCTION

Libraries exist in a social context and adapt to shifts in structures and consciousness. This keeps the missions of libraries meaningful

Laura Pattison currently works at the New York State Library in Albany, NY.

[Haworth co-indexing entry note]: "Acquisition of Feminist Books in Community College and Public Libraries: A Discussion and a Study," Pattison, Laura. Co-published simultaneously in *The Acquisitions Librarian* (The Haworth Press, Inc.) No. 9/10, 1993, pp. 309-322; and: *Multicultural Acquisitions* (ed: Karen Parrish and Bill Katz) The Haworth Press, Inc., 1993, pp. 309-322. Multiple copies of this article/chapter may be purchased from The Haworth Document Delivery Center. Call 1-800-3-HAWORTH (1-800-342-9678) between 9:00 - 5:00 (EST) and ask for DOCUMENT DELIVERY CENTER.

and is a necessity for political and fiscal viability. Selection of materials for library collections must reflect the changing demographies and requirements of users, who continually adapt to new conditions or perceptions of their lives. At some points, retrospective and current collection development activity may be necessary to extend and hasten the library's response to a changed condition or awareness.

Discussions of multiculturalism and diversity, taking place on many levels of society simultaneously, represent a change in consciousness, or rather a changed level of action taken as a result of longstanding critiques. Academic libraries have been impacted by challenges to the canon and changes in curricular materials. However, all libraries must address the questions raised by diversity discussions. It is important in this context for libraries to assess whether their collections have kept pace with a major influence of the twentieth century, the changes in conditions and awareness due to feminism.

In the last thirty years, feminism and the women's movement have had tremendous impact on individuals, institutions, and the "collective consciousness." It has been and will continue to be important for libraries to address the influence of feminism, in order to fully serve their communities of users. The women's movement has led to, and been stimulated by, a tremendous increase in numbers of books published by and about women. DuBois states that:

> feminist scholars are engaged in almost an archaeological endeavor–that of discovering and uncovering the actual facts of women's lives and experience, facts that have been hidden, inaccessible, suppressed, distorted, misunderstood, ignored.[1]

The digging process above has uncovered information and literature in need of publication. It has also revealed that many previously published works were not well distributed or are out of print. Libraries must thus not only consider the volume of new feminist works in making acquisitions decisions but must recognize and respond to historical and current inequities in production and dissemination of feminist publications.

ACQUISITIONS AND SERVICES

In an article regarding public library response to the profusion of materials by and about women, Dagg touched on both of these challenges. The author's primary focus in this case was library purchases of books written by women, regardless of subject, but feminist books were included in the discussion. In a study of acquisition of fiction and non-fiction books by six Canadian public libraries, it was found that in all cases, fewer purchases of books by women were made than of books by men.[2] Dagg described problems of access to women's materials rooted in discrimination in publishing and book reviewing. These difficulties make it all the more important for libraries to take initiative when purchasing materials by and about women, representing these in selection and acquisition policies and activities.

Feminist voices are essential to women first, as a validation of experiences and contributions too long invisible in our cultural record. But feminist works, through critiques of society and articulation of alternatives, can offer visions of an equitable society, healthier for women, children and men. According to the ALA *Library Bill of Rights,* library resources should be provided for all the people a library serves.[3] These resources should represent all points of view on current and historical issues. All members of society are diminished by lack of access to feminist publications. An ARBA review of a bibliography of women's studies material emphasizes the need for all libraries to reshape their existing collection policies to reflect the reality that the selection and purchase of "woman-related materials" will improve the total collection.[4]

The dynamic of changing user demands and library service was discussed by Parikh and Broidy who describe the women's movement as an excellent example of community impact upon the goals of the public library.[5] Because the women's movement has encouraged women to reclaim their lives and their history, there is potential for increased use of resources in libraries, *if women find these institutions responsive.* Libraries cannot afford to remain isolated from a popular movement with real and answerable information needs.[6] The authors state that adequate service, including provision of current materials on women, is achievable only when libraries integrate women's concerns into the full range of their activities, including acquisitions, cataloging functions, indexing, collection development, and programming. Parikh and Broidy call on academic libraries to play an activist role in supporting women's studies programs and serving female users. According to Schuman and Detlefsen, librarians have a vital role to play by recognizing the process of consciousness raising and the very real, everyday issues that oppress women.[7]

The responsibility of libraries to collect and make available information by women was discussed as well in an article by Emery. The context for collection development activities in academic libraries is once again, the growth of women's studies and the expansion of literature dealing with women. According to Emery, many teachers, scholars and librarians have failed to keep pace with the trends and implications of this expansion.[8] The author emphasized the need for librarians working in collection development and reference, in particular, to understand the parameters, origins, and research potential of a "revolution of interest in women."[9] It is the role of the academic library to make these materials available to the academic community and inform students and scholars of both the existence of these holdings and of a willingness to make feminist materials and services available. Emery states that the librarian holds ultimate responsibility for developing adequate library resources to support the women's studies curriculum, reference service and bibliographic instruction.[10]

REMEDIES AND EVALUATION

Williamson, Rafter and Cohen-Rose, directly addressed the responsibilities outlined above. They described the "mainstreaming" approach, used at Northeastern and Swarthmore to integrate women's studies materials into standard courses. The goal of mainstreaming is to build women's studies collections and increase access to these. The mainstreaming method was developed due to the belief that separate women's studies courses could no longer adequately expose students to the vast amount of information available on women.[11] To remedy this problem, library personnel supervised student researchers in the production of bibliographies of women's studies materials for individual professors and courses. In this way, resources were identified for curricular and collection development purposes, facilitating increased awareness and potentially use of women's studies materials. The program illustrates the efforts of two academic libraries to both improve services to their community of users and take initiative in responding to changes in the volume and nature of feminist materials for acquisition purposes.

For most libraries, evaluation of the current collection will precede the setting of collection development goals. A 1978 study at Arizona State University combined quantitative description of the women's studies and other collections with survey techniques, used to determine student and faculty satisfaction with the extent of and access to materials.[12] Data was collected by checking a total of nine bibliographies against library holdings. The study described below was completed using a similar method to obtain current data on the acquisitions of feminist books by nine public and community college libraries.

THE STUDY

An extensive literature search was undertaken to locate two or more authoritative core bibliographies. Though many bibliographies of feminist materials exist, most were not appropriate for use in this study, being either too general or specific, not current or unannotated. The bibliography which was chosen for use actually consists of reduced sections of two related bibliographies: *Women's Studies: A Recommended Core Bibliography*[13] and *Women's Studies: A Recommended Core Bibliography: 1980-85.*[14]

The bibliographies above were published "to offer a checklist against which libraries can evaluate their holdings."[15] The sections in each which were chosen for use are titled, "Women's Movement and Feminist Theory." Lists of titles in these sections are included at the end of this article. The non-fiction titles selected for study from the bibliographies shared these characteristics: publication in the United States; subject matter on women or feminism in the United States; publication between 1975-1985.

Collections of four community colleges and five public libraries were assessed for purposes of the study. These libraries are members of a regional library council and contribute holdings to a CD-ROM union catalog. All community colleges in the council were included in the study. Public libraries in the council that serve twenty-five to fifty thousand users were also examined.

To measure acquisition of books listed in the bibliographies selected for use, titles were compared with the holding of the libraries studied. The shared CD-ROM catalog was utilized to efficiently make this comparison, allowing simultaneous searching of the library collections. Books were searched by title, and by author if no citation was found with a title search. Data obtained through bibliographic checking of the nine libraries is summarized in three tables below. These tables display data comparing: percentage of match in the libraries studied; differences between the community college and public libraries; number of libraries acquiring books searched. For the most part, figures reflect total percentages for libraries studied rather than data regarding acquisition of particular titles included on the bibliographies used.

Table I provides figures representing title matches between the bibliographies and library collections. These figures allow comparison of individual library data as well as analysis of differences between the community college and public libraries studied. Both types of libraries exhibited a range of percentage of match between the bibliographies and the collection holdings. The range was broader by 4.1 percentage points in the case of public libraries. Community college libraries divided evenly, with two libraries showing percentages above the median (10.25) and two falling below. Four of the five public libraries, however, fell below the public library median (11.66). The lowest percentage of match was

TABLE I. MATCH OF INDIVIDUAL LIBRARIES WITH BIBLIOGRAPHY

| | Community College | | | | | Public | | | | |
	#1	#2	#3	#4		#1	#2	#3	#4	#5
Titles Matching Bibliography	0	5.0	21.0	21.0		2.0	5.0	27.0	10.0	12.0
Percentage of Match with Bibliography	0	5.2	21.9	21.9		2.1	5.2	28.1	10.4	12.5
Median	10.25					11.66				
Range	0 - 21.9					2.1 - 28.1				

found in the community college category; the highest percent noted for a public library. This high percentage, however provided the only instance where the match exceeded twenty-five percent, or one quarter of the total titles on the core bibliographies.

A complete evaluation of a library's selection of feminist materials would require further data collection and consideration of the particularities of each library. However, the percentages of match may indicate a situation requiring attention. One community college library had acquired none of the titles, bringing to one-third the number of libraries studied who had less than ten percent of the titles in their collection. In all cases except one, more than three quarters of books listed on the bibliographies were not purchased by the libraries studied.

When using the above method of collection assessment, it is necessary to consider potential limitations of the bibliographies utilized, to fully evaluate results. The titles examined were drawn from extensive bibliographies intended perhaps for academic collections. To determine, thus, if the bibliography was more appropriate for either the community college or public library, totals were combined for each type of library (see Table II).

The figures above indicate numbers and percentages of titles found only in the community college or public libraries studied. Figures are also given to show overlap between the two types of libraries, either for titles found or not found in either. The percentage of titles found in community college libraries alone is seen to be just one percent higher than the percentage found only in public libraries. The fact, however, that 56.3% of titles were found in *neither* type of library examined does not support the idea that the bibliography was more appropriate for either the community college or public libraries studied.

While analysis was generally not completed for individual titles, to further examine if low percentages were due to library acquisi-

TABLE II. COMPARISON OF COMMUNITY COLLEGE AND PUBLIC LIBRARY DATA

	Community College Only	Public Only	Neither	Both
Titles Matching Bibliography	12	11	54	19
Percentage of Match with Bibliography	12.5	11.5	56.3	19.8

tions or limitations of the bibliography, titles found in *neither* type of library were examined. Some of these titles are listed below:

- Daly, *Beyond God the Father*
- Dworkin, *Men Possessing Women*
- Hooks, *Black Women and Feminism*
- Morgan, *Going Too Far: the personal chronicle of a feminist*
- Smith, *Home Girls: a black feminist anthology*
- Spender, *Women of Ideas and what men have done to them*

These *are* important and well-known feminist titles, that should have been found in at least one, if not more, community college or public library.

Table III below includes calculations made in an effort to further assess the percentages of match with titles in the bibliography. The figures in Table III illustrate commonalities among libraries. It can be seen that approximately two-thirds of the titles were found in none of the libraries examined. When a title was found, it was most likely to be part of the collection of only one community college or public library. Both community college and public libraries had smaller percentages of titles held by two or three libraries. Only in the case of public libraries were titles found in the collections of four of the libraries studied.

CONCLUSION

A complete evaluation of the response of these libraries to the impact of the feminist movement would require placing the data

TABLE III. DUPLICATION OF TITLES IN PUBLIC AND COMMUNITY COLLEGE LIBRARIES

Number of Libraries with Title	Total Public	Total Community College
None	66	65
One	15	18
Two	8	10
Three	4	3
Four	2	0
Five	1	NA

collected in the context of library mission, user demand and library services to women. In addition, availability of feminist materials other than non-fiction books was not assessed in this study. Feminist literature or periodicals, for example, might constitute a significant part of a libraries' feminist collection. Evaluation of subject coverage in feminist books acquired could be an alternative to measuring title selection. All of the above factors could be considered in future studies.

Further research would be beneficial, as well, using alternate or compiled bibliographies, or different methods, to examine acquisition of a range of feminist titles. In this study, it was understood that library collections might contain many feminist titles not included in the bibliography used for study. The parameters of title selection excluded some early feminist classics and titles exemplifying the international context of the feminist movement. However, the assessment of both the community and public library collections examined did indicate a need for attention to collection development policies regarding feminist non-fiction books. Collection assessment of this nature is a necessary first step in evaluating library response to the impact of feminism. Use studies could precede or follow such assessment. Initiative on the part of libraries is necessary to ensure that collections reflect the impact of feminism on society and benefit from the increased availability of feminist materials, a positive development for all library users.

NOTES

1. Mark W. Emery, "Considerations regarding women's studies collection development in academic libraries," *Collection Management*, v.10, n.1-2 (1988), 87.

2. Anne Innis Dagg, "Books by women neglected," *Canadian Library Journal*, v.44, n.2 (April 1987), 66.

3. American Library Association. *Library Bill of Rights*. Chicago: American Library Association, 1990.

4. Bohdan S. Wynar, (ed.) *American Reference Books Annual*, 1980, 341.

5. Neel Parikh and Ellen Broidy, "Women's issues: the library response," *Wilson Library Bulletin*, (December 1982), 295.

6. *Ibid.*, 295.

7. Pat Schuman and Gay Detlefsen, "Sisterhood is serious: an annotated bibliography," *Library Journal*, v.96, n.15 (September 1, 1971), 2589.

8. Emery, op.cit., 87.

9. Emery, op.cit., 88.

10. Emery, op.cit., 90.

11. Susan G. Williamson, Nicole Hahn Rafter, and Amy Cohen-Rose, "Everyone wins: a collaborative model for mainstreaming women's studies," *Journal of Academic Librarianship*, v.15 (March 1989), 21.

12. Association of Research Libraries (Office of Management Systems), *Collection Description and Assessment in ARL Libraries*, SPEC KIT #87 (September 1982), ERIC, ED 235814.

13. Stineman, Esther F. *Women's Studies: a recommended core bibliography*. Littleton, CO: Libraries Unlimited, 1979.

14. Loeb, Catherine F., Susan E. Searing, Esther F. Stineman. *Women's Studies: a recommended core bibliography, 1980-85*. Littleton, CO: Libraries Unlimited, 1987.

15. "Current reviews for college libraries," *Choice*, v.24, n.10 (June 1987), 1536.

TITLES CHECKED
from Women's Studies:
A Recommended Core Bibliography (1979)

Blumhagen, Kathleen O'Connor and Walter D. Johnson, eds. *Women's Studies: An Interdisciplinary Collection*. Westport, CT: Greenwood Press, 1978.

Brown, Rita Mae. *A Plain Brown Rapper*. Oakland, CA: Diana Press, 1976.

Brownmiller, Susan. *Against Our Will: Men, Women, and Rape*. New York: Simon and Schuster, 1975.

Daly, Mary. *Beyond God the Father*. Boston: Beacon Press, 1973.

Deckard, Barbara Sinclair. *The Women's Movement: Political, Socioeconomic, and Psychological Issues*. New York: Harper and Row, 1975.

Delaney, Janice, et al. *The Curse: A Cultural History of Menstruation*. New York: E.P. Dutton, 1976.

DuBois, Ellen Carol, *Feminism and Suffrage: The Emergence of an Independent Women's Movement in America, 1848-1869*. Ithaca, NY: Cornell University Press, 1978.

Dworkin, Andrea, *Our Blood: Prophecies and Discourses on Sexual Politics*. New York: Harper and Row, 1976.

Eisenstein, Zillah R., ed. *Capitalist Patriarchy and the Case for Socialist Feminism*. New York: Monthly Review Press, 1978.

Freeman, Jo. *The Politics of Women's Liberation: A Case Study of an Emerging Social Movement and its Relation to the Policy Process*. New York: McKay, 1975.

Freeman, Jo, ed. *Women: A Feminist Perspective*. Palo Alto, CA: Mayfield, 1975.

Friedan, Betty. *It Changed My Life: Writings on the Women's Movement*. New York: Random House, 1976.

Gornick, Vivian. *Essays in Feminism.* New York: Harper and Row, 1978.

Hope, Karol, and Nancy Young, eds. *Momma: The Sourcebook for Single Mothers.* New York: New American Library, 1976.

International Tribunal on Crimes against Women, Brussels, 1976. *Crimes against Women: Proceedings of the International Tribunal.* Comp. and ed. by Diana E.H. Russell and Nicole Van de Ven. Millbrae, CA: Les Femmes, 1976.

Jaggar, Alison M., and Paula Rothenberg Struhl, eds. *Feminist Frameworks: Alternative Theoretical Accounts of the Relations Between Women and Men.* New York: McGraw-Hill, 1978.

Lipshitz, Susan, ed. *Tearing the Veil: Essays on Femininity.* Boston: Routledge and Kegan Paul, 1978.

Morgan, Robin. *Going Too Far: The Personal Chronicle of a Feminist.* New York: Random House, 1977.

Redstockings. *Feminist Revolution.* New York: Random House, 1976.

Reed, Evelyn. *Sexism and Science.* New York: Pathfinder Press, 1978.

Reid, Inez Smith. *"Together" Black Women.* New York: Third Press, 1975.

Rich, Adrienne Cecile. *Of Woman Born: Motherhood as Experience and Institution.* New York: Norton, 1976.

Ruether, Rosemary Radford. *New Woman, New Earth: Sexist Ideologies and Human Liberation.* New York: Seabury Press, 1975.

Saffioti, Heleieth Iara Bongiovani. *Women in Class Society.* New York: Monthly Review Press, 1978.

West, Uta, ed. *Women in a Changing World.* New York: McGraw-Hill, 1975.

Yates, Gayle Graham. *What Women Want: The Ideas of the Movement.* Cambridge, MA: Harvard University Press, 1975.

Zaretsky, Eli. *Capitalism, the Family and Personal Life.* New York: Harper and Row, 1976.

TITLES CHECKED
from Women's Studies:
A Recommended Core Bibliography, 1980-85 (1987)

Abel, Elizabeth, and Emily K. Abel, eds. *The Signs Reader: Women, Gender & Scholarship.* Chicago: University of Chicago Press, 1983.

Barrett, Michele and Mary McIntosh. *The Anti-Social Family.* New York: Schocken Books, 1983.

Beck, Evelyn Torton, ed. *Nice Jewish Girls: A Lesbian Anthology.* Watertown, MA: Persephone Press, 1982, repr. Trumansburg, NY: Crossing Press, 1984.

Bell, Susan Groag, and Karne M. Offen, eds. *Women, the Family, and Freedom: The Debate in Documents.* Stanford, CA: Stanford University Press, 1983.

Brody, Michal, ed. *Are We There Yet? A Continuing Story of Lavender Women, A Chicago Lesbian Newspaper,* 1971-76. Iowa City: Aunt Lute Book Company, 1985.

Browne, Susan et al. *With the Power of Each Breath: A Disabled Women's Anthology.* Pittsburgh: Cleis Press, 1985.

Bulkin, Elly et al. *Yours in Struggle: Three Feminist Perspectives on Anti-Semitism and Racism.* Brooklyn, NY: Long Haul Press, 1984.

Burstyn, Varda, ed. *Women Against Censorship.* Seattle, WA: University of Washington Press/Douglas and McIntyre, 1985.

Cavin, Susan. *Lesbian Origins.* San Francisco: Ism Press, 1985.

Chernin, Kim. *The Obsession: Reflections on the Tyranny of Slenderness.* New York: Harper and Row, 1981.

Cochran, Jo, J.T. Stewart, and Maysumi Tsutakawa. *Gathering Ground.* Seattle, WA: Seal Press, 1984.

Coward, Rosalind. *Patriarchal Precedents: Sexuality and Social Relations.* Boston: Routledge and Kegan Paul, 1983.

Delacoste, Frederique and Felice Newman, eds. *Fight Back! Feminist Resistance to Male Violence.* Minneapolis: Cleis Press, 1981.

Delphy, Christine. *Close to Home: A Materialist Analysis of Women's Oppression.* Edited by Diana Leonard. Amherst, MA: University of Massachusetts Press, 1984.

Donovan, Josephine. *Feminist Theory: The Intellectual Traditions of American Feminism.* New York: Ungar, 1985.

DuBois, Ellen Carol et al. *Feminist Scholarship: Kindling in the Groves of Academe.* Urbana, IL: University of Illinois Press, 1985.

Dworkin, Andrea. *Pornography: Men Possessing Women.* NY: Putnam, 1981.

Eichler, Margrit and Hilda Scott, eds. *Women in Futures Research.* New York: Pergamon Press, 1982.

Eisenstein, Hester. *Contemporary Feminist Thought.* Boston: G.K. Hall, 1983.

Eisenstein, Hester and Alice Jardine. *The Future of Difference.* NY: Barnard College Women's Center; Boston: G.K.Hall, 1980.

Eisenstein, Zilla R. *The Radical Future of Liberal Feminism.* New York: Longman, 1981.

Ferguson, Kathy E. *The Feminist Case Against Bureaucracy.* Philadelphia: Temple University Press, 1984.

Ferree, Myra Marx and Beth B. Hess. *Controversy and Coalition: The New Feminist Movement.* Boston: Twayne, 1985.

Friedan, Betty. *The Second Stage.* New York: Summit Books, 1982.

Fritz, Leah. *Dreamers and Dealers: An Intimate Appraisal of the Women's Movement.* Boston: Beacon Press, 1979.

Frye, Marilyn. *The Politics of Reality: Essays in Feminist Theory.* Trumansburg, NY: Crossing Press, 1983.

Greer, Germaine. *Sex and Destiny: The Politics of Human Fertility.* New York: Harper and Row, 1984.

Griffin, Susan. *Made From This Earth: An Anthology of Writings.* New York: Harper and Row, 1982.

Griffin, Susan. *Woman and Nature: The Roaring Inside Her.* New York: Harper and Row, 1978.

Griffin, Susan. *Rape: The Power of Consciousness.* New York: Harper and Row, 1979.

Griffin, Susan. *Pornography and Silence: Culture's Revenge Against Nature*. New York: Harper and Row, 1981.

Harstock, Nancy C.M. *Money, Sex and Power: Toward a Feminist Historical Materialism*. New York: Longman, 1983.

Heide, Wilma Scott. *Feminism for the Health of It*. Buffalo, NY: Margaretdaughters, 1985.

Hooks, Bell. *Ain't I a Woman: Black Women and Feminism*. Boston: South End Press, 1981.

Hull, Gloria T. et al., eds. *All the Women Are White, All the Blacks Are Men, But Some of Us Are Brave: Black Women's Studies*. Old Westbury, NY: Feminist Press, 1982.

Hunter College Women's Studies Collective, *Women's Realities, Women's Choices; An Introduction to Women's Studies*. New York: Oxford University Press, 1983.

Irigaray, Luce. *Speculum of the Other Woman*. Ithaca, NY: Cornell University Press, 1985.

Joseph, Gloria T. and Jill Lewis. *Common Differences: Conflict in Black and White Feminist Perspectives*. 2nd ed., Boston: South End Press, 1986.

Keohane, Nannerl O., Michelle Z. Rosaldo and Barbara C. Gelpi. *Signs—Feminist Theory: A Critique of Ideology*. Chicago: University of Chicago Press, 1982.

Kimball, Gayle, ed. *Women's Culture: The Women's Renaissance of the Seventies*. Metuchen, NJ: Scarecrow Press, 1981.

Koen, Susan and Nina Swaim. *Ain't Nowhere We Can Run: A Handbook for Women on the Nuclear Mentality*. Rev. ed. Norwich, VT: Women Against Nuclear Development (WAND); distr. Trumansburg, NY: Crossing Press, 1982.

Lederer, Laura, ed. *Take Back the Night: Women on Pornography*. New York: Morrow, 1980.

Leghorn, Lisa and Katherine Parker. *Woman's Worth: Sexual Economics and the World of Women*. Boston: Routledge and Kegan Paul, 1981.

McAllister, Pam, ed. *Reweaving the Web of Life: Feminism and Nonviolence*. Philadelphia: New Society Publishers, 1982.

Merchant, Carolyn. *The Death of Nature: Women, Ecology, and the Scientific Revolution*. San Francisco: Harper and Row, 1980.

Meulenblet, Anja et al., eds. *A Creative Tension: Key Issues of Socialist-Feminism*. Boston: South End Press, 1984.

Meyerding, Jane, ed. *We Are All Part of One Another*. Philadelphia: New Society Publishers, 1984.

Mitchell, Juliet. *Women: The Longest Revolution: Essays on Feminism, Literature and Psychoanalysis*. New York: Pantheon Books, 1984.

Moraga, Cherrie and Gloria Anzaldua, eds. *This Bridge Called My Back: Writings By Radical Women of Color*. Second ed. New York: Kitchen Table, Women of Color Press, 1983.

Morgan, Robin. *The Anatomy of Freedom: Feminism, Physics, and Global Politics*. Garden City, NY: Anchor Press/Doubleday, 1982.

O'Brien, Mary. *The Politics of Reproduction*. Boston: Routledge and Kegan Paul, 1981.

Petchesky, Rosalind Pollack. *Abortion and Woman's Choice: The State, Sexuality, and Reproductive Freedom*. Boston: Northeastern University Press, 1984.

The Quest Staff. *Building Feminist Theory: Essays from Quest*. New York: Longman, 1981.

Reardon, Betty A. *Sexism and the War System*. New York: Teachers College Press, 1985.

Richardson, Laurel and Verta Taylor. *Feminist Frontiers: Rethinking Sex, Gender, and Society*. Redding, MA: Addison-Wesley, 1983.

Root, Jane. *Pictures of Women: Sexuality*. Edited by Jane Hawksley. Boston: Pandora Press, 1984.

Rowland, Robyn, ed. *Women Who Do and Women Who Don't Join the Women's Movement*. Boston: Routledge and Kegan Paul, 1984.

Sargent, Lydia, ed. *Women and Revolution: A Discussion of the Unhappy Marriage of Marxism and Feminism*. Boston: South End Press, 1981.

Schechter, Susan. *Women and Male Violence: The Visions and Struggles of the Battered Women's Movement*. Boston: South End Press, 1982.

Schoenfielder, Lisa and Barb Wieser, eds. *Shadow on a Tightrope: Writings by Women on Fat Oppression*. Iowa City: Aunt Lute Book Company, 1983.

Smith, Barbara. *Home Girls: A Black Feminist Anthology*. Latham, NY: Kitchen Table, Women of Color Press, 1983.

Snitow, Ann et al., eds. *Powers of Desire: The Politics of Sexuality*. New York: Monthly Review Press, 1983.

Spender, Dale, ed. *Feminist Theorists: Three Centuries of Key Women Thinkers*. New York: Pantheon Books, 1983.

Spender, Dale. *Women of Ideas and What Men Have Done to Them*. Boston: Routledge and Kegan Paul, 1982.

Steinem, Gloria. *Outrageous Acts and Everyday Rebellions*. New York: Holt, Rinehart and Winston, 1983.

Swerdlow, Amy and Hanna Lessinger, eds. *Class, Race, and Sex: The Dynamics of Control*. New York: Barnard College Women's Center; Boston: G.K. Hall, 1983.

Thorne, Barrie and Marilyn Yalom, eds. *Rethinking the Family: Some Feminist Questions*. New York: Longman, 1982.

Treblicot, Joyce, ed. *Mothering: Essays in Feminist Theory*. Totowa, NJ: Rowman and Allanheld, 1983.

Treichler, Paula A. et al., eds. *For Alma Mater: Theory and Practice in Feminist Scholarship*. Urbana, IL: University of Illinois Press, 1985.

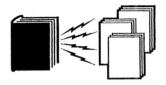

Haworth
DOCUMENT DELIVERY
SERVICE
and Local Photocopying Royalty Payment Form

This new service provides (a) a single-article order form for any article from a Haworth journal and (b) a convenient royalty payment form for local photocopying (not applicable to photocopies intended for resale).

- *Time Saving:* No running around from library to library to find a specific article.
- *Cost Effective:* All costs are kept down to a minimum.
- *Fast Delivery:* Choose from several options, including same-day FAX.
- *No Copyright Hassles:* You will be supplied by the original publisher.
- *Easy Payment:* Choose from several easy payment methods.

Open Accounts Welcome for ...
- Library Interlibrary Loan Departments
- Library Network/Consortia Wishing to Provide Single-Article Services
- Indexing/Abstracting Services with Single Article Provision Services
- Document Provision Brokers and Freelance Information Service Providers

MAIL or *FAX* THIS ENTIRE ORDER FORM TO:

Attn: **Marianne Arnold**
Haworth Document Delivery Service
The Haworth Press, Inc.
10 Alice Street
Binghamton, NY 13904-1580

or FAX: (607) 722-1424
or CALL: 1-800-3-HAWORTH
(1-800-342-9678; 9am-5pm EST)

PLEASE SEND ME PHOTOCOPIES OF THE FOLLOWING SINGLE ARTICLES:

1) Journal Title: _____
   Vol/Issue/Year: _____Starting & Ending Pages:_____
Article Title:_____
_____

2) Journal Title: _____
   Vol/Issue/Year: _____Starting & Ending Pages:_____
Article Title:_____
_____

3) Journal Title: _____
   Vol/Issue/Year: _____Starting & Ending Pages:_____.
Article Title:_____
_____

4) Journal Title: _____
   Vol/Issue/Year: _____Starting & Ending Pages:_____
Article Title:_____

(See other side for Costs and Payment Information)

COSTS: Please figure your cost to order quality copies of an article.

1. Set-up charge per article: $8.00
   ($8.00 × number of separate articles) _____

2. Photocopying charge for each article:

    1-10 pages: $1.00 _____

    11-19 pages: $3.00 _____

    20-29 pages: $5.00 _____

    30+ pages: $2.00/10 pages _____

3. Flexicover (optional): $2.00/article _____

4. Postage & Handling: US: $1.00 for the first article/

    $.50 each additional article _____

    Federal Express: $25.00 _____

    Outside US: $2.00 for first article/

    $.50 each additional article _____

5. Same-day FAX service: $.35 per page _____

6. Local Photocopying Royalty Payment: should you wish to copy the article yourself. Not intended for photocopies made for resale. $1.50 per article per copy (i.e. 10 articles x $1.50 each = $15.00) _____

GRAND TOTAL: _____

METHOD OF PAYMENT: (please check one)

❏ Check enclosed   ❏ Please ship and bill. PO # _____
(sorry we can ship and bill to bookstores only! All others must pre-pay)

❏ Charge to my credit card: ❏ Visa;   ❏ MasterCard; ❏ American Express;

Account Number: _____   Expiration date: _____

Signature: *X* _____   Name: _____

Institution: _____   Address: _____

City: _____   State: _____   Zip: _____

Phone Number: _____   FAX Number: _____

MAIL or *FAX* THIS ENTIRE ORDER FORM TO:

Attn: **Marianne Arnold**
Haworth Document Delivery Service
The Haworth Press, Inc.
10 Alice Street
Binghamton, NY 13904-1580

or **FAX:** (607) 722-1424
or **CALL:** 1-800-3-HAWORTH
(1-800-342-9678; 9am-5pm EST)